What Is a God?

What Is a God?

Anthropomorphic and Non-Anthropomorphic Aspects of Deity in Ancient Mesopotamia

Edited by
BARBARA NEVLING PORTER

Published for
THE CASCO BAY ASSYRIOLOGICAL INSTITUTE
and distributed by
Eisenbrauns
Winona Lake, Indiana
2009

Copyright © 2009 by The Casco Bay Assyriological Institute.
All rights reserved.
Printed in the United States of America.

Distributed by Eisenbrauns
Winona Lake, Indiana, U.S.A.

www.eisenbrauns.com

Transactions of the Casco Bay Assyriological Institute, volume 2

Library of Congress Cataloging-in-Publication Data

What is a god? : anthropomorphic and non-anthropomorphic aspects of deity in ancient Mesopotamia / edited by Barbara Nevling Porter.
      p. cm. — (Transactions of the Casco Bay Assyriological Institute ; 2)
Proceedings of a conference held in Sept. 2004 in Chebeague, Me.
Includes bibliographical references.
ISBN 978-0-9674250-1-6 (hardback : alk. paper)
  1. Mesopotamia—Religion—Congresses. 2. God—Congresses.
I. Porter, Barbara N. II. Title. III. Series
BL2350.I7W43   2009
299′.21—dc22

                                              2009017520

The paper used in this publication meets the minimum requirements of the American National Standard for Information Sciences—Permanence of Paper for Printed Library Materials, ANSI Z39.48–1984. ♾™

For William W. Hallo

in thanks for his friendship, his scholarship, and his generosity

Contents

Acknowledgments ix

Abbreviations xi

Introduction 1
    Barbara N. Porter

Die Geschöpfe des Prometheus,
        Or How and Why Did the Sumerians Create their Gods? 15
    Herman Vanstiphout

"The Stars Their Likenesses": Perspectives on the Relation Between
        Celestial Bodies and Gods in Ancient Mesopotamia 41
    Francesca Rochberg

In the Likeness of Man: Reflections on the Anthropocentric
        Perception of the Divine in Mesopotamian Art 93
    Tallay Ornan

Blessings from a Crown, Offerings to a Drum: Were There
        Non-Anthropomorphic Deities in Ancient Mesopotamia? 153
    Barbara N. Porter

Highlights of the Discussion 195

Acknowledgments

This book and the collaborative research project from which it grew would not have been possible without the help of many colleagues, friends, and institutions. It is a pleasure to be able to thank them here once again.

Major financial support for the project was provided by the Collaborative Research Grants program of the National Endowment for the Humanities, an agency of the United States government. I am most grateful to them for their help. Any views, findings, conclusions, or recommendations expressed in this publication do not necessarily reflect those of the National Endowment for the Humanities. In addition, the project received generous gifts from Dr. Jean Curran and Prof. Jeffrey Sosnaud and from the The Assyrian Foundation of America. James K. Nevling generously offered his guarantee of sufficient funding for the project. Marian Morgan gave her house once again as a setting for the conference's discussions. Jamie and Banu KomLosy and the Sunset House Bed and Breakfast housed and fed the participants with their characteristic warmth and contributed financially to the project, as well.

I would also like to thank the many individuals and institutions who provided photographs or permission to reproduce photographs and drawings to illustrate the book. They include James Eisenbraun of Eisenbrauns, Winona Lake, Indiana; The Bible Lands Museum, Jerusalem; The British School of Archaeology in Iraq, London; The Israel Museum, Jerusalem; The Istanbul Archaeological Museum, Istanbul; the Staatliche Museen zu Berlin, Vorderasiatisches Museum; the Trustees of the British Museum, London; The Museum of Fine Arts, Boston; The Neo-Assyrian Text Corpus Project, Helsinki; the Royal Netherlands Academy of Arts and Sciences, Amsterdam; Eli Raz, Ein Gedi; Othmar Keel and the series Orbis Biblicus et Orientalis; and Diana Stein-Wuenscher. I am also grateful to Mark McGee for expertly improving the sound of the discussion tapes and to Pnina Arad for producing the drawings needed for the book.

I am, as always, indebted to more colleagues, friends, and family members than I could ever list for their encouragement, patient ears, and sound advice. Jim Eisenbraun's friendly and skillful support made publication of the book a much easier task. I remain much indebted to the Harvard Semitic Museum and my colleagues there for their advice and encouragement, for rich impromptu discussions of topics ranging from ancient beds to deified mountains, and for continuing to make the extraordinary research facilities of Harvard University available to me. I am particularly grateful to Irene Winter, Bob Hunt, Henk Versnel, Anne Porter and Seth Porter for their support and tactful advice at every stage of the project. Above all, I thank my kind and able husband, Michael H. Porter, for all he did to solve my myriad computer problems, help with planning and grant writing, serve as gracious host and ingenious logistical problem-solver during the conference, help design the book, and offer me his unstinting help and support in every way for all these years.

Abbreviations

AfO	*Archiv für Orientforschung*
AHw	W. von Soden, *Akkadisches Handwörterbuch* (Wiesbaden, 1965–81)
ANEP	James B. Pritchard, ed., *The Ancient Near East in Pictures* (Princeton, 1954)
AJA	*American Journal of Archaeology*
AOAT	Alter Orient und Altes Testament
ANET	James B. Pritchard,ed., *Ancient Near Eastern Texts* (Princeton, 1955)
BaM	Baghdader Mitteilungen
BASOR	Bulletin of the American Schools of Oriental Research
BMS	L.W. King, *Babylonian Magic and Sorcery* (London, 1896)
CAD	*The Assyrian Dictionary of the Oriental Institute of the University of Chicago* (Chicago: 1956ff.)
CT	Cuneiform Texts from Babylonian Tablets . . . in the British Museum
DN	divine name
ETCSL	J. A. Black, G. Cunningham, J. Ebeling, E. Fluckiger-Hawker, E. Robson, J. Taylor, and G. Zólyomi, *The Electronic Text Corpus of Sumerian Literature* (Oxford, 1998–)
JAOS	*Journal of the American Oriental Society*
JCS	*Journal of Cuneiform Studies*
JSOTS	*Journal for the Study of the Old Testament*, Supplement Series
KAR	Erich Ebeling, *Keilschrifttexte aus Aššur religiösen Inhalts* (Leipzig, 1923)
KAV	O. Schroeder, *Keilschrifttexte aus Aššur verschiedenen Inhalts* (Leipzig, 1920)
LAS	Simo Parpola, *Letters from Assyrian Scholars to the Kings Esarhaddon and Assurbanipal. Part I: Texts,* AOAT 5/1 (Neukirchen, 1970)
MDOG	Mitteilungen der Deutschen Orient-Gesellschaft
MDP I	Jacques de Morgan, *Récherches archéologiques, premiere série, Mémoires de la Délégation en Perse I* (Paris, 1900)
N.A.B.U.	Nouvelles Assyriologiques Brèves et Utilitaires
OBO	Orbis Biblicus et Orientalis
OBO.SA	Orbis Biblicus et Orientalis, series archaeologica
OECT	Oxford Editions of Cuneiform Texts
OIP	Oriental Institute Publications (Chicago)
PKG	W. Orthmann, ed., *Der Alte Orient*, Propyläen Kunstgeschichte 14 (Berlin, 1975)
RA	*Revue d'assyriologie et d'archéologie orientale*
RIME	Royal Inscriptions of Mesopotamia, Early Periods
RLA	*Reallexikon der Assyriologie*, E. Ebeling, B. Meissner, et al., eds. (Berlin, 1938ff.)

III R	H.C. Rawlinson with George Smith, *The Cuneiform Inscriptions of Western Asia*, 3 (London, 1870)
IVR/1	H.C. Rawlinson with George Smith, *The Cuneiform Inscriptions of Western Asia*, 4/1 (London, 1875)
IVR/2	H.C. Rawlinson with T. G.Pinches, *The Cuneiform Inscriptions of Western Asia*, 4/2 (London, 1891)
SAA	State Archives of Assyria
SAALT	State Archives of Assyria Literary Texts
SAAS	State Archives of Assyria Studies
STT	O.R. Gurney and J.J. Finkelstein, *The Sultantepe Tablets* , I (London, 1957); O.R. Gurney and P. Hulin, *The Sultantepe Tablets*, II (London, 1964)
TCL	Textes cunéiformes. Musée du Louvre. (Paris)
TCS	Texts from Cuneiform Sources
UVB	*Vorläufiger Bericht über die . . . Ausgrabungen in Uruk-Warka* (Berlin, 1930 ff.)
WVDOG	Wissenschaftliche Veröffentlichungen der Deutschen Orient-Gesellschaft
ZA	*Zeitschrift für Assyriologie*

N.B.: Words in the Akkadian language appear in italics in lower case in these essays, and Sumerian words used as logograms in an Akkadian language text appear in roman small capitals. Sumerian words used in a Sumerian language text appear here either in roman type, letter-spaced, or in capitals, according to the preference of the individual author. Personal names in either language have been treated as English words except in instances in which their meaning or cultural affinity is under consideration.

Introduction

Barbara N. Porter

How did the ancient peoples of Mesopotamia imagine their gods? Did they think of them as impersonal forces of nature, as powerfully charged stones or animals, as lofty planets moving through the sky, as divine persons of tremendous power, or perhaps as a combination of these, divine entities of shifting forms or differing natures? How, in their opinion, did such divine powers, or beings, or entities behave? Could human beings interact with all of Mesopotamia's gods, whatever their form or nature?

Since the early days of Assyriological studies, most scholars have argued that ancient Mesopotamians imagined their divinities primarily in anthropomorphic form, as great divine beings with personalities and active lives, much like humans in their form and behavior.

This understanding of the gods of ancient Mesopotamia has been shaped to a large extent by the way the gods of Mesopotamia appear in Mesopotamian myths, hymns, and prayers, texts in which the gods are vividly represented as divine persons whose actions take place on a cosmic stage, but who are described and addressed in human terms, as lords and ladies, kings and queens, warriors and healers, judges or viziers or servants, sons and daughters, wives and husbands. The continuing emphasis today on the anthropomorphic nature of the gods of Mesopotamia is exemplified in the work of scholars such as Thorkild Jacobsen, Jean Bottéro, and (to a lesser degree) Wilfred G. Lambert, all major voices in the study of ancient Mesopotamian religion in recent times.

Jacobsen, for example, in his study of the historical development of Mesopotamian religious beliefs and practices entitled *The Treasures of Darkness*, argues that although Mesopotamian religion probably began with the worship of gods as cosmic and natural powers envisioned in "situationally determined, nonhuman, forms," this was followed at a very early time by the "victory of the human over the nonhuman forms," so that "with the beginning of the third millennium, from Early Dynastic onward, the human form came to dominate almost completely, leaving to the older forms the somewhat ambiguous role of divine 'emblems' only."[1]

Bottéro, in his survey of Mesopotamian religion entitled *Religion in Ancient Mesopotamia*, comes to the conclusion that the ancient Mesopotamians were

---

1. Thorkild Jacobsen, *The Treasures of Darkness: A History of Mesopotamian Religion* (New Haven and London: Yale University Press, 1976), p. 9.

"resolutely polytheistic and anthropomorphist from the beginning."[2] "Well before writing and history," he suggests, "the ancient Mesopotamians, in order to dispel the innumerable secrets behind things of this world, were inclined to place many figures behind those things, imaginary figures based on their own models, although obviously well above them, like an amplified projection of themselves. Each figure was believed to be responsible for certain natural phenomena and for certain human concepts . . . . In other words, the ancient Mesopotamians doubled their universe with a parallel universe of supernatural personalities whose names reflected their roles: An was Heaven, and the god who presided over Heaven; Utu/Šamaš was the sun and the sun god; Ašnan was grain and the goddess who watched over it. . . ."[3] While this initial statement seems to suggest that natural phenomena such as sun and grain were non-anthropomorphic forms of the gods in question, Bottéro argues later that this was not in fact the case. He suggests that while heavenly bodies such as the sun and moon "were often more or less identified with the divinities who represented and ruled over them," nevertheless, "a true divination of the stars, making them equal to the gods, never seems to have been formally recognized . . . ."[4] Similarly, he suggests, "palpable realities superior to humans," such as mountains and bodies of water, were "endowed with a supernatural character" but remained "inferior to the gods themselves . . . ."[5] And the evil forces referred to as demons, "even though their divine character was declared by the divine determinative affixed to their names," were not quite gods, but entities thought of as "superior to humans and inferior to the gods."[6] Having dismissed such non-anthropomorphic entities in various ways as being not quite gods, Bottéro concludes that in ancient Mesopotamia, "the gods' image was thus basically anthropomorphic."[7]

Wilfred G. Lambert, while granting a somewhat larger role in Mesopotamian religion to non-anthropomorphic entities than either Jacobsen or Bottéro, also argues for "the prevailing anthropomorphic conception" of the gods in Mesopotamia.[8] Describing how temple life, for example, was organized to reflect the idea that temples were the "houses" of the great god resident in them, with the other gods of that temple considered to be that great god's family, servants, and courtiers, an arrangement that echoed the organization of the great households of the Mesopotamian elite, [9] Lambert concludes that "the official pantheon of Sumer

---

2. Jean Bottéro, *Religion in Ancient Mesopotamia*, trans. Teresa Lavender Fagan (Chicago and London: University of Chicago Press, 2001, first published as *La plus vieille religion: En Mésopotamie*; Paris, Editions Gallimard, 1998), p. 44.
3. Jacobsen, *Religion*, p. 44.
4. *Religion*, p. 63.
5. *Ibid.*
6. *Ibid.*
7. *Religion*, p. 64.
8. W. G. Lambert, "Gott: B. Nach akkadischen Texten," RLA 3, p. 544b.

and Babylon is easily seen as the outcome of reflection on the universe: these ancients were surrounded by forces of nature, real or imagined, which they identified as persons of superhuman power."[10] Lambert adds, however, that "there was always some ambiguity about the precise relationship of the deity to the aspect of nature, whether, for example, the sun god was in very fact the actual fiery ball ... or whether he was not of human form ... directing the actual solar body."[11] Elsewhere he suggests that this apparent ambiguity was instead a reflection of the different levels of theological sophistication of individuals within the society, arguing that only ordinary, uneducated people in Mesopotamia believed that planets were actually gods, while educated and more sophisticated Mesopotamians believed the gods to be anthropomorphic in form and understood the natural phenomena associated with them, such as planets, to be simply manifestations of those anthropomorphic gods. The scholars who shaped the official theology of the state temples, and the members of the elite for whom they wrote, he suggests, made a

> distinction between the very god and his several manifestations.... The simple might be content to see the sun in the sky and to acknowledge it as Šamaš, but the theologians knew that Šamaš lived in the heavens in human form, like a king surrounded by family and court.[12]

In addition, Lambert surveys evidence that appears to suggest the Mesopotamians also believed in some gods that were only half anthropomorphic, or even entirely non-anthropomorphic, in form. The various fantastic composite creatures, such as the bull-man and scorpion-man, he readily accepts as genuine minor gods, despite their half-animal form.[13] Although he also points out that there is evidence of some entirely non-anthropomorphic gods in certain personal names and in magical incantations, he dismisses this as referring to long-discarded ancient beliefs, traces of which were still evident in these conservative genres. Like Jacobsen, he sees the evidence for most non-anthropomorphic gods as "archaic matter," reflecting a very early time before the systematization of Sumerian and Babylonian religion.[14] The single exception, in Lambert's opinion, was the worship of certain temples, parts of temples, and objects belonging to gods, which he characterizes as a regional phenomenon limited to southern Mesopotamia.[15] Like Jacobsen and Bottéro, Lambert's survey of Mesopotamian religion quite correctly

---

9. W. G. Lambert, "Ancient Mesopotamian Gods: Superstition, Philosophy, Theology," *Revue de l'histoire des religions* 207/2 (1990), pp. 117–18.
10. Lambert, "Ancient Mesopotamian Gods," p. 120.
11. *Ibid.*
12. Lambert, RLA 3, p. 544b.
13. Lambert, "Ancient Mesopotamian Gods," p. 129.
14. Lambert, "Ancient Mesopotamian Gods," pp. 125–27.
15. Lambert, "Ancient Mesopotamian Gods," pp. 128–29.

focuses most of its attention on the anthropomorphic gods and forms of gods that dominate much of the literature. His recognition of the worship of a small number of half-anthropomorphic and non-anthropomorphic gods in addition has received little attention from most scholars of Mesopotamian religion.

Not surprisingly, contemporary textbooks on ancient Mesopotamia and handbooks on Mesopotamian religion reflect the anthropomorphic emphasis of such specialists. W. von Soden's authoritative introduction to ancient Mesopotamia, for example, bases its account of Mesopotamian religion on the premise that "the terrestrial world was carried over to the primarily heavenly world of the gods.... all Mesopotamian deities had a human form,"[16] G. Roux's handbook *Ancient Iraq*, still a staple of introductory courses, states simply that in early Mesopotamia, "divine society was conceived as a replica of human society.... The heavens were populated with hundreds of supremely powerful manlike beings," a religious concept that he argues changed "surprisingly little" in later periods.[17] Jeremy Black and Anthony Green reflect a widely shared scholarly consensus when they comment in their brief illustrated dictionary of the gods, demons, and symbols of Mesopotamia that

> The gods of the ancient Mesopotamians, in historical times, were almost without exception anthropomorphic, male or female. It seems that they were imagined as of gigantic size and of superhuman powers, although the power of all the gods was by no means equal: some were relatively minor or of restricted influence. They shared the emotions and foibles of mankind.[18]

Despite such statements, however, a surprising amount of evidence suggests that ancient Mesopotamian ideas of deity were not so exclusively anthropomorphic as is usually assumed. Certainly Mesopotamian "gods" (DINGIR in Sumerian and *ilu* in Akkadian) as they appear in myths, hymns, and prayers do in many ways resemble the familiar, largely anthropomorphic deities of the ancient Greeks, Romans, and Norsemen, and the single god of the Hebrews. But there is evidence even in many of these same texts that Mesopotamians, including members of the intellectual elite, persistently imagined a great many of their gods, including the most important ones, as occuring in non-anthropomorphic forms as well. A hymn to Nanna, god of the moon, for example, addresses him as "Nanna, great lord, light shining in the clear skies," while another hymn says to him, "On

---

16. Wolfram von Soden, *The Ancient Orient: An Introduction to the Study of the Ancient Near East*, trans. Donald G. Schley (Grand Rapids, Michigan: Wm. B. Eerdmans, 1994, German edition 1985), p. 175.

17. Georges Roux, *Ancient Iraq* (Harmondsworth, Middlesex, England: Penguin Books, 1964), pp. 88 and 190.

18. Jeremy Black and Anthony Green, *Gods, Demons and Symbols of Ancient Mesopotamia: An Illustrated Dictionary* (Austin, Texas: University of Texas Press in cooperation with British Museum Press, 1992), p. 93.

the broad firmament of heaven . . . you spread light, the darkness you illumine, upon your rising wait the Anunnaki gods."[19] In passages such as these, the moon god, although addressed as a great lord, is described in terms that suggest he was at least partly envisioned as being the moon itself, rising, setting, and giving off light to the earth. In a second example, Nidaba, the goddess of reeds, grasses, and grain, is addressed anthropomorphically in one hymn as "the able housekeeper of An, lady" and then extolled with the words, "Milady, you are the food of (the temple) Ekur, you are the drink of (the temple) Eanna . . . Nidaba, you are the beer." The same text adds, "Nidaba, where you are not heaped up people are not settled, cities are not built."[20] Nidaba appears here both as a divine lady and as piled-up grain and the food produced from it, as if these were all thought of as alternative forms of the goddess. An even more complex concept of deity is suggested by a later Assyrian hymn to the god Ninurta. It begins by addressing Ninurta as an anthropomorphically conceived divine person, "Ninurta, the warrior," but then goes on to describe him as a huge cosmic being whose face and facial features are the sun and other stars (themselves identified here as gods), whose head is the storm god Adad, whose neck is the divine ruler and judge Marduk, and whose other body parts are deities associated with contentment, healing, agricultural plenty and so on, down to his feet. Ninurta, presented here as the ideal god, appears in this description as a formidable composite of differing forms and powers, a "package" that includes an anthropomorphic deity, planets and stars, natural forces, qualities, and activities, each an *ilu* in its own right.[21]

The importance of non-anthropomorphic forms and images to Mesopotamian conceptions of the divine is even more strongly suggested when we move on from hymns and prayers to consider evidence drawn from other literary genres and from visual imagery. Texts giving instructions for the performance of particular rituals, for example, suggest that some gods were envisioned in several forms, only one of them anthropomorphic, and that certain gods had no anthropomorphic form at all. One Assyrian ritual text, for example, describes the procedure for a ritual in which the king and a priest present food offerings to gods that appear to have been represented by statues in anthropomorphic form, to some of the same gods in the form of crowns, stars, and other material objects, and also to gods identified, for example, as a lion, light, various city gates, temple doors, and the locks of those doors, in most cases with the DINGIR sign identifying a god written before their names.[22] Another Assyrian text lists materials used in a variety of

---

19. Jacobsen, *Treasures*, pp. 122–23.
20. Jacobsen, *Treasures*, p. 10.
21. For a translation, with bibliography, see Benjamin R. Foster, *Before the Muses: An Anthology of Akkadian Literature*, 2nd edition, vol II (Bethesda, Maryland: CDL Press, 1996), pp. 619–20.
22. Brigitte Menzel, *Assyrische Tempel* (Rome: Biblical Institute Press, 1981), II, no. 54 (K. 252), pp. T 113–25.

rituals, such as conch, lapis lazuli, gold, and cedar, equating each with a particular god; whether such materials in some way represented those gods or were viewed as embodying them remains unclear.[23] Administrative records from Sumerian temples include records of food offerings presented to a variety of objects, such as beds, chariots, harps, and weapons, again frequently marked with a preceding DINGIR sign.[24] Letters and astronomical reports sent to the king of Assyria by his royal astronomers and astrologers seem to refer to planets and stars both as celestial bodies and as gods; a letter discussing the moon comments, for example, "If there is a (lunar) eclipse in month III on the 14th day and the god in his eclipse becomes dark on the east side. . . ."[25] In another letter, discussing the ominous significance of appearances of the moon, sun, and various stars together, the astronomer concludes his prediction of planetary movements with the comment, "On the 14th day one god will [be seen] with another; let the king be happy." [26] Visual images, as well, represent the gods of Mesopotamia not only as divine persons who look much like human beings, but also as objects or animals such as a scorpion, a crown, a temple, the crescent moon, or a writing stylus.[27] Whether such creatures and objects were understood as emblems of anthropomorphic gods, as alternate non-anthropomorphic forms of such gods, or as independently divine objects and animals remains to be established.

Such evidence makes one wonder if the long-standing emphasis on the anthropomorphic nature of Mesopotamian gods has perhaps led us to underestimate the complexity of Mesopotamian concepts of the divine. If so, this over-simplification is due in part to the balkanized nature of Assyriology, a young field in which experts in a particular literary genre or chronological period have tended to work together in relative isolation, focusing on the complexities of their own types of evidence and often unaware of issues or advances in other sub-specialties. As a result, the memorably anthropomorphic images of gods in prayers, hymns, and myths, on which specialists in religion have tended to focus, have largely shaped current understanding of Mesopotamian gods, while the often different images of gods that appear in sources such as astronomical reports, ritual instructions, lexical lists and visual imagery have played a much more minor role.

The relative isolation of the specialties is regrettable, but understandable. Texts such as those dealing with astronomy or ritual are difficult for non-specialists to

---

23. Alasdair Livingstone, *Mystical and Mythological Explanatory Works of Assyrian and Babylonian Scholars* (Oxford: Clarendon Press, 1986), pp. 175–87, with commentary on possible reasons for associating the god with the materials.

24. For a survey and discussion of these numerous texts, with bibliography, see my chapter in this volume.

25. Hermann Hunger, *Astrological Reports to Assyrian Kings*, State Archives of Assyria VIII (Helsinki: Neo-Assyrian Text Corpus Project and Helsinki U. Press, 1992), p. 5, no. 4, line 1.

26. Hunger, *Reports*, p. 220, no 383, reverse, line 9.

27. For some typical examples, see the illustrations in Black and Green, *Gods, Demons, passim.*

read because the scribes who composed them wrote in their own specialty's cuneiform "shorthand" and employed that field's specialized vocabulary. In addition, technical problems can make interpretation of the texts difficult for anyone but an expert; astronomical texts, for example, discuss constellations whose shape and position have shifted over the ages, making them difficult to identify even for scholars adept in astronomy and mathematics. Understanding medical texts demands medical expertise to identify the diseases under discussion and the likely effect of the treatments the texts prescribe. Correctly identifying the plants and minerals named in medical and ritual texts presents an equally daunting problem. To complicate matters further, reliable copies and up-to-date editions of many groups of texts are only now being published after years of preparatory study, so that many texts have been largely inaccessible to all but a few scholars. Archaeological evidence and visual imagery present their own complexities and require years of training and experience to interpret knowledgably. Because of such problems, no single scholar is master of all the relevant types of evidence for understanding Mesopotamia's gods.

Recently, however, as new editions of key texts are published and as our understanding of the subtleties of the relevant ancient languages and technical fields improves, a few specialists in each discipline have begun to reassess the long-accepted concept of Mesopotamia's gods as almost entirely anthropomorphic. Such discussions, however, have remained largely confined to small groups of experts and have not yet had much impact on the field as a whole. A few scholars of ancient Mesopotamian astronomy, for example, working with newly published editions of Mesopotamian astronomical handbooks, reports, and letters, have been discussing whether an ancient field of inquiry that referred to the objects of its study as both "stars" and "gods" should be understood as an observational science, a theological endeavor, a field of magical inquiry, or an intricate combination of these (for us, separate) ways of thinking, a question whose answer lies partly in developing a better understanding of what Mesopotamian astronomers intended to convey when they referred to various planets and stars as "gods."[28]

Several philologists, on their part, have recently begun to explore a variety of texts that seem to reflect a belief in non-anthropomorphic deities or forms of deity. Gebhard Selz, for example, in a paper read at a 1997 conference on Sumerian gods, weighed the implications of the inclusion of various animals and material objects in early lexical texts listing entities that are labeled as gods, and considered these, for example, in the light of temple records that report the presentation of offerings to non-anthropomorphic entities such as harps, spears,

---

28. See, for example, Francesca Rochberg, "Personifications and Metaphors in Babylonian Celestial *Omina*," *Journal of the American Oriental Society* 116.3 (1996), pp. 475–85; David Brown, *Mesopotamian Planetary Astronomy-Astrology*, Cuneiform Monographs 18 (Groningen: Styx Publications, 2000).

thrones, fire, and various metals.[29] In 1986, Alasdair Livingstone published a study of esoteric texts that appear to equate particular great gods with certain tangible objects, numbers, kinds of wood, metals, semi-precious stones and plants.[30] In 1999, Stefan Maul (who later became a participant in the collaborative research project whose results are published here) gave a lecture at Harvard University in which he argued that some gods of Mesopotamia were represented by, or in some sense even equated with, particular metals, focusing on the goddess Ishtar as his principle example.[31]

A few art historians as well have been exploring in new ways the significance of visual imagery for understanding Mesopotamian ideas about the forms and nature of gods. Irene J. Winter, for example, has noted in a recent article that the rituals performed to transform gods' statues into living deities were also performed on royal statues and on other types of visual imagery, raising the possibility that carvings we have long understood to be visual representations of gods in some cases may themselves have been thought of by Mesopotamians as living gods.[32] Tallay Ornan, who like Maul became a participant in the present project, argues in a recent book that while the visual representation of deities changed over time in Mesopotamia, increasingly eschewing anthropomorphic forms, the mental image of the gods as anthropomorphic in form and nature remained the same (a theory that she explores farther in her contribution here).[33]

As such specialized studies continued to appear, it seemed that the time had come to try to bring such potentially revolutionary ideas to the attention of the field as a whole, so that they might play a larger role in the mainstream discussion of religion in Mesopotamia. With that in mind, The Casco Bay Assyriological Institute invited a small team of scholars, each expert in a different aspect of Mesopotamian studies, to collaborate in reassessing current ideas of how the Mesopotamians imagined their gods, and to begin to create a revised model of Mesopotamia's gods that would reflect the full complexity of the ancient evidence.

---

29. Gebhard Selz, "The Holy Drum, the Spear, and the Harp: Towards an Understanding of the Problems of Deification in the Third Millennium Mesopotamia," in I. L. Finkel and M. J. Geller, eds., *Sumerian Gods and Their Representations*, Cuneiform Monographs 7 (Groningen: Styx Publications, 1997), pp. 167–213.

30. Livingstone, *Mystical and Mythological Explanatory Texts*, pp. 92–112 and 171–204.

31. Entitled "Constructions of Divinity: Thoughts on the Notions of God in the Ancient Near East," and presented on February 19, 1999 to the workshop on Religions of Ancient Mesopotamia and Adjacent Areas, organized by the Department of Near Eastern Languages and Civilizations. For recent developments in his argument, see note 1 in the chapter on the conference discussions, below.

32. I. J. Winter, "'Idols of the King': Royal Images as Recipients of Ritual Action in Ancient Mesopotamia," *Journal of Ritual Studies* 6 (1992), pp. 13–42.

33. Now published as Tallay Ornan, *The Triumph of the Symbol: Pictorial Representation of Deities in Mesopotamia and the Biblical Image Ban*, Orbis Biblicus et Orientalis 213 (Fribourg: Academic Press, and Göttingen: Vandenhoeck and Ruprecht, in cooperation with the Israel Exploration Society, 2005).

Each of the five participants in the project was asked to prepare a substantial essay on the forms and nature of the gods of ancient Mesopotamia, based on how gods are represented in the particular ancient materials in which that scholar is an expert. After these papers had been circulated among the participants, we met in September of 2004 in the quiet of Chebeague Island, Maine, for five days of intense discussion. To encourage an easy exchange of opinions, we worked without an audience, freeing us from the gladiatorial aspect of many academic conferences. In the months that followed, the participants all revised their papers as they saw fit in the light of the conference discussions and further research. The chapters that follow are the result of that intense, and warmly collaborative, experience.

The project participants are a remarkable group of people, well qualified to present and evaluate the evidence of their respective specialties. Francesca Rochberg, a specialist in Mesopotamian astronomy and now a professor of Near Eastern studies at the University of California at Berkeley, is a MacArthur fellow, editor of a new edition of the section on lunar eclipses in the Mesopotamian astrological text *Enuma Anu Enlil* and author of numerous books and articles. Her charge for the project was to draw on Mesopotamian astronomical and astrological treatises, letters, and reports to consider the implications of their references to celestial bodies as gods and gods as celestial bodies, and to analyze the relationship of gods to celestial bodies and astral phenomena, as seen through Mesopotamian eyes.

Herman L. J. Vanstiphout, a specialist in Sumerian literature and professor of Assyriology (now retired) at the University of Groningen in the Netherlands, has written extensively about Sumerian and Akkadian myths and literary texts, and has recently published a new edition and translation of the *Epic of Gilgamesh*, a king said to be "two-thirds god." His task was to reassess the nature of gods as they are represented in myths and literary texts, exploring issues such as who and what could become a god in Mesopotamia, what gods looked like, how they spent their time (and what kind of time that was), and what impact they had on human beings and the cosmos (and vice versa).

Tallay Ornan, a specialist in ancient Near Eastern art, was at the time the project began the Rodney E. Soher Curator of Western Asiatic Antiquities at the Israel Museum in Jerusalem. She was also a lecturer at The Hebrew University, Jerusalem, where she has since become a full-time faculty member at the Institute of Archaeology and the Ancient Near East. She has written extensively on the depiction of gods in Mesopotamian and West Semitic seals and is the author of a recent book examining the preference for non-anthropomorphic depictions of gods in second millennium visual imagery in Mesopotamia. Her responsibility was to survey and explore the meaning and significance of anthropomorphic and non-anthropomorphic representations of gods in Mesopotamian visual imagery.

Barbara Nevling Porter, a historian specializing in Neo-Assyrian royal inscriptions, visual imagery, and religion, is an independent scholar, a research associate of the Harvard Semitic Museum, and the director of the Casco Bay Assyriological Institute. She is the author of several books and numerous articles on religion, politics, and iconography, and directed and participated in the Casco Bay Assyriological Institute's earlier conference, "One God or Many? Concepts of Divinity in the Ancient World." Her charge (in addition to organizing and directing the conference and preparing its papers for publication) was to survey and evaluate the evidence for non-anthropomorphic deities in Mesopotamia.

Stefan M. Maul, a philologist specializing in Akkadian texts, is professor of Assyriology at the University of Heidelberg, Germany. He is a member of the advisory board of the German Archaeological Institute, an editor of the journal *Revue Assyriologique*, a winner of the prestigious Leibniz prize, and the founder and director of a research institute engaged in studying and publishing the cuneiform literary texts from the ancient Assyrian city of Assur. As an expert in the archaeological and documentary evidence for ritual practice who has published editions of two types of ritual texts, his task was to survey and evaluate the textual and archaeological evidence suggesting that the metals, precious stones and plants used in rituals were in some way equated with particular gods.

Unfortunately, a serious injury prevented Prof. Maul from completing his paper and from attending the conference. However, the text of the unpublished lecture mentioned above in which he had discussed evidence for identifying certain great gods with particular metals, was circulated among the participants and served as a written contribution to the conference. Supplemented by two published essays in which he had approached the topic from other directions, it was the focus of one conference discussion session. Although Prof. Maul could not participate in these discussions personally, his papers provoked lively debate, helping us to identify and explore key areas of disagreement.

The discussion of every paper, in fact, revealed areas of disagreement between the participants. Identifying and clarifying those issues may well prove to be the project's most important contribution to future research. The areas in which we differ help to pinpoint the areas of ambiguity and contradiction in the ancient evidence. They also made us aware of subtle underlying differences in our methodological approaches and in our sense of the meaning of the words that play a central role in the discussion. Although I hasten to add that we agreed on a great many points, I suspect that the issues on which we still disagree are more important: they point to problems that future studies must address if we are ever to understand the nature of Mesopotamian gods.

It became clear almost immediately, for example, that (as we had anticipated) the different genres or media on which each participant focused had led us to draw quite different conclusions about how Mesopotamians envisioned the gods. Clearly, the choice of a particular genre to some extent determined how the gods were addressed and represented. But what caused those differences between genres and what is their significance for understanding the dominant religious beliefs of Mesopotamia? Do different literary or visual genres, for example, reflect the theological beliefs of different groups in the society? Is one genre a more authoritative source of information about contemporary belief and practice than another genre? Were different visual media, such as cylinder seals and palace bas reliefs, governed by different rules of decorum about how the gods could be represented? Was myth a genre that permitted speculation or even criticism of the gods, while genres such as hymns and prayers required respectful praise? Do some genres of evidence reflect contemporary ideas, while others preserve early, possibly outdated, theological concepts? Were ritual instruction texts factual records of contemporary religious practice, idealizing fictional accounts, or even white papers promoting a revision of the forms of worship? Why do some genres of astronomical texts refer to gods as *controlling* the planets while others refer instead to planets as *being* gods? Although we wrestled with such questions, we came to no final agreement about the answers to them; it became abundantly clear, however, that the differences in how different genres represent the gods are of crucial importance for our question. Not only do the representations of gods in different genres suggest that there was no single, monolithic "idea of what a god was" in ancient Mesopotamia, even within a single chronological period and area, they also make it abundantly clear that we must understand more about each genre in question, its rules and conventions, its authors, its uses, and its intended purpose or impact, if we are really to understand how Mesopotamians envisioned their gods.

As the discussion of the papers progressed, it also became clear that despite our efforts at establishing definitions, we had significant (and often unrecognized) differences about the meaning of several terms central to the discussion including the words "god" and "anthropomorphic"! Implicit differences in the way we were using the word "god" became a particularly thorny issue and one that was never entirely resolved. Our discussions about it raised a further list of difficult questions. When a particular participant used the word "god," for example, or argued that something was not a "real god" did he or she (in each case) mean the word "god" as we, the modern observers, understand that term (and if so, how *do* we understand that term?) or as ancient Mesopotamians understood it? And if the latter, which ancient Mesopotamians? Did the idea of the nature of gods differ in different periods, in different regions, or in different cultural groups? Do we, the modern observers of ancient Mesopotamia, understand a "god" to be by definition an entity not perceptible to the senses? If so, does it follow that all representations (visual and verbal) of a god are of necessity metaphoric descriptions, not literal depictions of the form or forms of a god? If so, did Mesopotamians share this point of view and think consciously of gods as being represented metonymically, or did they imagine their gods as literally having a particular form and appearance (or forms and appearances), even if they remained invisible? *Did* gods remain invisible, in Mesopotamian opinion? Does the word "god" refer to an entity that must be a "being"? If so, does the idea that an entity is a being imply that it is alive? That it is of necessity cognizant? Must a god be omniscient? Must it have intentions? Must it be able (and inclined) to act upon other beings or entities? Must it have personality? Can a god be a phenomenon of nature, or a "first mover" or the impersonal embodiment of a concept such as "justice," or is a god by definition an animate being somewhat like a human "person"?

We discovered there were problems with related terms as well. Although Webster's dictionary offers the word "deity" as a synonym for "god," for example, most of us used the words "deity" and "divinities" in our chapters in ways that implied we understand those words to mean something subtly different from the words "god" and "gods," yet none of us ever explicitly addressed the nature of that difference. In addition, we debated whether the ancient words DINGIR and *ilu* really are Mesopotamian equivalents of the word "god"' or whether that translation should be abandoned. And we wrestled with whether calling an entity "divine" implies that it is a god.

Even the term "anthropomorphic" proved controversial. We differed in our opinions of the degree to which an entity has to resemble the human in order to be thought anthropomorphic. If an entity has been given a proper name, is it therefore thought of as being anthropomorphic, for example? If its form is that of an object, but it can speak, is it anthropomorphic? If it is presented with food, does that indicate it is thought of as anthropomorphic, or does that simply suggest it was thought of as alive? If it is represented as having a personality, is it anthropomorphic, or do other living things have personalities also? (Or do dogs and similar living things have personality attributed to them only because they also are being anthropomorphized by observers, as two participants at one point contended?) If an entity is sometimes represented as anthropomorphic, should we conclude that it is always thought of as anthropomorphic, even if differently represented at other times? Are Mesopotamian gods better described as "anthropoid" than "anthropomorphic"? Is the term "anthropocentric" perhaps more accurate, as Ornan argues here? Vanstiphout deals with the issue partly by coining another term, "substantialities," arguing that Mesopotamian gods appear to have had simultaneously several "substantialities," one immaterial, one anthropomorphic, and one (or more) that of a material object such as a planet. What it means to say that an entity was envisioned as "anthropomorphic" and what criteria identify it as such are issues that need further clarification, despite our strenuous efforts.

Another central issue that we debated at length without reaching full agreement is the nature of human categorization and its implications for understanding Mesopotamian ideas about gods. Do all categories leak, for example? Are all things that are placed in a single category by humans thought of as being things of the same type, or do they more typically have one essential characteristic, or one of several possible characteristics, in common? For that matter, do all humans approach the task of categorizing in the same ways? The issue of categorization and how it is done in various human societies has already been the subject of an extensive debate in the fields of anthropology and linguistics; the literature now emerging from those debates played no direct role in the conference discussions but may in time help Assyriologists to clarify how the ancient Mesopotamians thought about their categories of DINGIR and *ilu* and how those terms relate to modern religious categories and terminologies.

As the conference progressed, it became increasingly clear that the participants in the conference had different ideas about how ancient Mesopotamians categorized, particularly in their use of determinatives, the linguistic markers written before a word in ancient Sumerian or Akkadian to indicate the category to which the named entity belonged, categories which included such things as "males," "plants," "things made of wood," and (the crucial category for us) "gods." Did labeling a word with the DINGIR determinative (the written sign representing the word usually translated 'god') mean that the Mesopotamian writer understood the entity so labeled to *be* a DINGIR (whatever a DINGIR may be)? Or did labeling with the DINGIR determinative instead mark that entity as sharing one (or several?) (or one of several?) qualities considered to be characteristic of a god? If so, what were these characteristics or qualities? Overwhelming power? Sanctity? Holiness? Or something else altogether? How broad a spectrum of difference was permitted among entities referred to as DINGIRs and *ilu*s? Did omission of the determinative before the name of an entity imply that entity was (in that situation, at least) not considered to be a DINGIR, or had ceased to be a DINGIR, or was the omission of the determinative instead simply optional? On these issues, central to our discussions, the jury is still out.

If our papers and our hours of intense discussion have left many central issues unresolved, they have, I think, succeeded in opening the way to a reassessment of what a "god" was in Mesopotamian eyes. The point of the chapters that follow is not to offer a single, agreed-upon model of the gods as Mesopotamians understood them, but rather to reopen the debate about how Mesopotamians thought about the divine, exploring the question in the light of widely assorted evidence—much of it for too long overlooked, undervalued, or dismissed as incomprehensible. It is my hope that when others have read these chapters, they will be moved to join the debate, contributing their own ideas and expertise to a growing reassessment of Mesopotamian concepts of deity.

Die Geschöpfe des Prometheus, Or How and Why Did the Sumerians Create Their Gods?

Herman Vanstiphout
University of Groningen (ret.)

> La crainte de dire et de redire ce qui va sans dire
> est souvent mauvaise conseillère.
> (Edmond Sollberger)

Introductory: A Defence of Poetry

The arguments that will be proposed in this paper are based almost exclusively on the rich resources of classical Sumerian literature. I realise that none of the three terms, *classical*, *Sumerian* and *literature*, is beyond dispute.

By *classical* I mean basically the Nippur and Ur curricular texts. Since this group of texts was regarded as being somehow normative in the educational programme of the e d u b a, and since they remained so from the time of the early Isin kings[1] (at the very latest) at least until Samsu-iluna's period,[2] they certainly are deserving of the adjective "classical." Their canonical status is indicated by three facts: the structure and composition of the curriculum is nearly identical in the main "catalogues";[3] in the material we have from the two foremost academies in Nippur and Ur, which constitutes the bulk of Sumerian literature as we know it, the curricular function[4] can generally be established on the basis of the actual

---

1. The Isin Dynasty, being the earliest successors to the Ur III Empire, ruled over the larger part of Babylonia from 2017 to 1794 BCE. The reigns which concern us most are those of Išbi-Erra (2017–1985 BCE), Išme-Dagan (1953–1935 BCE) and Lipit-Eštar (1934–1924 BCE).

2. Samsu-Iluna was the successor of Hammurapi on the throne of Babylon(ia). He reigned from 1750–1712 BCE. In a number of cases the exemplars dated to the tenth year of Samsu-Iluna seem to present a "canonical" text, as can be judged from the exercise extracts taken from this version. Also the formats (carefully executed tablets or prisms) so dated speak for a high degree of canonicity.

3. These "catalogues" are tablets listing the opening lines of a set of compositions. The concept of "title" was unknown; the opening lines had this function, much as Papal *bullae* still do. For more information on the catalogues, see H. Vanstiphout, "The Old Babylonian Literary Canon: Structure, Function and Intention," in Gillis J. Dorleijn and H. Vanstiphout, eds., *Cultural Repertoires: Structure, Function and Dynamics*, (Leuven : Peeters, 2003), pp. 1–28.

4. For the curriculum as such, see most recently Vanstiphout, "Canon," which cites much of the earlier literature on the subject. For the curricular functions of various tablet types and of literary texts

numbers and different tablet types representing the individual compositions;[5] the emerging picture is not invalidated by smaller finds from other places, such as Isin and Uruk.[6] All the evidence available at present—and it is quite abundant—seems to point to a large set of texts that had official sanction in the educational system, which seems to be sufficient reason for us to take it seriously as a source for and product of common, yet informed, opinion.

The term *Sumerian* is to be understood in a cultural and sociohistorical way, and not as an ethnic designation.[7] Certainly, the spoken language had been defunct for some centuries before the great flowering of the Old Babylonian e d u b a.[8] Yet within a completely (or at the very least overwhelmingly) Akkadophone environment, Sumerian remained not only the vehicle, but also to a large degree the target language, of the education system—which may go a long way toward explaining why already in Old Babylonian times the grasp of linguistic essentials was so strong and subtle.[9] What is more, the subject matter of this Sumerian literature, produced largely by Akkadian speakers, is basically concerned with Sumerian traditions, values and reminiscences—or perhaps better,

---

in particular, see S. Tinney, "Texts, Tablets, and Teaching: Scribal Education in Nipper and Ur," *Expedition* 40/2 (1998), pp. 40–50 and *idem*, "On the Curricular Setting of Sumerian Literature," *Iraq* 61 (1999), pp. 159–72.

5. That is to say that (a) there are far more exemplars of copies, complete or partial, of the compositions represented in the catalogues than of other texts; (b) this difference in frequency is statistically meaningful in that it is not a difference in scale, but a basically different pattern (a composition from the catalogues, consisting of 70 lines, may well survive in 30 or more "manuscripts"; compositions not known from the catalogues, and of comparable length, hardly ever reach the number of 5 "manuscripts"); (c) many, though not all, "canonical" compositions include a significant number of unmistakable "exercise" tablets among their "manuscripts"; the non-canonical works hardly ever include even one.

6. See e.g., the remarkable set of "lentil" exercise tablets from Uruk, representing lines from the texts that were members of the "Tetrad," the four easy pieces which were studied at the very beginning of teaching "real" Sumerian. See Tinney, "Curricular Setting," *passim*.

7. In a forthcoming article, "Where (and Who) Are the Sumerians?", which was first read at the 2002 Rencontre in Leiden, I have tried to demonstrate that the concept of ethnicity is completely absent from the normative curriculum—and hence the official ideology of the Old Babylonian school.

8. This is the view commonly held these days. Yet it should not be taken in any absolute sense. There is incontrovertible evidence that at least a significant part of "scribal" education was dedicated to "spoken" or perhaps even "colloquial" Sumerian. What is more, would there be any point to the *Disputations*, apart from their rollicking jollity, if Sumerian had been regarded as a mummified and sanctified, and therefore surely dead, language? And what about the *Tale of the Illiterate Doctor of Isin*—a cruel sneer in any case (see B. Foster, *Before the Muses* [Bethesda, MD: CDL Press, 1993], pp. 835–36)? How "dead" was Latin in Western Europe anyway, at least until the eighteenth century, being for a large part *the* language of law, learning and religion? If Bram Stoker had not already given it a specific connotation, the term "undead" would do very well for Latin and for Sumerian.

9. See in general the masterful study by J. Black, *Sumerian Grammar in Babylonian Theory* (Rome: Pontifical Biblical Institute, 1991²), and Maryanna Wolf and Rebecca Kennedy, "How the Origins of Written Language Instruct Us to Teach: A Response to Steven Strauss," *Educational Researcher* (March 2003), pp. 26–30.

with traditions, values and reminiscences harking back to the "historical" Sumerian past, and therefore perceived as Sumerian. "Sumerian" had by then become a cultural and intellectual term, referring to what has been called felicitously a "culturally constructed group identity."[10]

Lastly, the term *literature* would probably have thrown even the literati of the early second millennium. Niek Veldhuis has recently argued cogently[11] that what we understand as being literature or poetry was a branch of scribal education, just as much as were lexical lists, mathematics, etc.[12] Everything that was taught in the e d u b a was perceived to hang together, and the whole of instruction did have a name: n a m - d u b s a r a or *ṭupšarrūtu* 'scribal craft/lore/knowledge/wisdom.' This basic or underlying unity of the arts and sciences—and ultimately wisdom— was perceived quite explicitly to reside in the cuneiform signs themselves. The sign was the repository, and therefore the expression, of all kinds of "meanings," whether linguistic, cross-linguistic, aesthetic, fundamental, applied, extended, restricted, symbolic, iconic . . . the single sign is all these, and more. Therefore any assemblage of signs—or "text"—can and does have a multiplicity of meanings, just as do the "natural" signs or the configurations thereof, which together make up the universe. The universe is a (cuneiform) text, and a cuneiform text holds the key to the understanding of the universe.[13]

My choice of material is not a case of mere elective affinity (or affectation). There are good reasons for it. As I pointed out above, for quite some centuries the system, structure and contents of scribal education probably received official sanction and national[14] acceptance; indeed, there was no alternative to it. This

---

10. I leave aside the highly important question of how widespread and/or pervasive this identity was in the whole of the social fabric, that is, outside the group that had constructed it and endeavoured to perpetuate and enforce it. The reason is that we will probably never know, since the instrument used for it (writing) was in the almost exclusive possession of the construction workers themselves.

11. Niek Veldhuis, "Sumerian Literature," in Dorleijn & Vanstiphout, *Cultural Repertoires*, pp. 29–44.

12. Although there is at least one small witness for a division between what might be called arts and maths—or business school. Proverb 2:50 says: "The scribe of accounts is weak on the tablet / the scribe of tablets is weak with accounts." See Bendt Alster, *Proverbs of Ancient Sumer* (Bethesda, MD: CDL Press, 1997), pp. 54–55 and 364–65.

13. See H. Vanstiphout, "The *n*th Degree of Writing at Nineveh," *Iraq* 66 (2004), pp. 51–54. Note that writing/reading (i.e., the recognition of the signs) dominates our *understanding* of the text or the universe. It does not *classify* them. The reason why not was already expressed forcefully by Borges: "notoriamente no hay clasificación del universo que no sea arbitraria y conjetural. La razón es muy simple: no sabemos qué cosa es el universo." Jorge Luis Borges, "El idioma analítico de John Wilkins," in *idem*, *Obras completas* (Buenos Aires: Emecé editores, 1974), p. 708.

14. Although there were not as yet "nations," let alone nationalities, in the modern sense. See Vanstiphout, "Where are the Sumerians?" For the invention of "national identities," see Anne-Marie Thiesse, *La création des identités nationales: Europe XVIIIe-XXe siècle* (Paris: Éditions du Seuil, 1999).

implies that what was produced by this education reflected, and in a significant way shaped, the dominant ideology in all its aspects, including that pertaining to religious matters, such as the interpretation of the essence, function, meaning and relevance of the mental construction we (and they) refer to as 'gods.'

Two more remarks deserve to be made. First of all, this literary material was the intellectual sustenance and daily business of a restricted group of highly educated people, but the system was also the only way in which "culture," expressed by the twin terms nam-dubsara, meaning 'the lore of all that is written, how to read it, and how to write it,' and nam-lu-ulu, meaning 'how to become a complete human being' or, literally translated, 'humaniora,'[15] was made available, albeit only in part, to the larger number of bureaucrats that constituted the backbone of the sometimes over-organised state. Apparently the Babylonians did not set much store by small government, and "intellectual" (dub-sar!) was not yet a term of abuse. Also, it should count for something that all this thinking and writing came from those who were judged to be the best minds, and certainly the best schooled intellects, of their times.

In the second place, the use of these literary texts implied the preservation of their traditional culture—or at least of what they thought was their cultural heritage—as well as the constant rethinking and re-interpretation and restatement of the same. But it also shows in many instances the use or re-use or re-reading of their past as they perceived it, in order to present a blueprint of society, state, and ethical values as they should be.[16] For all these reasons it seemed a good idea to look at the literary material in order to understand what they thought about gods. This material is the only way in which they speak to us directly.

[1] A natural history of gods

The *origin* of the species "god"[17] as such is hardly ever mentioned in our material; in other words, the texts rarely speak about how the first gods came into being. There is, however, sometimes an indication of the moment in time when this important event took place: right after the earth was separated from the sky. There

---

15. See the illuminating paper by Zweder von Martels, "The Kaleidoscope of the Past: Reflections on the Reception and Cultural Implications of the Term *studia humanitatis*," in Dorleijn & Vanstiphout, *Cultural Repertoires*, pp. 87–104, which discusses the terms "humanist," "humanism" and "humaniora" in early modern times, i.e. three and a half millennia after the Mesopotamians discovered the concept and coined the phrase.

16. A splendid example is the *Matter of Aratta*, for which see now Herman Vanstiphout, *Epics of Sumerian Kings: The Matter of Aratta*, Writings from the Ancient World 20 (Atlanta: Society of Biblical Literature, 2003). All these tales are ultimately about Sumer's technical, moral and cultural superiority over all the other regions and the obligations towards the world this entails, what may be expressed as "the Blackheads' burden."

17. I use "god" as a generic term which includes goddesses. The gender distinction is only made where it is relevant.

are some compositions that use this theme right at the beginning, which is convenient since these texts are mostly about beginnings or very ancient times anyway. Thus the *Lugalbanda Story* begins with the lines:

> [In the days long past, when heaven was sundered from earth][18],
> [In the days] long past, [when] all *needs* [*were provided for*],
> [In the days] long past, [when] after the *first* harvest barley [*was eaten*],
> [When *boundaries*] were laid out, when plots were measured out,
> [When *marker stones*] were put up and inscribed with their names,[19]
> etc.

The somewhat weird *Hymn to the Hoe*[20] starts as follows:

> Did the Lord not make manifest every thing as it should be?
> The Lord who never alters the destinies he has decided,
> Enlil, who made sprout the seed of the Land[21] out of the earth,
> Did he not hasten to separate heaven from earth?
> Did he not hasten to separate earth from heaven?
> And, in order to make mankind thrive (there) where 'flesh came into being,'[22]
> Did he not fix the axis of the world in Duranki?[23]

In the *Debate between Silver and Copper* we find the lines:

> (Copper speaks:)
> "After the heavens were separated from the earth,
> There was no drinking water;
> In order that the people should eat food,
> My father Enlil created me in a single day,
> And then the Tigris charged like a great wild bull."[24]

There is an interesting difficulty here: in one tradition—a very minor one—it is said that n a m m u, the mother of them all, first bore divine sky (a n) and divine

---

18. The first line is only known indirectly. Italics indicate uncertain translations or restorations.
19. See Vanstiphout, *Epics*, p. 105.
20. Felicitously dubbed "an exercise in *al*-literation" by J. V. Kinnier Wilson.
21. 'Land,' with capital *L*, is k a l a m in Sumerian. This always stands for Sumer /Babylonia.
22. This is a kenning for the (heavenly) place where everything started, but also for the earthly city of Nippur.
23. D u r a n k i, lit., 'the axis of heaven and earth,' besides being another kenning for Nippur, is also an obvious way of bridging the chasm between heaven and earth that resulted from their separation. For the text see D. O. Edzard, "U 7804//UET VI/1 26: 'Gedicht von der Hacke'," in Andrew George and I. L. Finkel, eds., *Wisdom, Gods and Literature: Studies in Assyriology in Honour of W. G. Lambert* (Winona Lake: Eisenbrauns, 2000), pp. 131-35, with earlier literature. There is as yet no complete edition.
24. Unfortunately the reconstruction of the whole composition is as yet still impossible. The lines are from "segment D." There is even some doubt as to whether the existing fragments belong to a single composition, or to two or more treating the same subject matter.

earth (ki). Since the sign for nammu is also the sign for engur, the idea seems to be that the whole cosmos ultimately grew out of the primordial subterranean water, which is engur. This seems hard to envisage, but there it is. Another popular formula indicating the beginning of everything is the mention of Enlil or the gods in general deciding the destinies. The *Debate between Bird and Fish* starts,

> In those ancient days, when the good destinies were decreed,
> And after An and Enlil had set the rules of heaven and earth . . . [25]

And the first line of *Gudea's Cylinder Inscription* might be seen as an attempt at combining the two formulae:

> On the day when in heaven and on earth the fates were decreed . . . [26]

In any case, this first day of the existence of the universe as we know it saw also the beginning of a species of beings whom we call gods, and their society is organised pretty much on the lines of normal, human societies. They have families, different kinds of interactive relationships, a kind of hierarchy, and a "family history," expressed by different genealogies.[27]

The two major *genealogies* can be found in the diagram drawn up by Black and Green.[28] But these diagrams include only the great gods, omitting the sometimes huge extended families and households that grew around one or a pair of primary gods, including not only children and grandchildren, but also all kinds of dependants, clients, servants etc. While these genealogies are certainly the most authoritative ones, there were many local variants, so that one cannot meaningfully speak of "one" pantheon. However all that may be, the overall scheme seems to be one in which the group of gods is headed by the sky-god An (who in most cases is a *deus otiosus* if not *absconditus*[29]) followed by ten "great gods" with their husbands or wives, who have equal status. These are:[30]

---

25. See provisionally Samuel N. Kramer, "Sumerische Litteraire Teksten uit Ur," *Phoenix* 10 (1964), pp. 99–108.

26. See now Dietz O. Edzard, *Gudea and His Dynasty*, The Royal Inscriptions of Mesopotamia: Early Periods, 3.1 (Toronto: University of Toronto Press, 1997), pp. 58–101.

27. An unresolved difficulty remains: were the gods already there when heaven and earth were separated, or did they come into being at the moment of separation? It is reasonable to suppose that the deciding of destinies was the work of the gods. But is that the same event as the separation?

28. Jeremy Black and Anthony Green, *Gods, Demons and Symbols of Ancient Mesopotamia*, (London: British Museum Press, 1992), p. 87.

29. But not always: in the traditions about *Gilgameš and the Bull of Heaven* he does have a part to play. It is a minor but still essential part: he gives Inana the use of the Bull for destroying Uruk and Gilgameš. This is fitting, since at least in this version he is not only Inana's father, but also the god of Uruk, together with Inana.

30. The "main" deity is mentioned first. The husband or wife is added in brackets. Female deities are underlined. The deity's main functions and/or stellar forms appear in the third column. The fourth column lists the cities of their main cult—and their earthly residence.

Utu	(Šerida)	sun	Larsa, Sippar
Nanna(r)	(Ningal)	moon	Ur
Iškur	(Šala)	storm, lightning	Karkara
Enki	(Damgalnuna)	wisdom	Eridug
Martu	--[31]	nomads!	--[32]
Nusku	--	minister of Enlil, fire, light	--[33]
Inana	(Dumuzid)	sexuality, warfare, controversy, Venus	Uruk
Ereškigal	1[34](Nergal) 2 (Enlil) 3 (Ninazu)	netherworld	--[35]
Bau[36]	1 (Ningirsu) 2 (Zababa)	--	Lagaš
Enlil[37]	(Ninlil)	chief executive[38]	Nippur

This list is, of course, much too simple, if not downright misleading. Yet it reveals three significant aspects of divinity that will occupy us further. First, there is the principle of divine couples united in marriage and all that this entails; second, there is the somewhat lopsided and very incomplete distribution of functions; third, there is the close relationship between a god and his city.

The *growth* of the divine population therefore depends on the institution of *marriage*, and therefore on *birthing*, and therefore on *sexuality*. In fact, the deeds of the gods as they appear in the record deal with procreation much more than with creation. Generally this highly important topic is treated in two ways: an insistence on predominantly male sexuality, and a kind of aetiology of the institution of marriage as a civil instrument. As to the first, there is somewhat conflicting

---

31. Although there is a remarkable tale about Martu's marriage. See S. N. Kramer, "The Marriage of Martu," in J. Klein & A. Skaist, eds., *Bar-Ilan Studies in Assyriology Dedicated to Pinhas Artzi* (Bar-Ilan University Press, 1990), pp. 11–25 and J. Klein, "The *Marriage of Martu*: The Urbanization of 'Barbaric' Nomads," *Michmanim* 9 (1996), pp. 83–96; *idem*, "The God Martu in Sumerian Literature," in Irving Finkel and M. J. Geller, eds., *Sumerian Gods and Their Representations*, Cuneiform Monographs 7 (Groningen: Styx, 1997), pp. 99–116. In later traditions he seems to be married to *Bēlet-ṣēri* (Akkadian: 'lady of the desert').

32. As explained by column 3!

33. As explained by column 3!

34. The different husbands represent different traditions, not a series of marriages.

35. As explained by column 3!

36. Or *Baba*.

37. Particularly for Enlil's family there is a widespread alternative genealogy. See Black & Green, *Gods, Demons*, p. 87.

38. This is probably secondary, the more so since I believe that Michalowski's interpretation of Enlil as an *interpretatio sumerica* of a term related to the Akkadian word for 'god' (*ilum*) is very plausible. See Piotr Michalowski, "The Unbearable Lightness of Enlil," in J. Prosecký, ed., *Intellectual Life of the Ancient Near East* (Prague: Academy of Sciences of the Czech Republic, Oriental Institute, 1998), pp. 237–47.

evidence. In *Enki and Ninhursaŋ*[39] we see a somewhat droll picture of a lusty god impregnating[40] first the earth, thus creating the marshland. In the marshes he impregnates Nin-hursaŋ, who gives birth to Nin-sar. He then impregnates Nin-sar, who gives birth to Nin-kura. Nin-kura gives birth to Uttu. Thereupon Nin-hursaŋ takes Enki's semen away from Uttu's thighs and grows some plants from it. Enki eats them and falls ill, whereupon Nin-hursaŋ bears a series of medicinal beings that cure Enki. There are some peculiarities to this text: the copulation scenes can be seen as normal in terms of animal or human sexual behaviour—although Enki's arousal seems to be that of a superhuman (or superman). But the pregnancies are miraculously short: nine days instead of nine months. Also the questions remain as to how Nin-hursaŋ extracts Enki's semen from Uttu's womb, and how she herself gets pregnant again, of an octet! Another feature consists in the fact that the sequence of copulations leading to birthings is framed in terms of the *carré d'amour*[41] consisting of (A) a lusty lover, (B) the longed-for girl, (C) a representative of the girl's family opposing irregular love-making, and (D) a helper of the lover. The main tasks of (D) are to arrange trysts between lover and girl, and to see to it that goods of any kind are transferred from (A) to (B) or, perhaps more importantly to (C)—thus regulating the affair. This is the classic structure of any well-regulated marriage, so that the story is about marriage as an institution as well. The same can be said about two stories in which Enlil woos and wins Ninlil,[42] and the motif even underlies the *Marriage of Martu*,[43] albeit with a peculiar twist.

About the *food* of the gods not much is said in our sources—yet what there is, is not without importance. The concept of a kind of sustenance that is specifically reserved for the gods, and perhaps ensures their immortality, such as the Homeric nectar and ambrosia, seems to be absent.[44] On the contrary, when the gods are

---

39. For which see now most conveniently Pascal Attinger, "Enki et Nin-hursaga," *Zeitschrift für Assyriologie* 74 (1984), pp. 1–52, and the Oxford website www-etcsl.orient.ox.ac.uk/section1/b111.htm.

40. For the copulation motif, see J.S. Cooper, "Enki's Member: Eros and Irrigation in Sumerian Literature," in H. Behrens et al., eds., *DUMU-E₂-DUB-BA-A.: Studies in Honor of Å.W. Sjöberg* (Philadelphia: University Museum, Babylonian Section, 1989), pp. 87–90. In fact, as we will see later, copulation and impregnation by a male deity (usually Enlil or Enki) is possibly the first form of divine creation. For Uttu, see H. Vanstiphout, "A *double entendre* concerning Uttu," *N.A.B.U.* (1990/2, no. 57), pp. 40–44, and *idem*, "Once Again: Sex and Weaving," *N.A.B.U.* (1990/2, no. 60), pp. 45–46.

41. See H. Vanstiphout, "*Un carré d'amour sumérien*, Or Ways to Win a Woman," in J.M. Durand, ed., *La femme dans le proche-orient antique* (Paris: ERC, 1987), pp. 163–78.

42. See H. Behrens, *Enlil und Ninlil: Ein sumerischer Mythos aus Nippur* (Rome: Pontifical Biblical Institute, 1978) with the recension of J.S. Cooper in *Journal of Cuneiform Studies* 32 (1980), pp. 175–88, and M. Civil, "Enlil and Ninlil: The Marriage of Sud," in *Journal of the American Oriental Society* 103 (1983), pp. 43–66. In the latter story Ninlil is named Sud.

43. See S.N. Kramer, "The Marriage" and J. Klein, "The *Marriage*."

44. Two remarks seem to be called for. In the first place Gelb's famous dictum that "we shall never find out what is the food of the gods if we do not find out what is the daily food of the labourers" is

dining, they do so on food that is commonly produced by toil of earthlings. There are good illustrations of divine dependence on food produced by humans. Thus there is the feast Lugalbanda[45] prepares for the gods after they have rescued him from death. The text is quite clear:

> At the rising of the Sun,
> Lugalbanda, invoking the name of Enlil,
> Made An, Enlil, Enki and Ninhursaŋ
> Sit down for a banquet at the slaughtering pit,
> The place in the highlands he had prepared.
> The banquet was set, the libations poured out;
> Dark beer, strong drink, white beer,
> Wine, drinks pleasing to the palate,
> He poured out over the plain as a libation.
> He cut the meat of the brown goats
> And roasted the dark livers;
> Like incense put on the fire, he let the smoke rise.
> As if Dumuzid himself had brought the tastiest bits from the cattle-pen
> So the food prepared by Lugalbanda
> Was eaten with relish by An, Enlil, Enki and Ninhursaŋ.[46]

It is a great pity that the Sumerian version of the *Flood Story* is so fragmentary that we do not know whether this also had Zi-usudra presenting the gods with a banquet, as Uta-napištim does in the Babylonian text, but it is quite reasonable to think that he did. Also, the *Debate between Ewe and Grain* starts with Enki's proposal that the gods should send down Ewe and Grain from the Holy Mound:

> On that day, at the birthplace of the gods,
> Their very own home, on the Holy Mound, they created Ewe and Grain.
> Having gathered them in the banquet hall of the gods,
> Of the bounty of Ewe and Grain
> Did the Anuna gods of the Holy Mound
> Partake, but they were not sated;

---

not only unfortunate; it is completely beside the mark, since the evidence we *do* have is that the same food was meant for both groups. Secondly I should point out that there may be one instance which contradicts my statement: Adapa is offered the food and drink "of life" in heaven. His refusal means that he will not find immortality.

45. It must be noted that Lugalbanda is a mere mortal, not a god. Yet he communes with the gods in this episode, quite literally, and the whole story is about his elevation to a kind of saintly saviour of his people, or, in other words, to a superman—but not a superhuman. Of course, this adds much poignancy to the story.

See Herman Vanstiphout, "Reflections on the Dream of Lugalbanda (A Typological and Interpretative Analysis of LH 322–65)," in J. Prosecký, *Intellectual Life*, pp. 397–412, and *idem*, "Sanctus Lugalbanda," in Tzvi Abusch, ed., *Riches Hidden in Secret Places: Ancient Near Eastern Studies in Memory of Thorkild Jacobsen* (Winona Lake, IN: Eisenbrauns 2002), pp. 259–89.

46. Lines 371–85 of *Lugalbanda in the Wilderness*. See now Vanstiphout, *Epics*, p. 125.

> Of the sweet milk of their holy sheepfold
> Did the Anuna gods of the Holy Mound
> Drink, but were not sated.
> For their own well-being in the holy sheepfold
> They gave them to mankind as sustenance.
> On that day Enki spoke to Enlil:
> "Father Enlil, now that Ewe and Grain
> Have been created on the Holy Mound,
> Let us send them down from the Holy Mound!"[47]
> And Enki and Enlil, having spoken their holy word
> Made Ewe and Grain descend from the Holy Mound.[48]

The picture thus seems to be that the gods had much the same preferences in matters culinary (and sexual) as ordinary human beings. But then this cannot come as a surprise: the evidence of food offerings to the gods overwhelmingly proves that the gods do indeed eat—and procreate—in the same manner as we mortals do.

Like any other species, the gods have a *territory* and a *time-slot*. One would expect the divine *territory* to be the whole natural world—both visible and invisible. In any case the notion of a separate supernatural world does not seem to exist. Yet there is a definite and separate subnatural world: the Netherworld. This is, however, restricted to those divinities that rule there, specifically to Ereškigal and her clan, to Dumuzid half the time, and, perhaps, to the older "slain gods," or dingirugge, of whom we know next to nothing, and who might well be very restricted and esoteric theological *fiorituri* to the general system. The reason for this is simple: gods do not normally die. Excepting the Netherworld, the whole natural world constitutes the divine territory. But this territory itself is divided into four different parts, whose geographical or cosmological arrangement is not very clear.[49] These are: the skies (or heaven), the inhabited earth, the subterranean ocean, and the parts of the earth unknown to and unreachable by humans. This latter part may be called "the shadow side." The location of the gods' abodes is mostly twofold: their true home address is either in heaven or in the subterranean ocean, and their secondary address is their temple(s) on earth. Just as their heavenly station need not be fixed in all cases, so can they roam freely all over earth, yet the notion of omnipresence, so typical for the religions of the Book, seems absent: on some occasions they have to travel, helped by their human subjects, from

---

47. 'Send down' is to be taken as 'send down to earth'.

48. Lines 26–42 of the *Debate between Ewe and Grain*. See Bendt Alster and H. Vanstiphout, "Lahar and Ashnan: Presentation and Analysis of a Sumerian Disputation," *Acta Sumerologica* 9 (1987), pp. 1–87, and Herman Vanstiphout, "The Banquet Scene in the Sumerian Literary Debates," *Res Orientales* 4 (1992), pp. 37–63.

49. For the cosmology, see the succinct, precise but unfortunately "orientalist" statement by Wilfred G. Lambert, "Babylonian Cosmology," in Carmen Blacker and M. Loewe, eds., *Ancient Cosmologies*, (London: Allen & Unwin, 1975), pp. 42–62.

one city to another. The gods do not inhabit the "shadow side" as such, though they control it; it is the realm of the monsters and other unnatural creatures that can and do repeatedly invade the inhabited earth.[50]

The *time-slot* allotted to the gods has a kind of built-in contradiction. There is a definite beginning, in that their first manifestation occurs at the separation of heaven and earth, at which time all the destinies were fixed. Therefore divine "time" can be represented as an arrow. But there is no *Götterdämmerung*; on the contrary, time becomes a circle without beginning or end—a feature that is regularly alluded to, and even underlies the Babylonian philosophy of (political) history, as can be seen, e.g., in the *Sumerian King List*[51] and in the conclusions to the *"Historical" Lamentations*.[52] Indeed, the technical term for the cycle of history, by which principle the worldly overlordship regularly "turns" from one city to another, is bala, lit. 'spindle.' In a totally different vein, the cyclical nature of time is also illustrated by the never-ending cycle of life and death of Dumuzid, the only great god who dies[53]—and is resurrected every year. Thus "history" in its widest meaning, *viz.* the history of everything, including deities, mankind and the universe, is a combination of the metaphors "arrow" and "cycle." After the single initial moment, or a short burst of unilinear unique events,[54] time's cycle begins: this cycle, as far as the gods and global human history (transcending the individual fates of mortal men) are concerned, consists of the recursive patterns that reappear in a world that remains essentially unchanged.[55]

Finally, what *shape* do the gods assume? From a number of data we can infer that they had a shape that was at the very least humanoid. They insist on houses—in cities—that are based on normal human architecture, and as far as we know, this was the case in their heavenly mansions as well as in their earthly dwellings.[56]

---

50. For the "shadow side" see Franz Wiggermann, "Scenes from the Shadow Side," in Marianne Vogelzang and H. Vanstiphout, eds., *Mesopotamian Poetic Language: Sumerian and Akkadian*, Cuneiform Monographs 6 (Groningen: Styx, 1996), pp. 207–30.

51. See Thorkild Jacobsen, *The Sumerian King List*, Assyriological Studies 11 (Chicago: University of Chicago Press, 1939)—still a monumental masterpiece—and the recent study by Jean-Jacques Glassner, *Chroniques mésopotamiennes* (Paris: Les belles lettres, 1993), pp. 43–51.

52. In all of these the final songs not only pray for a return of the happy days that preceded the catastrophe; they are certain that this will happen. The *Nippur Lament* (see Steve Tinney, *The Nippur Lament: Royal Rhetoric and Divine Legitimation in the Reign of Išme-Dagan of Isin [1953–1935 B.C.]*, Occasional Publications of the Samuel Noah Kramer Fund 16 [Philadelphia: University of Pennsylvania Museum, 1995]), even devotes far more text to the restoration than to the destruction.

53. In fact, one might perhaps legitimately question his death. The texts merely say that he is taken away to the Netherworld.

54. Such as the creation acts, or the fixing of destinies of "all things that are necessary."

55. For the principles involved in the basic dichotomy of arrow and cycle in respect to geological time, see the fascinating study by Stephen Jay Gould, *Time's Arrow, Time's Cycle: Myth and Metaphor in the Discovery of Geological Time* (Cambridge, Mass.: Harvard University Press, 1987).

56. We can infer this—indirectly—from the fact that the *Collection of Temple Hymns* (which do not give any architectural details, but are clearly about the existing, earthly temples) takes the position

Also their family structure, their family life, their sexuality, their food and drink preferences, their clothes, their finery, their weapons and other utensils, their means of transport, etc., are identical to those of the human species. This means that it would be very hard to recognise a god if one should meet one in the street. But with one important exception this never happens, or at least there are no reports of encounters between god and man. The exception is, of course, Inana, whose ambitions, lust for sexual experience and penchant for pitting rival lovers against each other are the topic of some important poems. In these poems she regularly appears to humans—albeit that these are, or become, heroes[57]—although in the *Šukaletuda* story,[58] she appears as a Lilith-like demon bringing utter doom to the naïve lover. Therefore it seems that generally the gods may have a (super)human shape, but that they also remain invisible in their heaven. This brings us to a difficulty: what is the status of the statues of the gods? We know that they were regarded as somehow identical to the gods themselves: they are clothed and fed and generally cared for as if they were living beings. But the rituals and other references (poorly understood though they are) make clear that this is merely pious make-believe. There may have been a moment in ritual at which the statue undergoes a transubstantiation[59] and turns into the living god, but we have no evidence

---

that the earthly home is a reflection or even a true copy of the "ideal" heavenly house. This idea is clearly expressed in the much later *Enūma eliš*. For the *Temple Hymns* see Åke W. Sjöberg, *The Collection of the Sumerian Temple Hymns*, Texts from Cuneiform Sources 3 (Locust Valley, NY: J. J. Augustin, 1969).

57. For Inana's character see Herman Vanstiphout, "Inanna/Ishtar as a Figure of Controversy," in H. Kippenberg, ed., *Struggles of Gods: Papers of the Groningen Work Group for the Study of the History of Religions*, Religion and Reason 31 (Berlin-New York-Amsterdam: de Gruyter, 1984), pp. 225–38. For her appearing to humans, see e.g., the *Bull-of-Heaven* episode in *Gilgameš*, where she appears on the walls of Uruk; *The Return of Lugalbanda*, where she sits in state to receive Lugalbanda and hands him the the solution to Enmerkar's problem; and *Enmerkar and Ensuhgirana*, where she appears as the insatiable lover of Enmerkar. See Vanstiphout, *Epics*, pp. 154–59, vv. 338–417 and *ibid.*, pp. 32–35, vv. 77–113. Note, by the way, that she is referred to as "my sister" by Enmerkar.

58. See Konrad Volk, *Inanna und Šukaletuda: Zur historisch-politischen Deutung eines sumerischen Literaturwerkes*, SANTAG 3 (Wiesbaden: Harrassowitz, 1995).

59. The rituals known as *mīs pî* and *pēt pî* ('washing the mouth' and 'opening the mouth') are generally understood as evidence for a kind of transubstantiation. But as far as I know these are much later than the Old Babylonian period. Still, there is perhaps some slight evidence of early forms of the same idea. Even in the Presargonic Sumerian texts from Lagash (roughly 2500–2375 BCE), the verb TUD 'to bear (children)' is commonly used for the making of a divine statue, and in the later texts, such as the rituals alluded to above, the Akkadian counterpart of TUD, *walādu*, is used. But that is all there is. For TUD in this sense, see already H. Vanstiphout, "Political Ideology in Early Sumer," *Orientalia Lovaniensia Periodica* 2 (1970), pp. 13–14 with footnote 30, and now V. A. Hurowitz, "The Mesopotamian God-Image, From Womb to Tomb," *Journal of the American Oriental Society* 123 (2003), pp. 147–57, who quotes much earlier literature. Highly intriguing are the lines from the Sumerian poem about Inana's descent to the Netherworld, which Hurowitz quotes there. The goddess pleads with Enlil not to let her die, and adds, "let not *your good metal* be covered with dust of the Netherworld" and comparable lines about "*your good lapis lazuli*" and "*your boxwood*." Hurowitz understands these lines as referring to the cult statue of the goddess, being identified with the goddess.

for that.[60] Yet there are a few sparse indications of gods appearing in disguise. First there is Enlil, who disguises himself three times in order to seduce Ninlil. But this happens within the divine society, and so it should perhaps not be counted. There is also the possibility—not more than that—that in the *City Laments,* the Storm that ravages the city is none other than Enlil. But here the question may be whether this is really meant to be so, or whether this is simply a very dense use of transference: the instrument becomes the actor and vice versa.[61] But apart from these literary devices there is only the cautionary tale about *Enlil and Namzidtara,* where Enlil appears as a raven.[62] Of course, there is also the fact that in many cases one or another attribute of a god can refer to the god himself, but these instances are also mere poetic tricks. This leaves us with one large category. For many, though not all, gods there is a general second category of representation, or of shape: they are also identified *by* and *as* their stars or other heavenly bodies. I shall not dwell on this, since it is the topic of another contribution to this volume.

[2] Divine properties and powers

Perhaps the first specifically divine property is the one mentioned at the end of the preceding section. Gods seem to possess three different kinds of *substantiality*. First, they do have a human-like, material physicality, albeit that theirs is in all respects greater and more powerful than the human version. Second, they also possess its antithesis: an identity or personality that is purely immaterial, although it may be thought to be immanent in the material world as well. And third, in most cases they have also a stellar or perhaps better, a cosmic existence, which is material enough, but not corporeal.[63] The first kind we can generally know only by surmise, inference or transference. The second one was perhaps deemed to be visible in its effects: the living world in its different aspects seems to prove this immanent presence of the immaterial gods.[64] The third one is, by its materiality, the

---

60. In fact, we do not really know how these statues looked, even in the late periods. We might have known, if Nebuchadnezzar I had left Marduk's statue in Susa, together with the Hammurapi code and the Naram-Sin Stela.

61. It might be useful to collect more examples of this and other uses of metaphor. Jeremy Black's splendid study (Jeremy Black, *Reading Sumerian Poetry* [London: The Athlone Press, 1998)] has shown the way to a sophisticated study of metaphor. I mention just one interesting aspect: the very dense and artificial language of the *Temple Hymns* in many cases consist of a subtle, refined and elegant metaphorical twist, whereby an effect or object of a description in fact hides the real target of the metaphor, and thereby enhances its greatness and expands its significance. The classical example of this technique is found in a modern Hymn to Rome by the poet Fausto Salvatori. The refrain is: "Sole che sorgi libero e giocondo / Sul colle nostro i tuoi cavalli doma; / Tu non vedrai nessuna cosa al mondo / Maggior di Roma."

62. See Miguel Civil, "Enlil and Namzitarra," *Archiv für Orientforschung* 25 (1974), pp. 65–71.

63. In a way Enki's "existence" as the sweet water subterranean ocean also falls in this category.

64. In other words, the natural world has a kind of dual existence, in that all of its features are at the same time simply natural facts, but also emanations of the appropriate divinity. This is very possibly

only truly reliable way of knowing the gods. The interesting point is meanwhile that the gods can switch between these modes of existence at will or at whim. This does not matter, since their individuality, their oneness remains the same and consists of all three modes. The switch is merely a matter of manifestation. Yet there are subtle differences between the effects these three modes can produce. Most of the "original" elements constituting the world as we know it, and especially human civilisation based upon the world as it was created, are ascribed to the creative actions of the gods in their corporeal existence. The rules and ordinations now governing the world and especially human society depend upon the gods' immanent and thereby omnipresent existence. The sidereal existence, which is basically cyclical, shows that they are still present and active, and that we should study their "ways"—literally—in order to perceive their wishes, warnings and knowledge, and then act accordingly.

Thus *omnipresence* is surely one of their most important properties. This omnipresence is not only manifest in the three modes of existence as sketched above; it also works in space as well as in time. They are present in the skies (sidereal) and on earth (in the creation period and still now: corporeal) and everywhere (immanence). But they were present at the very beginning of the world; they are still here; and they will always be here.

This future omnipresence takes on—quite understandably—the form of *immortality*. This is why the arrow of time has become a cycle of time. There are, however, two drawbacks to immortality. The first one is the matter of ageing. However, this only appears to be a problem: given the cyclical nature of divine time, and since there can be no ending, a process of ageing, or of decay, is really unthinkable. They remain forever as they were in their pristine, creative period. Since time is an unending circle, they do not age; so the Struldbruggs' problem does not arise.[65] The second drawback would be a very human one: that of boredom. But that one they have solved in a uniquely Mesopotamian way. After their original creation, they have divided their creation into distinct departments and drawn up the rules governing them. And by delegation, the actual realisation of these unending and endlessly repeating tasks is left to a great extent to their human servants. The gods are now merely the supervisors and guarantors of what must be done and the guarantors of acceptable results. Also the cyclical character

---

simply restated in the notion that all aspects of the natural world come under the authority of a specific god. This is why and how Enki has organised the world! This is also the reason why the universe can be understood or "read" as a cuneiform text: the universe is nothing but a tablet (or perhaps better, a long series of list-like tablets) written by the gods. Nor is this peculiar to Mesopotamia. In all three religions of the Book, one can find many instances of apologetic or doctrinal discourse treating the "Book of Nature" as irrefutable evidence for the existence of god—such as in the argument of the watchmaker, who now has turned out to be blind.

65. See Jonathan Swift, *Gulliver's Travels,* Part III: A Voyage to Laputa, Balnibarbi, Glubbdubdrib, Luggnagg and Japan (Chapter 10).

of time has been effectuated even on earth: the cycle of the seasons is perceived, quite logically, as necessary, as anyone can see every year.

There are two more properties usually ascribed to the single god of the religions of the Book: *omniscience* and *omnipotence*. We cannot know, of course, whether the Babylonians perceived the inanity of these properties. They are manifestly a physical impossibility, but what is more, they are *logically* impossible, since they obviously cancel each other out. But on the practical level, the Babylonians solved the problem by the simple means of a *division of labour*, which implies division of power, and ultimately division of responsibility and authority. This is stated quite clearly in one of the basic texts for our understanding of the divine running of the universe—and still more practically—of the Land. This is the text known as *How Enki Ordered the World*.[66] The third part of this poem is illuminating for our purposes. In this part Enki undertakes an inspection tour of the Land, creating some implements, organising the work to be done, and allotting the responsibility for each sector to a different individual god. Thus he starts out with the infrastructure, including:

- the main water courses;
- the marshlands;
- the sealand;
- the rainfall;
- irrigation and work in the fields;
- the tending of crops;
- construction work and architecture;
- management of wild and domestic animals;
- management of arable land and other resources.

A couple of quotations would not be amiss.

He organised plough, yoke and team;
Great prince Enki gave the oxen that follow . . . ;
He opened the holy furrows
And made the barley grow on the cultivated field.
And the Lord who wears the diadem, the symbol of the plains,
Him of the agricultural implements, the farmer of Enlil,

---

66. There is no complete edition as yet. For a provisional text reconstruction see Herman Vanstiphout, "De Enki-Administratie, of waarom de wereld zo in elkaar zit," *Revue belge de philologie et d'histoire/Belgisch Tijdschrift voor Filologie en Geschiedenis* 77/1 (1999), pp 5–51 (especially pp. 28–51) and *idem*, "Why Did Enki Organize the World?" in Finkel & Geller, *Sumerian Gods*, pp. 117–34. See also the discussions by Richard E. Averbeck, "Daily Life and Culture in Enki and the World Order and other Sumerian Literary Compositions," in R. E. Averbeck, M. W. Chavalas, and D. B. Weisberg, eds., *Life and Culture in the Ancient Near East* (Bethesda, MD : CDL Press, 2003), pp. 23–61, and *idem*, "Myth, Ritual and Order in 'Enki and the World Order'," *Journal of the American Oriental Society* 123 (2003), pp. 757–71.

> Enkimdu, responsible for ditches and dykes
> Did Enki appoint in charge of all this.[67]

Or again:

> The great prince bound a string to the hoe, and constructed brick moulds;
> He penetrated the mud(?) like finest oil;
> And him whose sharp-toothed hoe is like a scavenging snake,
> Whose well-placed brick mould is like a well-stacked heap
>   of hulled grain to the ewes,
> Kulla, who forms(?) the bricks of the Land,
> Did Enki appoint in charge of all this.[68]

This text is of great importance, for it describes in great detail how the Land was to be governed and run, and how Enki had originally organised all this. This system of delegating power, dividing labour, and allotting responsibility within the possibilities of the appointee not only obviated strife between the gods, but also made an efficient scheme for the welfare of the Land, the happiness of the human race, and hence, the feeding of the gods. It is very important to note that, ultimately, divine authority appears to be based on the expert skill of the god in question.

Therefore one might well understand divine power or authority in terms of *guardianship* and *responsibility*. The gods are supposed to take action only from this perspective, and their interventions took place, once again, in the primeval period, when the world was made. The actual and recurring labour is undertaken by human forces, working by the rules drawn up aeons ago by the responsible gods themselves. The system of specialisation, delegation, division of labour, responsibility and accountability filters down from the all-highest gods to the simple labourer, under the benign guardianship of a specialist god for each and every way of life.

Of course, this division of power and of labour can only be effective if there is a high degree of *co-operation*. This is also provided for in the divine ordinances. Although here our material is not so abundant as on some other points, there is some good evidence for a system of yearly consultations among the Great Gods. This was supposed to happen in Nippur—earthly home of the chief executive—under the presidency of Enlil and at the occasion of the New Year festival. Some of the processional texts describing the journey of a god to Nippur may even reflect an annual enacting of these government meetings: it is possible that statues of the gods did indeed travel to Nippur once a year in order to lay down the political programme for the coming year. Possibly the event also had the character of a "State of the Union" speech. It is indeed reasonable to read large parts of the

---

67. How Enki Ordered the World, vv. 318–25.
68. How Enki Ordered the World, vv. 335–40.

great hymn to Enlil known as *Enlil sudraše* [69] in this way. The division of labour and of responsibility has still another feature. The gods also share responsibility for the rule of the Land in its entirety. This is because the great gods have divided the Land among themselves: each one resides in a particular city of which he or she is the *city god*, and for which he or she is responsible. This system, under which the city god is the divine ruler of the city, but also the protector and the guardian of that city, can be seen most clearly in two kinds of document. First, in the *Collection of Temple Hymns*, it is clearly stated that the god has chosen that city as his preferred abode, and even built the temple:

> [. . .], shrine where the destinies are fixed,
> [. . .], foundation upon which the ziggurat rises,
> [. . .], dwelling of Enlil,
> [. . .], your right hand and your left are Ki-engi and Ki-uri,[70]
> House of Enlil, your interior is cool, your exterior decides the fates,
> Your door post and your lintel are a lofty mountain;
> Your pilasters, a noble hill;
> Your top is the [. . .] top of your princely dais;
> Your fundament serves heaven and earth.
> Your prince, great prince Enlil, the good lord,
> The lord of the confines of heaven, the lord who decides the fates,
> Great mountain Enlil has built his house on your close,
> O Nippur, and there he sits on the throne.[71]

The other documents are the *City Laments*. In this genre the city god is often held responsible for the misfortune of the city; he/she expresses the sorrows of the city, and he/she is urged to ensure a better future.

> Mother Ningal,[72] as if she were an enemy, now stands outside her city.
> The woman cries bitterly over her devastated house;
> Over her devastated shrine Ur she cries bitterly:
> "An has verily cursed my city; thus my city is destroyed;
> Enlil has verily overturned my house, and struck it with the hoe.
> On those from below he hurled fire! Alas, my city is destroyed!
> Enlil has flung flames on those from above!
> Outside the city the outlying districts are destroyed: I cry, 'Woe! My city!'
> Inside the city the inner city is destroyed: I cry, 'Woe! My city!'

---

69. There is no dependable edition. Adam Falkenstein's edition, *Sumerische Götterlieder* (Heidelberg: Carl Winter Universitätsverlag, 1959), pp. 5–79, is still useful.

70. Ki-engi and Ki-uri are the "native" Sumerian terms for Sumer and Akkad, i.e. the south and the north of Babylonia.

71. Lines 25–36 of the *Collection*. See Sjöberg, *Collection*, p. 18.

72. Wife of Nanna, city god of Ur.

> My houses outside the city are destroyed: I cry, 'Woe! My houses!'
> My houses in the inner city are destroyed: I cry: 'Woe! My houses!'"[73]

And near the end of the poem we read:

> Mother Ningal, return like a cow to your pen, like a sheep to your fold!
> Like a cow to your pen of yore, like a sheep to your fold!
> Like a young child to your room, my queen, to your house!
> May An, king of the gods, decree, "It is enough!" to you!
> May Enlil, king of all the lands, now decree your fate!
> May he restore your city; rule (again) as its queen!
> May he restore Nippur; rule (again) as its queen!
> May he restore Ur; rule (again) as its queen!
> May he restore Isin; rule (again) as its queen![74]

As a last instance of divine power we may discuss the gods' *power to create*. It is worth noticing that this act of creation seems to be treated in two different ways, perhaps to be connected with two different steps in the process of creating. As we have seen above, Enki's main task consisted of organising. But before he did that, he had created in a totally different manner the twin rivers:

> He raises his member, he ejaculates;
> He [fills] the Tigris with sparkling water.[75]
> As the grazing cow mooing for her calf in the byre
> (Would be) by a potent bull, he [penetrates?] the Euphrates with all his force.
> He raises his member, brings the gift to the bride.
> He fills the womb of the Tigris with joy, as the wild bull does, and [. . .]
>   the birth.
> The water he thus brought was sparkling, and sweet as wine;
> The grain he thus brought was heavy; people eat it.[76]

The same motif is found at the beginning of the *Debate Between Winter and Summer*:

> He copulated with the great hills, he gave the mountain its share.
> He filled its womb with Summer and Winter, the plenitude and life of the Land.
> As Enlil copulated with the earth, there was a roar like a bull's.
> The hill spent the day at that place and at night she opened her loins.
> She bore Summer and Winter as smoothly as fine oil.

---

73. *Ur Lament*, vv. 254–64. See still Samuel N. Kramer, *Lamentation over the Destruction of Ur*, Assyriological Studies 12 (Chicago: Chicago University Press, 1940).

74. *Ur Lament*, vv. 378–86.

75. Sumerian has the same word (A) for 'water' and 'semen'.

76. *Enki Organises the World,* vv. 253–60. See Vanstiphout, "How Did Enki," p. 120, and generally Cooper, "Enki's Member."

He fed them pure plants on the terraces of the hills like great bulls.
He nourished them in the pastures of the hills.[77]

Yet, as has been noted above, there is another method of primary creation: the gods can and do create primordial things by sending them down from heaven, where they presumably already exist, to earth, as happens in the debate between *Ewe and Grain*.[78] The same method is used in the tale *How Grain Came to Sumer*:

> Mankind used to eat grass with their mouths like sheep,
> For in those days they did not know grain, or barley, or flax.
> An brought these things down from the midst of heaven;
> Enlil lifted his eyes as the stag lifts its antlers when climbing a cliff;
> He looked to the south, and saw the wide sea;
> He looked to the north and saw the mountain of fragrant cedars.
> He piled up all the barley and gave it to the mountain;
> He piled up the bounty of the Land, gave the innuha barley to the mountain;
> He barred the access to the open hills;
> He [closed?] its lock which heaven and earth [. . .]
> He [fastened] its bolt [. . .]
> Then Nin-azu [. . .]
> Said to his brother Nin-mada:
> "Let us go to the mountain [. . .]
> To the mountain where barley and flax grow [. . .]
> The rolling river, where water wells up from the earth;
> Let us fetch the [barley from its mountain];
> Let us [introduce?] the innuha barley into Sumer,
> For Sumer knows no barley; let us introduce grain [into it]"[79]

Still, there remains a vexing problem in connection with the powers of a god. Is there a *limit* to these powers? There is, of course, the organisational scheme, in which each god's competence, and therefore power, is confined or restricted by the competencies of his colleagues. But within their own competencies, are they really omnipotent, and, what is more, completely free in their actions? A basic concept in Sumerian thought, hitherto not discussed, is the concept of ME—which is also, and more simply, the Sumerian verb 'to be.' Everything that exists in the world, from the material to the organisational to the social to the performative, etc., has its ME. The concept is hard to circumscribe, let alone define. It is, perhaps, somewhat akin to the Platonic "idea," but it has also been understood as 'divine

---

77. No edition available. The lines are 12–18.
78. See above, section [1], *apud* the food of the gods.
79. *How Grain Came to Sumer*, vv. 1–20. A provisional edition is available in Françoise Bruschweiler, *Inanna: La déesse triomphante et vaincue dans la cosmologie sumérienne*, Les cahiers du CEPOA 4 (Leuven : Peeters, 1987), pp. 54–57.

essence,'[80] although there are some problems with this terminology. It is never made clear whether the divine character of the ME belongs to the ME in its own right, or to the god who at any given moment is in possession of the ME, or simply to the fact that the ME belongs to the divine sphere. Very broadly speaking one might understand ME as the abstract but no less real quintessence of all things, procedures, action, interrelations . . . . Without its ME, nothing can exist. And the point of any kind of existing "thing" is to conform as closely as possible to its ideal, if unreachable, form, which is its ME. Now the relationship between the gods and the MEs is still problematic, and was manifestly equally so to the Babylonian thinkers as well. First there is the troublesome fact that nam-diŋir 'divinity' is itself one of the MES. Since a god is, then, a god only by virtue of this ME one can hardly say that the god is independent of the ME, or that he rules the ME. Secondly it is held that the MES are essentially unchangeable; yet some passages in the *City Laments* accuse the gods of changing the ME, or at least, of trying to.[81] Finally, there are gods that are more or less in charge of the MES. The best instance of this is the "myth" *Inana and Enki*,[82] wherein Inana by a not very subtle trick[83] steals the MES from Enki, into whose trust they had been given, and takes them home to her own city. The text gives a catalogue of 110 MES, which is repeated four times. Glassner[84] has suggested that this shortened list (for the MES may be thought to be infinite in number[85]) stands for those MES that are Inana's typical powers and features. This is attractive, but I doubt that it can be upheld, on the whole.[86] Probably related to this motif is the epithet sometimes used for Inana: me u_5-a. This is usually translated as "who rides the MES." I suggest that it means

---

80. See Antoine Cavigneaux, "L'essence divine," *Journal of Cuneiform Studies* 30 (1978), pp. 177–89. As a mere illustration of the power and meaning of syntax, I would translate ME in French as 'la divine essence,' and not as Cavigneaux has done. The point is that I think that the ME itself has divine essence, and that consequently the ME is *not* the essence of any individual god. In English, of course, it can be read both ways.

81. This might of course be understood in the light of the cyclical nature of history. See, e.g., the *Sumer and Ur Lament* (see Piotr Michalowski, *The Lamentation over the Destruction of Sumer and Ur*, Mesopotamian Civilizations 2 [Winona Lake, IN: Eisenbrauns, 1989], v. 493: "May An not change the MES of heaven, or the rules for treating people with justice," which may be understood as "May An never again attempt to . . . . " Note the dilemma: the MES are said to be those of heaven, yet An (= heaven) has changed them, which he apparently was not allowed to do.

82. See Gertrud Farber, *Der Mythos "Inanna und Enki" unter besonderer Berücksichtigung der Liste der ME,* Studia Pohl 10 (Rome: Biblical Institute Press, 1973), and Jean-Jacques Glassner, "Inanna et les me," in M. deJong Ellis, ed., *Nippur at the Centennial* (Philadelphia: University of Pennsylvania Museum, 1992), pp. 55–86.

83. She makes him drunk.

84. Glassner, "Inanna," p. 57.

85. The number šar$_2$, often used for the MES, is in most cases to be understood as 'infinity.'

86. As Glassner ("Inanna," p. 59) freely admits: "Ces termes, certes, n'apparaissent guère dans la littérature, associée à Inanna."

"who guides/steers the MEs,"[87] in the sense that she, as a goddess is responsible for the correct application of the MEs. It would seem, therefore, that the gods are not completely free agents with respect to the MEs. The MEs are the eternal and unchangeable first principles, or quintessences, of everything that exists. They are also the blueprints for everything that exists, in that they prescribe how it should exist. They do limit the divine powers.

[3] God and man

Lowering our sights from the most abstract concept of the universe-as-it-should-be-in-its-every-detail, we may now take a look at that part of the universe that concerns us most closely: mankind.

It is somewhat strange that the *creation of mankind* by the gods, although a rather well established fact, is not a popular theme in classical Sumerian literature. Pettinato studied the topic in some depth quite some time ago,[88] and maybe it should be taken up again. In our material it occurs as such only in a few stray allusions and in one complete text, *Enki and Ninmah*;[89] however, the creation of man is only one of the topics dealt with in this story, and not the most important one.

On the other hand, the *relations between mankind and the gods* are deemed to be of much interest. In the first instance, these relations are closely defined within the theory and practice of the system of the city-states, ideally co-operating in the government of the Land (kalam). In this system the city gods are for all purposes identified with their city, and this works both ways. The population of the city regards the god and his family, and house or temple, as the permanent entity that incarnates the spiritual and a-temporal personification of the city, as opposed to the ruler, who represents the temporal—in both meanings of that term[90]—power, but whose function and fate derive from and rely upon the god, ideally in close communion. In a way, the temporal ruler therefore acts in the name, and with the blessings, of the god, somewhat as his chief executive. On the other hand the god identifies himself very closely with the city (far less with the rulers!) as a whole. There are many instances of this in the *City Laments*, where a god or goddess bewails the city's misfortunes as his/her very own, sometimes even accuses his/her fellow gods, and in every case pleads with them, acting as

---

87. Interpreting u_5 not as *rakābu* in the G, but as *rukkubu* in the D.

88. Giovanni Pettinato, *Das altorientalische Menschenbild und die sumerischen und akkadischen Schöpfungsmythen*, Abhandlungen der Heidelberger Akademie der Wissenschaften, Philosophisch-historische Klasse, Jahrgang 1971, 1. Abhandlung (Heidelberg: Carl Winter Universitätsverlag, 1971).

89. There is no complete edition, although there is the dissertation by C. A. Benito, "'Enki and Ninmah' and 'Enki and the World Order'" (The University of Pennsylvania, Philadelphia, 1969), which is now very much outdated. The most relevant lines have been studied by Herbert Sauren, "Nammu und Enki," in Mark E. Cohen, D. Snell, and D. B. Weisberg, eds., *The Tablet and the Scroll: Near Eastern Studies in Honor of William W. Hallo* (Bethesda, MD: CDL Press, 1993), pp. 198–208.

90. I mean "secular" and "temporary."

both a substitute and a mediator/mediatrix for "his" or "her" population. On this level, the loyalty to and trust in the divine champion of the city is very important and outspoken. But just as clearly, the population expects of their champion the same loyalty and trust—and protection. More or less the same kind of relationship can be found in the attitude towards the gods, great and not so great,[91] in their capacity as responsible managers of the departments governing the natural world, such as irrigation, commerce, agriculture, building, etc., which were organised by Enki at the beginning of time. In a complex civilisation there are many different specialised tasks to be undertaken by man; and for each one of these tasks there is a divine director who theoretically can be approached for advice, help, and presumably also for receiving complaints and straightening out difficulties. The myriads of economic and administrative documents we have could perhaps one day be examined systematically from the point of view that the Enki administration is the theoretical scheme—or the protocol—from which all these documents ultimately stem. In both modes one might say that the divine world is regarded as a representation, but also as a model of and a model for the city or state, or even the natural world as a whole.

It is probably significant that in the rich literary material we now have from the classical period there is but one text that directly addresses the *personal relation* between a man and his god. This text, known as *Man and his God*,[92] is the first instance of the theme of the pious sufferer, which in later times and other literatures will become very popular. The text[93] is in effect one long monologue, consisting of a personal lament in which the sufferer complains to his god about the various forms of ill luck, sickness, poverty, and social isolation he has to endure. He then offers a prayer in the form of a penitential lament, and asks that his family and friends do likewise. The lament also includes a confession of sins, which he himself is not aware of having committed. At the end the god relents, and happiness is restored. The important point seems to be the notion that the sufferer feels it necessary to confess to sins of which he is not aware. This will occupy us again.

In the important texts that deal, in a very sophisticated way, with the Babylonians' self-perception in its cultural and "historical" sense, we find cases of *close personal contacts* between the "heroes" (for want of a better term) and the gods.

---

91. In the case of the most important gods we thus have the possibility of a double function: as city god and as department head.

92. See Samuel N. Kramer, "Man and His God: A Sumerian Variation on the 'Job' Motif," in Martin Noth and D.W. Thomas, eds., *Wisdom in Israel and the Ancient Near East: Studies Presented to Professor Harold Henry Rowley*, Supplements to Vetus Testamentum 3 (Leiden: Brill, 1955), pp. 170–82, and now Jacob Klein, "Man and his God," in William W. Hallo and K. Lawson Younger, Jr., eds., *The Context of Scripture*. Vol. I: *Canonical Compositions from the Biblical World* (Leiden: Brill, 1997), pp. 573–75.

93. Which apparently did not make the canon!

The *Aratta cycle* of poems[94] is very instructive in this regard. There we see a famous ruler, Enmerkar, or his son Lugalbanda, performing seemingly impossible deeds, sometimes with, but also without, the help of the gods. A few examples may serve to illustrate this. In *Enmerkar and the Lord of Aratta*, Enmerkar finds the solution to the impossible tasks technically with the help of Nisaba[95] and Enki,[96] but this divine help is very much downplayed. After all, Nisaba is the goddess of grain, and Enki, among other things, of all technical matters. Even so, in both cases the gods merit only a few lines. In stark contrast, Enmerkar's whole enterprise is undertaken, apparently of his own free will, at the express request[97] of Inana, whom he addresses as his sister[98] throughout![99] In *Enmerkar and Ensuhgirana* the *occasio litigandi* consists of the sexual favours of Inana, granted to Enmerkar from the beginning anyway, and the final solution is brought about by a competition between the bad wizard and the good fairy; it does not depend on these favours.[100] In the *Lugalbanda* stories, finally, Lugalbanda is saved from an ignominious death by the great luminaries after a series of prayers that are among the most moving lines of Sumerian poetry ever written.[101] His ultimate recovery, and his subsequent development into the only man who can save Enmerkar and Uruk, does *not* depend on divine help.[102] The case of Gilgameš is also instructive: he openly flouts the gods' decisions and regulations. The core message of the epic in its grandest formulation is that he reaches full humanity by accepting the only important difference between himself and the gods: mortality.[103] He is the ultimate humanist hero, in that "he who has seen and experienced everything" finally and proudly accepts the common fate of mankind. The lesson from the heroic tales, that are as much about human culture and human nature as about heroics in a military sense, is that real heroism consists in human endeavour: they do it themselves, sometimes even in spite of the gods.

---

94. See Vanstiphout, *Epics*, passim.
95. *Enmerkar and the Lord of Aratta*, ll. 319–21. Vanstiphout, *Epics*, pp. 74–75.
96. *Enmerkar and the Lord of Aratta*, l. 419. Vanstiphout, *Epics*, pp. 80–81.
97. Albeit in answer to Enmerkar's plea.
98. In these and other texts "sister" often stands for "lover."
99. *Enmerkar and the Lord of Aratta*, ll. 38–64 repeated as 80–104. Vanstiphout, *Epics*, pp. 58–63.
100. *Enmerkar and Ensuhgirana*, ll. 33–107 and 228–48. Vanstiphout, *Epics*, pp. 32–35 and 42–43.
101. *Lugalbanda in the Wilderness*, ll. 148–263. Vanstiphout, *Epics*, pp. 112–19.
102. For the finale of Lugalbanda's recovery and his elevation to a saviour-hero, see Vanstiphout, "Dream of Lugalbanda," and *idem*, "Sanctus Lugalbanda."
103. Reading Gilgameš always reminds me of some beautiful lines of the French poet Louis Aragon. In the darkest days of France under Nazi occupation he was near the point of suicide, saying, "Il n'aurait fallu qu'un moment de plus que la mort vienne." But then he suddenly was overwhelmed by "la réalité de l'immensité des choses humaines," upon which he became a member of the Communist Party.

Therefore one may well conclude that in the thinking of our intellectuals of four millennia ago the gods had but *little relevance for personal human destiny*—with the exception, perhaps, of the gods as symbols and representatives of mankind's own, human, urbane society. This may well be a telling point. The notion of sin does exist: sins and the confession of sins are mentioned in *Man and his God*. But the peculiar thing is that the "sinner" confesses to things he is not aware of. This is no wonder, for there are hardly any catalogues of sins. The reason may well be that "sin" as such was only defined and understood as a social misdemeanour or a crime. These matters are covered by civil and criminal law, not by theology.[104] As far as our documentation goes, there seems to be no difference between a socially defined crime, punishable by law, and a sin—or rather, the latter category does not seem to exist independently. Ethics, therefore, are a social category, and the gods were apparently not interested in thinking up lists of commandments and interdictions without social relevance, such as dietary rules, ethnic discriminations or sexual prohibitions. Upholding the social fabric, working within the rules of urban society, striving towards the greater welfare of the community, investing in intellectual endeavours, preserving and enhancing the literary heritage, developing critical faculties, puncturing empty pretensions, solving conflict by mediation or honest comparison—these are but a few of the ethical principles we find particularly in the typically intellectual e d u b a-literature.[105] And generally one does not need a "God-given" whimsical set of dos and don'ts in order to do that.

Conclusion

> Expedit esse deos, et ut expedit esse putemus
> (Ovid, *Ars Amatoria* 1.637)

It will probably be said that I have based my analysis on a relatively small corpus. In rebuttal I can propose three arguments. First, it is a real corpus, not a haphazard collection of texts accidentally gathered by the fortunes of modern discoveries, made legitimately or otherwise. The catalogues and the comparative analysis of distribution in terms of absolute numbers of tablets and of tablet types both argue in my favour. Second, taken as a whole, the corpus presents us with a relatively coherent group of texts—most of which respond to one or another of the questions I have raised. Third, most of the material, in the most material sense, comes from the two cities that were in about 1800 BCE and later, recogn-

---

104. One telling illustration: most popular commentaries on the stela of Hammurapi interpret the relief on top of the stela as depicting the god handing down the law code to the king. In fact, the god is merely handing down the symbols of civil power, which enable the king to enforce justice in his own capacity.

105. The point seems justified, because it was in these kinds of sub-literary products that they were talking about themselves.

ised as the centres *par excellence* of the literary heritage, and they were apparently still in working order. Therefore I submit that my case is a legitimate one. I do not pretend to speak for the *whole* of society, for *all* the scribal centres, or for *all* kinds of written material. But this is not my fault; nor is it the fault of gaps in our documentation; nor is it the fault of lack of scope in the material. It is the fault, if fault there is, of the ancient scribes themselves. The range, structure and articulation of the core corpus of higher literary production are what they have given us. Therefore I plead that it is legitimate to use this material in order to present an approach to the problem that the convenor of this conference set us. A subsidiary argument might be that the group of people responsible for creating these texts and for the way of thinking illustrated in them, may be reckoned to be among the best educated and articulate people of their times—which is not to say that they were the most powerful, or the most prestigious, or the most revered.

At this point the reader may well ask where Prometheus comes in, who are his creatures, and what he has to do with Babylonia anyway. Succinctly put, my answer is that the Old Babylonian school is Prometheus, and that his creatures are the gods as they appear in this literature. Prometheus, as we know, is himself of doubtful and hesitating divinity; he takes the part of mankind, which he, in some versions of the story, had created. But in my metaphor the creatures of this Babylonian Prometheus are the gods as seen in a new light. The ideology of the e d u b a is clear on the point that it creates, if not mankind, then at least humanity (n a m - l u - u l u). And in the same reading of the metaphor, I regard the e d u b a's re-interpretation of the gods as perhaps an intended and explicit effort to humanise the gods themselves.

Let me try to reconstruct the main lines of the process or evolution in thought as I think it happened. We do not as yet know as much as we would like to about the earlier stages of Sumerian writing. But what we know seems to present the following picture. In the beginning the gods were mainly deified forces or elements of nature: water, sky, grain, animals, earth....

Soon some of these deities, who may have different names while standing for the same natural force, were related to individual cities. By an ongoing process of interrelations and attempts at scaling up on the territorial and political level, at a certain point there arose a system whereby some of these deities, while remaining bound to their cities, took on national significance, presumably in the wake of the growing importance of their cities. Just one instance may be relevant: An, the sky-god, is also the city god of Uruk, and Uruk is one of the first, if not the very first, city of metropolitan size and ambition. Partly already during the early dynastic period, and certainly during the Akkad and Ur III periods, the state or even "Empire" took form over the whole territory, and the successor states to Ur III shared the ideology which was by then firmly ensconced.

Possibly, even probably, already in the Ur III period, and certainly by the early years of the Isin dynasty, these political and cultural evolutions were given a new expression in the works of school literature. Thus the *primitive period*, wherein the gods do their creative work, including sometimes the creation of mankind, was relegated to a few texts about Enlil and Enki ejaculating Sumer into prosperity, or to very short introductions to texts with a totally different purpose. But this was soon followed by the *period of organisation*: a group of texts now laid stress on the creation or invention of social institutions, such as marriage, trade, agriculture etc., leading up to Enki's masterpiece of organising the whole world (which means Sumer, and *vice versa*). Then come two new developments: stories about famous heroes of the past (though they are still closely related to the divine tribe) take over centre stage, and the gods begin to loose their exclusivity and mastery. The human heroes are no longer exclusively dependent upon the gods. But also the near identity of the city god and the virtual city is stressed more and more, so that the god becomes a mere symbol, or even a representative, of the city. Thus the *human aspect* becomes steadily more important in the gods themselves, and also on a more abstract plane. Theoretically inclined as they sometimes were, the scribes began to give more and more importance to the general principles, or quintessences, or MEs, than to the gods as divine persons. The *scribes* even invented a special genre for this: they began to compose debates between two almost quodlibetal phenomena in which each one is basically defending its own ME against the other. The god who is supposed to judge them cannot reach a decision on merit, so he awards victory to the most skilful debater. The scribes have won out: their craft in a dead language and an elitist diction is what these debates are really about. This thumbnail sketch is not to be read as a history of Sumerian literature: all these different stages are present at the same time, sometimes even in the same composition. The surmised "historicity" of sorts is in most cases itself an invention of the scribes.

It should not be overlooked that in many, if not most, of the pieces belonging to the great curriculum one can detect traces or even outright statements about the gods that are heavily ironic. Is this evidence of a kind of familiarity with the divine tribe, or is it an expression of a lurking scepticism? We do not know, but I would like to think that our scribes by and large agreed with Ovid: "It might come in handy if gods should happen to exist, so it is convenient that we believe they do exist."

"The Stars Their Likenesses"

Perspectives on the Relation Between Celestial Bodies and Gods in Ancient Mesopotamia

Francesca Rochberg
University of California, Berkeley

> There is a very ancient tradition in the form of a myth, that the stars are gods and that the divine embraces the whole of nature.
> (Aristotle *Metaphysics* XII.viii.19)[1]

One would like very much to know what ancient myth Aristotle had in mind in the epigraph quoted above that expressed the idea that the stars were gods. Whether the origins of the tradition to which Aristotle refers could be ancient Near Eastern is to some extent dependent upon our interpretations of the evidence to be presented below. To provide the reader some guidance to this discussion of the heavens and heavenly bodies and their relation to the gods of Sumer, Assyria and Babylonia, the following gives an outline of the aspects of the subject that will be treated here:

I. Historical and Historiographical Background
II. Interpretative Perspectives on the Mesopotamian Conception of Divinity in the Heavens

---

1. Cf. Cicero *De Natura Deorum* II.xxxvii 95, quoting from a lost dialogue of Aristotle, "De Philosophia": "If there were beings who had always lived beneath the earth, in comfortable, well-lit dwellings, decorated with statues and pictures and furnished with all the luxuries enjoyed by persons thought to be supremely happy, and who though they had never come forth above the ground had learnt by report and by hearsay of the existence of certain deities or divine powers; and then if at some time the jaws of the earth were opened and they were able to escape from their hidden abode and to come forth into the regions which we inhabit; when they suddenly had sight of the earth and the seas and the sky, and came to know of the vast clouds and mighty winds, and beheld the sun, and realized not only its size and beauty but also its potency in causing the day by shedding light over all the sky, and, after night had darkened the earth, they then saw the whole sky spangled and adorned with stars, and the changing phases of the moon's light, now waxing and now waning, and the risings and settings of all these heavenly bodies and their courses fixed and changeless throughout all eternity— when they saw these things, surely they would think that the gods exist and that these mighty marvels are their handiwork."

III. Perspective 1. Gods as Celestial Bodies: The Astral Nature of Mesopotamian Deities

IV.1. Perspective 2. Celestial Bodies as Gods: The Stars as Images and Manifestations of Gods

IV.2. Perspective 3. Celestial Bodies as Gods: Personifications of Stars as Gods

V. Contemplation of the Divine Heaven: The Unification of Perspectives

Before proceeding, some definition of terms may be helpful. In what follows, the term *deity* or *god* will represent a personalized being denoted by a personal name and written with the divine determinative. The determinative DINGIR, itself a word meaning "god," serves as a classifying mark for those beings so determined as "gods." In the present discussion, it has not been an objective to define the meaning of the word "god" (dingir/*ilu*) in Mesopotamian terms. Here it is simply taken that personal divine names, such as ᵈSin, or ᵈIštar, written with the divine determinative, are identifiable as gods, regardless of what that means in a theological sense. I assume that the definition or description of such gods requires the use of representation (symbol, emblem, transferred language). Therefore, if we say that Ištar is Venus, or Ištar is the Bow Star, or Ištar is love or warfare, we still have not said what Ištar "is," but only how she can be represented. More importantly, such representation does not afford us any idea about a Mesopotamian definition of "god."

The names of gods are to be distinguished from the designations of the heavenly bodies, which are also written with the divine determinative. In this case, the determinative indicates that these entities belong to the category "divine," hence are divine things by their association to particular deities. For example, the name of the moon-god ᵈSin represents the divine being known from god-lists such as An = *Anum,* a divine being whose relation to other deities is known from a divine genealogy and whose character is known from a mythology. As such, this god does not exist in the perceptible world, but is represented by a variety of things in the perceptible world, one of which is the moon. Because of its association with the god ᵈSin, the moon is designated by writings, such as the numeral 30 or the word "crescent" (*uškāru*), that can be written with the divine determinative, hence ᵈ30 or ᵈ*uškāru*, indicating that the moon is a kind of divine "thing." Although the distinction between the moon and the moon-god can be made in accordance with the use of determinatives, the fact that the moon is also sometimes denoted not only by means of the divine name itself, ᵈSin, but also by the word "god" (*ilu*), points to an ambiguity in the Mesopotamian understanding of the relation between moon and moon-god. This ambiguity permits both the reference to the moon as the moon-god and as the divine visible lunar object. Parallels are evident with respect to other deified celestial objects and their associated divinities.

I. Historical and Historiographical Background

The idea of the starry sky as the abode of gods is in evidence across a wide geographical as well as chronological span of ancient Near Eastern and Mediterranean history, from third millennium Sumerian mythology and the first Akkadian celestial omens of the second millennium to the "astralized" iconography of deities in first millennium Syro-Palestine,[2] the "visible gods" of Plato[3] and the divine powers of the heavenly bodies in the Greek and Greco-Egyptian magical papyri of the late Hellenistic period.[4] "This fundamental aspect of ancient religion," as the editors of *Prayer, Magic, and the Stars in the Ancient and Late Antique World* (2003) point out, "has only recently begun to receive the attention it deserves, particularly in the fields of Classical Studies and Late Antiquity. There has been more recognition of the prominence of the stars in Mesopotamian religion, where the first cuneiform sign used to designate the word 'god' appears in the image of a star."[5] The association of god and star seems to be as old as writing itself. The pictogram of a (usually) 8-pointed star, later to denote in the cuneiform script the words dingir/*ilu* 'god' and an/*šamê* 'sky' as well as the sky god An/*Anu*, is already attested as the divine determinative in archaic Sumerian script (Uruk IVa period).[6] The pictographic writing for the word "star" (mul) in turn was made up of three AN-signs in a visual analog to a constellation. The MUL-sign, also attested in archaic script, not only depicts a cluster of stars, but also very likely conveys the idea that the stars were already conceived of as divine.

---

2. See Othmar Keel and Christoph Uehlinger, *Gods, Goddesses, and Images of God in Ancient Israel*, trans. Thomas H. Trapp (Minneapolis: Fortress Press,1998 [first publ. as *Göttinnen, Götter und Gottessymbole*, Fribourg: Herder Verlag, 1992]), chapter 8.

3. "But, it is, of course, the stars and the bodies we can perceive existing along with them that must be named first as *visible gods*, and the greatest, most worshipful, and clearsighted of them all." *Epinomis* 984 d (the emphasis here is mine). See A. E. Taylor, in E. Hamilton and H. Cairns, eds., *The Collected Dialogues*, Bollingen Series 71 (Princeton: Princeton University Press, 1961, 1989), p. 1526.

4. Many facets of the subject of the religious importance of the heavens in Greek, Greco-Roman and Christian thought are discussed in Alan Scott, *Origen and the Life of the Stars: A History of an Idea* (Oxford: Clarendon, 2001).

5. S. Noegel, J. Walker and B. Wheeler, eds., *Prayer, Magic and the Stars in the Ancient and Late Antique World* (University Park, Pennsylvania: Pennsylvania State University Press, 2003), p. 13. Jean Bottéro, *Religion in Ancient Mesopotamia*, trans. Teresa Lavender Fagan (Chicago: University of Chicago Press, 2001), p. 58, notes that the etymology of the word "god" (dingir/*ilu*) is unknown, although he takes the orthographic representation of the word as a star to indicate the superior, exalted, or transcendent nature of the gods, in keeping with his view that "the transcendence of the divine over the human is one of the fundamental truths of Mesopotamian religious thought" (p. 61).

6. See R. Labat, *Manuel d'épigraphie Akkadienne* (Paris: Geuthner, 1976, 5th ed.), no. 13, and Gebhard J. Selz, "'The Holy Drum, the Spear, and the Harp': Towards an Understanding of the Problems of Deification in Third Millennium Mesopotamia," in Finkel and Geller, *Sumerian Gods*, p. 169, 2.2.1 [8].

The widespread, if not ubiquitous, general association of the divine with heaven in the ancient Near Eastern and Mediterranean cultural arena took various forms in different places and over time. To illustrate the diversity in expressions of this idea, there is the statement of Cicero (first century B.C.E.) that

> contemplating the heavenly bodies the mind arrives at a knowledge of the gods, from which arises piety, with its comrades justice and the rest of the virtues, the sources of a life of happiness that vies with and resembles the divine existence and leaves us inferior to the celestial beings in nothing else save immortality, which is immaterial for happiness.[7]

This idea has Platonic roots, as Plato (or some member of the Academy) in *Epinomis* finds the source of wisdom, "the chiefest constituent of full virtue,"[8] in the heavens (*Ouranos*), the contemplation of which confers "number" upon man's rational faculty and from that, virtue in his soul. Why the contemplation of the heavenly bodies was thought to confer the virtues of piety and happiness is much later explained by Ptolemy (second century C.E.) in the introductory section of the *Almagest*, in which he places the celestial bodies with the eternal and unchanging, hence divine, part of the universe, and so,

> from the constancy, order, symmetry and calm which are associated with the divine, it makes its followers lovers of this divine beauty, accustoming them and reforming their natures, as it were, to a similar spiritual state.[9]

The Aristotelianism that underpins this variation on the theme of the heavens as divine stands in stark contrast to Mesopotamian belief, which while conceiving of a dualism in heaven and earth, did not correlate that separation with notions of eternity and change, perfection and corruption. One cannot pinpoint the origin of the particular Greek response to the heavenly bodies and the derived divine meaning of the geometry of the sphere in any similar expression in Mesopotamian religious or intellectual culture. Indeed, apart from the basic idea of the divine heaven, there is little else that relates Cicero's or Ptolemy's conception to the evidence from Mesopotamia, because a basic world-view was not shared. Such passages make clear that the notion of the divine, the placement of the divine in heaven, and what constitutes contemplation of that divine heaven are culture-specific, and that those ideas attested to in ancient Mesopotamia must be understood first within their own context before bringing them into a larger cultural or historical framework.

---

7. Cicero *De Natura Deorum* II lxi 153, trans. H. Rackham, Loeb Classical Library (Harvard University Press, 1933), p. 271.

8. Plato *Epinomis* 977d, trans. A. E. Taylor, in E. Hamilton and H. Cairns, eds., *The Collected Dialogues*, Bollingen Series 71 (Princeton: Princeton University Press, 1961, 1989), p. 1520.

9. Ptolemy Alm. I.1, G. J. Toomer, ed., *Ptolemy's Almagest* (New York, Berlin, Heidelberg and Tokyo: Springer Verlag, 1984), p. 37.

To be sure, the conception of gods as heavenly agents, which originated in ancient Mesopotamia, had a powerful legacy, but some early twentieth century attempts to trace this idea have become intellectual detritus. As a result, what was already a difficult interpretative problem with respect to textual evidence for gods as stars and stars as gods, became unduly fraught with tension from the fact that the whole matter of astral religion in ancient Mesopotamia was tainted by the legacy of the small but once influential group of Orientalists and Assyriologists known as the "Panbabylonists." This group, among them H. Winckler, A. Jeremias, P. Jensen, and E. F. Weidner, following an idea first promulgated by the comparative mythographer Eduard Stucken,[10] claimed that the source of a tendency to personify and allegorize the movements of heavenly bodies as mythic projections of the activities of deities was to be found in ancient Mesopotamia, from whence the phenomenon diffused throughout the ancient world as astral mythology and astral religion.[11] Effective for a short time during the early twentieth century as part of the newly erected bridge from the study of the Bible as the origins of Western religious thought to its even older Near Eastern context, astral mythology worked to reposition ancient Mesopotamia as the fount of civilization. Alfred Jeremias, for example, would "explain" details of the Biblical text in terms of Babylonian prototypes and these, wherever he could, in terms of astral configurations and mythological representations of such configurations derived from Stucken's *Astralmythen*.[12] Where the Panbabylonists misconceived the whole subject of the divinity of the heavens was in the way they coopted astronomy to explain myth, particularly by asserting the importance of the zodiac and the precession of the equinoxes in the third millennium B.C.E., although neither concept existed at that time.[13] Of course, that thesis proved to be speculative nonsense, as F. X. Kugler so perspicaciously showed.[14]

---

10. Within the field of the history of religion, no less a figure than J. Z. Smith noted that despite the Panbabylonists' being factually wrong in their textual interpretations and theoretically wrong about the nature of cultural diffusion, "they saw clearly the need to ground comparison and patterns in a historical process . . . saw clearly the power of pattern (and hence, of comparison) as a device for interpretation." See Jonathan Z. Smith, "In Comparison a Magic Dwells," in Kimberley C. Patton and Benjamin C. Ray, eds., *A Magic Still Dwells: Comparative Religion in the Postmodern Age* (Berkeley, Los Angeles, and London: University of California Press, 2000), pp. 33–34.

11. H. Zimmern could be counted among the Panbabylonists, but his work did not engage so much with astronomy as with the diffusion of the "Christusmyth" from Babylonia, as in his *Zum Streit um die Christusmythe: Das babylonische Material in seinem Hauptpunkten dargestellt* (Berlin: Reuther & Reichard, 1910).

12. A. Jeremias, *The Old Testament in the Light of the Ancient East* (London: Williams and Norgate and New York: G. P. Putnam's Sons, 1911).

13. Although textual evidence for the zodiac occurs by the early fifth century B.C.E., precession was never recognized in the Babylonian astronomical tradition. See O. Neugebauer, "The Alleged Babylonian Discovery of the Precession of the Equinoxes," *JAOS* 70 (1950), pp. 1–8.

14. See F. X. Kugler, *Im Bannkreis Babels: Panbabylonistische Konstruktionen und Religionsgeschichtliche Tatsachen* (Münster: Aschendorff, 1910) and *idem*, "Auf den Trümmern des Panbabylonismus," *Anthropos* 4 (1909), pp. 477–99.

Subsequently, the subject of Mesopotamian astral religion, or of any astral interpretation of mythological elements, became somewhat untouchable, as illustrated by B. Alster's comment in 1976 that "earlier generations of Assyriologists viewed Gilgameš as the hero of the sun. If one took this seriously today, one would run the risk of making a fool of oneself."[15] On the basis of his interest in the astral elements of Sumerian religion, Alster stationed himself rather defensively apart from Thorkild Jacobsen. Alster's ideas concerning astral religious subjects consequently were not met with any real dialogue, much less acceptance. The reluctance to treat this subject continued up to the appearance of Erica Reiner's 1995 study of astral magic, which offers a new first step into astral aspects of Mesopotamian religion. Ironically, the connections assumed by Panbabylonists between Mesopotamian thinking about the stars and the gods and that of subsequent ancient Mediterranean cultures may well have some merit, but on grounds different from those that supported the Panbabylonist program, and probably not much beyond the basic location of the divine in heaven. At any rate, such cultural connections remain to be studied and defined. The present paper does not comment on or respond to any particular part of the historiography of ancient Mesopotamian astral religion, but concerns only the most basic elements of the subject of divinity in the heavens, that is, how gods were stars, and conversely, how stars were gods.

II. Interpretative Perspectives on the Mesopotamian Conception of Divinity in the Heavens

Evidence for ancient Mesopotamian ideas of divinity in the heavens can be organized in accordance with a number of perspectives on the subject reflected in different types of texts. The evidence presented in the following discussion is selective. Many more examples could be cited from available texts, but an exhaustive survey has not been an objective here. Instead I shall focus on three perspectives on divinity in the heavens, a classification which I believe would not be changed by the addition of further examples. First, evident primarily in mythological texts is the perspective in which the gods are seen as celestial bodies. In this first perspective, which focuses on the astral nature of some deities, e.g., Inana as the planet Venus or Nanna/Suen as the moon, the divine is understood to be visibly embodied by a planet (or star). This first perspective necessarily takes the deity as its principal referent. In the second perspective celestial bodies are viewed as images of gods, i.e., as worldly objects that manifest divine agency and give perceptible form to certain deities. The primary referent in this case is the celestial object. Omen texts and other astronomical treatments of stars, constella-

---

15. B. Alster, "Early Patterns in Mesopotamian Literature," in B. Eichler, ed., *Kramer Anniversary Volume*, AOAT 25 (Neukirchen-Vluyn: Butzon & Bercker Kevelaer, 1976), p. 16, note 11.

tions, and planets provide the major sources for this perspective. In the third perspective the focus is on the divine nature of some of the heavenly bodies, e.g., on the sun as the sun-god, the moon as the moon-god, on Venus as Ištar, and on many other stars identified with other deities. This could be said to amount to the same idea as that of the first "perspective," i.e., the idea of divine embodiment, and ultimately it is. For discussion's sake, however, it is important to recognize that there is a difference in the way the idea is articulated in context, with the principal referent being the celestial body, not the god. This perspective is adopted primarily in the genre of prayer, although examples may be found in omen texts as well. The key element in passages that take this third perspective is personification, in this case meaning that a celestial body is personified and so referred to as a god in an anthropomorphic way. The three perspectives, then, can be defined and differentiated in terms of whether a given passage speaks of 1) a god, 2) a star or other celestial body, or 3) a personified star or other celestial body.

The "perspectives" defined in this way can be separated in terms of their expression in different literary contexts. But variations in manner of speaking may point to real differences in the conception of divinity in heaven. Regardless of whether a single conception is merely refracted in different contexts or whether theological differences can legitimately be constructed, my purpose in separating these "perspectives" is to aid in the discussion of the variety of texts that speak of divinity in the heavens in each of these ways.

A number of genres of texts are used here as sources for investigating the question of the placement of the divine in heaven in Mesopotamian religion. Mythology is one such genre, but here I regard the genre of "astral myth" as a modern misnomer, although no doubt some elements in a number of myths may have astral referents, as W. Heimpel has argued, for example, of a particular passage in *Inana's Descent*.[16] On the whole, however, the stories concerning deities in Sumerian and Akkadian mythology cannot be read as, or reduced to, explanations of astronomical phenomena; because such mythological stories do not attempt to explain phenomena, there is no confusion between inanimate phenomena of nature and personalized divinity.[17] The idea that such stories could be read in that way,

---

16. Wolfgang Heimpel, "A Catalog of Near Eastern Venus Deities," *Syro-Mesopotamian Studies* 4 (1982), pp. 9–22. Cf. the reading of the text in terms of the temple statue in A. George, "Inanna's Descent to the Netherworld," *JCS* 37 (1985), pp. 109–113, and G. Buccellati, "The Descent of Inanna as a Ritual Journey to Kutha?" *Syro-Mesopotamian Studies* 4/3 (1982), pp. 53–57.

17. I do not see the logic of J. Z. Smith's claim that myth commits "a self-conscious category mistake. That is to say that the discrepancy of myth is not an error but the very source of its power." See "Good News is No News: Aretology and Gospel," in his *Map is Not Territory: Studies in the History of Religions* (Leiden: Brill, 1978), p. 206. Unless it can be shown that mythic stories of gods are attempts to explain physical phenomena, either deliberately or for lack of another way to do it, there are no grounds for the charge of having committed either an unconscious or self-conscious category mistake.

however, underlay not only the *Astralmythen* of Eduard Stucken and Ernst Siecke, but also in large part Sir James Frazer's *The Golden Bough*, in which the intellectualist analysis of myth presupposed that ancient (or "primitive") myth represented the only means of explaining nature available to people not cognitively equipped to deal with their questions about the physical world by other means, especially not rational, "scientific" ones. The symbology of myth of course can encode and put into a narrative frame sequences of events in nature, and such myths share a mode of discourse with other religious texts whose referents are celestial bodies considered as gods. The motivating question of this paper is not how the motions and appearances of the heavenly bodies were understood mechanically by ancient Mesopotamian scribes and scholars and where this fails in the form of myth, but rather where, in the many expressions of interest in and understanding of celestial phenomena, the heavenly bodies were associated with or personified as gods. The other relevant genres utilized here are rituals, incantations, cultic commentaries, texts concerning celestial divination (omens as well as letters or reports) and other, non-divinatory astronomical works, such as the compilation MUL.APIN and the later astronomical Diaries. For purposes of presentation, these text genres will help to separate the three perspectives just defined, as the "religious" or mythological works refer primarily to gods, while the "scientific," i.e., astrological/astronomical, works refer primarily to stars, constellations and planets (although such distinctions are not hard and fast). As already noted, the three perspectives will each be treated separately for the purpose of discussion, but the legitimacy of their status as representing separate views will be addressed in the concluding section.

III. Perspective 1. Gods as Celestial Bodies: The Astral Nature of Mesopotamian Deities

The first perspective on the nature and relation of the gods to the heavenly bodies focuses on the astral nature of some of the Mesopotamian gods, and is evident in narrative contexts such as myths and also in hymns or prayers to gods. J. J. van Dijk noted[18] that as a result of the dualism of the Sumerian world-view, i.e., the separation between above and below, the same deity sometimes had both a chthonic and an astral manifestation, e.g., ᵈama-ušumgal '(divine) sovereign mother' and ᵈama-ušumgal-an-na '(divine) sovereign mother of heaven,' or ᵈgeštin '(divine) vine' and ᵈgeštin-an-na '(divine) vine of heaven.' Perhaps this dualistic practice underlies historically and conceptually the astral locus of the divine, giving rise as well to the idea of celestial bodies being physical manifestations of deities. The idea seems implicit in the practice of naming (mainly astral) gods DN 'of heaven' (*ša šamê*), attested from the Old to Neo-Babylonian

---

18. J. J. van Dijk, "Gott" in RLA 3 (1969), p. 536.

periods, as in the deities Šamaš-of-Heaven, Adad-of-Heaven, Sin-of-Heaven, and even Anu-of-Heaven.[19]

An aspect of the conception of the divine that is significant for understanding the relation between deity and star is the idea of awesome divine radiance, expressed in both Sumerian and Akkadian religious discourse by the term me.lám/ *melammu* (or perhaps mé-lim₅/*melimmu*[20]). In Sumerian liturgy, for example, the radiance of the goddess Inana is a principal element of her description as the planet Venus:

> I shall greet the great lady of heaven, Inana! I shall greet the holy torch who fills the heavens, the light, Inana, her who shines like daylight, the great lady of heaven, Inana! . . . the respected one who fills heaven and earth with her huge brilliance.[21]

In the composition *Lugalbanda in the Mountain Cave*, the moon-god Suen is referred to as "the astral holy bull-calf" who "shines in the heavens like the morning star" and "spreads bright light in the night."[22] Radiant light continues to be a basic characteristic of the divine in later Babylonian mythology, e.g., in *Enūma Eliš* VI 156, Marduk's ninth name is *Namru* 'Bright One,' "the shining god who illumines our ways," and in Tablet VII 126, his forty-ninth name is *Nēbiru* 'Ford', "the star which in the skies is brilliant." The synonymy of astral luminosity and divine radiance is perhaps most obviously evident in the case of the sun-god Šamaš/the sun in the statement, "you, Šamaš, have covered the heavens and all the countries with your radiance (*melammu*)."[23] So too was his wife Aya the personification of the morning light, or goddess of the dawn, as shown by her Sumerian name ᵈŠE₃.NIR.DA = ᵈ·ˢᵉ šer₇-da = *šērtu* 'dawn.'[24] The name of the temple of the sun-god Utu/Šamaš, é-babbar 'Shining (white, light) House,' further reflects the

---

19. See P. A. Beaulieu, *The Pantheon of Uruk During the Neo-Babylonian Period*, Cuneiform Monographs 23 (Leiden and Boston: Brill and Styx, 2003), p. 346. [Ed.: The conventional notation DN stands for the name of any god.]

20. See Dietz Otto Edzard, "The Names of the Sumerian Temples," in Finkel and Geller, *Sumerian Gods*, p. 162, note 15. See also A. L. Oppenheim, "Akkadian *pul(u)ḫ(t)u* and *melammu*," *JAOS* 63 (1943), pp. 31–34.

21. From *Iddin Dagan A* as given in J. A. Black, G. Cunningham, J. Ebeling, E. Fluckiger-Hawker, E. Robson, J. Taylor, and G. Zólyomi, *The Electronic Text Corpus of Sumerian Literature* (hereafter ETCSL) (Oxford, 1998–), t.2.5.3.1:1–16. Cf. "(Ištar) brilliant torch of heaven and earth, radiance of the whole inhabited world" in L. W. King, *Enuma Elish: The Seven Tablets of Creation* (London: Luzac, 1902), vol. 2, pl. 78:35.

22. ETCSL t.1.8.2.1:202–204.

23. Stephen H. Langdon, *Babylonian Penitential Psalms*, Oxford Editions of Cuneiform Texts 6 (Paris: P. Geuthner, 1927), p. 52:9 f., cited in CAD s.v. *melammu*, lexical section.

24. See Marvin A. Powell, "Aia = Eos," in H. Behrens, D. Loding, and M. T. Roth, eds., *DUMU-E₂-DUB-BA-A: Studies in Honor of Åke W. Sjöberg*, Occasional Publications of the Samuel Noah Kramer Fund 11 (Philadelphia: University Museum, 1989), pp. 447–48.

idea of that god's great brilliance. And even though such descriptions as 'huge' (maḫ), 'bright' (kù) and 'awesome' (nί) are common in Sumerian temple names, in this case the temple certainly seems to be named for the principal feature of its patron god.

The brilliance and luminosity of a celestial body was seen as emblematic of its divine quality, and as a physical phenomenon such luminosity made the divine manifest in the world. Whether the idea of the gods' radiance originally stemmed from an astral association with individual deities, or was extended to such associations as a secondary effect of the notion of divine splendor, is probably not answerable. In the case of Inana, the astral aspect of the goddess seems to be original, and has been traced to Uruk IV by K. Szarzyńska in her study of Archaic Period cult offerings to two of the forms of the goddess, called Inana-húd (UD) 'Inana of the morning' and Inana-sig 'Inana of the evening.'[25] The divine name Inana itself, 'Lady of Heaven,' is furthermore etymologically suggestive of an astral deity,[26] and the name of her temple é-an-na 'House of Heaven'[27] evokes the same idea.

While radiance ranked as a principal attribute of the divine, the form given the deities in visual and mythological representation expressed an anthropomorphic image of the gods who populate Sumero-Akkadian mythology, but who were obviously not in that form visible in nature. The gods, being conceived of and imagined, not observed, may be differentiated from natural (perceptual) phenomena, yet the gods seem to have been viewed as immanent and active in the world of phenomena, as many instances of divine agency are preserved in Sumero-Akkadian mythology. For example, as forces over the basic parts of the physical world, the three great gods Anu, Enlil, and Ea were said to "inhabit" specific regions of the cosmos in their myths. Thus, in the myth of *Atra-ḫasīs*, the divine trinity cast lots, divided the universe, and came to be identified with heaven, earth, and the subterranean waters of Apsû, respectively.[28] Through this narrative account, the character of the principal Sumerian deities, An, Enlil, and Enki, is shown as that of forces within or over various parts of the world, such as the sky, the winds, the

---

25. K. Szarzyńska, "Offerings for the Goddess Inana in Archaic Uruk," *RA* 87 (1993), pp. 7–27. See also Beaulieu, *Pantheon*, pp. 103–4.

26. See G. Selz, "Thoughts on Inana(k), Ištar, In(n)in(a), Annunītum, and Anat, and the Origin of the Title 'Queen of Heaven'," *NIN: Journal of Gender Studies* 1 (2000), p. 30.

27. Edzard, "The Names of the Sumerian Temples," p. 162, has explained the relation of the temple name é-an-na to Inana as parallel to that of the temple name é-maḫ for Nin-maḫ. Thus the temple of 'Lady of Heaven' (*Nin-an-ak) was 'House of Heaven.'

28. W. G. Lambert and A. R. Millard, *Atra-Hasīs: The Babylonian Story of the Flood* (Oxford: Clarendon,1969), p. 43, Tablet I:7–16. Note that *Enūma Eliš* IV 141–146 contains a variant account of the regions of the great trinity: Anu in Heaven (Ašrata), Enlil in Ešarra (= Lower Heaven), and Ea in Ešgalla (= Apsû), and cf. *Enūma Eliš* V 119–122. The image of heavenly levels is further elaborated upon in AO 8196 iv 20–22 and KAR 307 obv. 30–38, discussed in W. Horowitz, *Mesopotamian Cosmic Geography* (Mesopotamian Civlizations 8; Winona Lake, Indiana: Eisenbrauns, 1998), pp. 3–4.

foothills and the sweet waters.[29] Celestial gods, such as Nanna, Utu, and Inana, similarly are made manifest in the luminaries and as the personalized powers in those natural phenomena.

Any discussion of the gods as celestial bodies must give due prominence to Nanna/Suen/Sin, the moon-god.[30] Two principal aspects of the moon-god emerge already in the hymns to Nanna ascribed to Enheduana:[31] his aspect first as the patron of the cattle herds and of dairy products,[32] and second, as the luminary Suen "who comes out from the bright (or "blue") sky" to "brighten the land"[33] and is called "ruler, fit for the clear sky." Another descriptive name, ^{d}giš-nu$_{11}$-gal 'alabaster,' suggests the lustrous white appearance of the lunar disk.[34] From this name was derived the name of the temples of Nanna-Suen at Ur, Babylon, and Bīt-Suenna (more often occurring, however, in the form é-kiš-nu-gál).[35]

The horns of the moon-god, found especially in descriptions of the appearance of the lunar crescent, refer at once to the celestial and pastoral aspects of the god. Hence the references to Nanna/Suen as a calf or bull can be understood as referring to both as well, as alluded to in the epithet of the hero "who like Sin creates the horns."[36] The conceptualization of the moon-god himself as a bull is exemplified in the incantation known as *The Cow of Sin, Called Geme-Sin*. There, the god as a wild bull loves and impregnates the cow Geme-Sin and facilitates her giving birth.[37] The association of the moon-god with cattle appears as well in the earliest iconography of the moon-god. D. Collon makes mention of a Late Uruk

---

29. T. Jacobsen, *The Treasures of Darkness: A History of Mesopotamian Religion* (New Haven and London: Yale University Press, 1976), p. 121.

30. The amalgamation of Nanna and Suen was complete by the late Akkadian period, according to Colbow, "More Insights into Representation of the Moon God," p. 21 note 11, and Å Sjöberg, *Der Mondgott Nanna-Su'en in der sumerischen Uberlieferung I Teil: Texte* (Uppsala: Almqvist & Wiksell,1960), pp. 10f.

31. Å.W. Sjöberg and E. Bergmann, *The Collection of the Sumerian Temple Hymns*, Texts from Cuneiform Sources 3 (Locust Valley, N.Y.: J. J. Augustin, 1969), Hymn no. 8: hymn to Ekišnugal and no. 37: hymn to é-ú-ru-um.

32. Suen could be represented by a calf, as in the dedication of the temple of Enlil in Nippur in N1542 obv. 3, "Carnelian calf, charmingly embelllished," M. G. Hall, "A Study of the Sumerian Moon-God, Nanna/Suen" (University of Pennsylvania Dissertation, 1985), pp. 848 and 850.

33. Sjöberg and Bergmann, *Sumerian Temple Hymns,* p. 45, Hymn no. 37, line 475 (an(!)-za-gìn-ta) and line 476 (kalam-e zalag-zalag-ge).

34. Hall, *Moon-God*, p. 510, from Hymn to Nanna, George A. Barton, *Miscellaneous Babylonian Inscriptions, Part I: Sumerian Religious Texts* [New Haven: Yale U. Press, 1918) 12, CBS 2225, col. I 12', and Hall's chapter 6 section III 13.1.1 and 1.3 on the name Suen and distinctions between the moon-gods of Nippur and Ur. For ^{d}giš-nu$_{11}$-gal, see RLA 3, p. 403 s.v. Gišnugal.

35. See A. R. George, *House Most High: The Temples of Ancient Mesopotamia* (Winona Lake, IN: Eisenbrauns, 1993), Gazeteer No. 653, 654, and 656, p. 114.

36. J. J. van Dijk, *Lugal ud me-lam-bi Nir-gal: Le récit épique et didactique des travaux de Ninurta* (Leiden: Brill, 1983), p. 70, line 143.

37. N. Veldhuis, *A Cow of Sîn* (Groningen: Styx Publications, 1991).

period seal from Choga Mish showing a god seated on a horned bull (throne) and a small figure beside him holding up the crescent standard, all arranged inside another (later-attested) emblem of the moon-god, the barge.[38] Another iconographic reference to the astral and pastoral aspects of Nanna/Suen/Sin is evident in Old Babylonian seals that show the moon-god standing atop criss-crossed bulls holding the crescent standard, or the variant which shows a seated god with his feet on a recumbent bull as he holds a crescent standard, as well as other iconographic associations of the crescent with the bull.[39]

The celestial manifestation of this deity is indicated by a passage in the *Lugalbanda Epic* (lines 199–209) which speaks of his resplendence and luminosity being "an ornament in the zenith" (line 207),[40] and of a crescent that gives direction to the rising sun (line 204), meaning presumably that on the day of last visibility, the crescent moon rises just before sunrise.[41] Here the power of the moon-god over his son Utu is conveyed. His great power as ruler and arbiter of good and evil is praised in this same poem (lines 213–225), and he is portrayed as an unapproachable king in remote heaven: "King/Suen, you whom no one can approach in the remote heaven."[42] Indeed, his vast power is expressed in similes such as "remote as the heavens, wide as the earth."[43] References to the variable appearance of the moon in its phases are found in hymnic poetry, e.g., from a tigi (song played on the harp) of Inana: "An gives birth to him for you each month on New-moon day like Suen."[44] This part of the moon-god's nature is also seen in Akkadian epithets, such as *Sin eddešû* 'perpetually renewing Sin'[45] or *inbu* 'fruit,' and is reflected also in the title of the hemerological series *Inbu bēl arḫim* 'Fruit (i.e., Sin), Lord of the Month.'[46] Such descriptions, although serving the

---

38. D. Collon, "Moon, Boats and Battle," in Finkel and Geller, *Sumerian Gods*, p. 12 and figure 7.
39. See Gudrun Colbow, "More Insights into Representation of the Moon God," in Finkel and Geller, *Sumerian Gods*, p. 25.
40. Cf. from *Enmerkar and the Lord of Aratta*, line 271: Nanna is "aloft in the zenith." See Hall, *Moon-God*, p. 534.
41. Line 204: a-a ^{d}nanna ^{d}utu-è-ra si-sá mu-na-an-sum "father Nanna gave direction to the rising sun." Hall, *Moon-God*, p. 530 and 705 translates 'new moon' (u_4-sakar), but as a new moon, the moon would set after the sun. The question is the meaning of si-sá and how the moon could give direction to the rising if at new moon the moon rises just after sunrise (and sets after sunset).
42. Hall, *Moon-God*, p. 530.
43. Sjöberg, *Mondgott*, p. 80, Text 7:1, and commentary pp. 83–4. Cf. the description of Ningirsu in Gudea Cylinder A v 13, cited above, note 21.
44. Hall, *Moon-God*, p. 516, C. J. Gadd, *Cuneiform Texts from Babylonian Tablets in the British Museum*, 36 (London: British Museum, 1921), (hereafter CT 36) T 36 pl. 33–34, BM 96739 rev. 25 (= 30).
45. [45] L. W. King, *Babylonian Magic and Sorcery* (London: Luzac, 1896), No. 1:2 (henceforth BMS), translated in B. R. Foster, *Before the Muses: An Anthology of Akkadian Literature*, 2 vols. (Bethesda, MD: CDL Press, 1993), p. 682.
46. See CAD s.v. *inbu*, meaning 1d. The explanatory work i.NAM.giš.ḫur.an.ki.a takes up the question of Sin-*inbu*. The fragmentary first line of K 2670 reads: DIŠ gurun ^{d}30 *áš-šu* [. . .] " 'Fruit'

purpose of glorifying the (moon)-god in religious literary contexts, also can be seen descriptively as more or less direct depictions of the moon, i.e., as being bright, distant, large, and changing shape with its phases.

Embedded in the origins of the Mesopotamian cultic calendar, as reflected in the semi-annual á-ki-ti festival celebrated at Ur from Pre-Sargonic times, is the astral nature of Nanna, patron deity of Ur. The ritual was synchronized with the equinoxes, calendric turning-points of the luni-solar year occurring during the first and seventh months of the Ur calendar year. M. Cohen's exegesis of the original astral religious nature of the festival in terms of the change in the length of daylight and night as affected by the equinoxes through the year and the related visibility of the sun and moon is not convincing, but he is no doubt correct in his analysis of the festival as "the arrival of Nanna into his city . . . an arrival which was reenacted by a triumphal entry of the statue of Nanna back into Ur from the á-ki-ti building."[47]

The moon-god's astral character dominates his portrayals in Akkadian hymns and prayers. Because the moon as a sign made known the "decisions" of the god

---

is Sin because [. . .]," for which see A. Livingstone, *Mystical and Mythological Explanatory Works of Assyrian and Babylonian Scholars* (Oxford: Clarendon Press, 1986), pp. 28 and 45. Text K 170+ line 1 is a bit more complete: [DIŠ gurun ᵈ3]0 mu ᵈa-nù im-bu-ú šum-š[u "Fruit is Sin because Anu called his name." See also in the same text, line 9: in the table of names of Sin, the verb *nabû* appears after the break, followed by *bēl purussê arhi* "lord of the decisions of the month," so presumably the text reads *inbu Sin Anu imbu* "fruit (is) what Anu called/named Sin." The best passage is K 2164+, obv. 13 (Livingstone, *Mystical*, p. 21): 30 [a.rá 30] 15 15 a.rá 4 60 60 ᵈa-nù im-bi gurun "0;30 [x 0;30] = 0;15 0;15 x 4 = 1 1 (is) Anu. He (Anu) called/named the fruit." This line is itself an explanation for the seventh day of the month, which is "a half of a half," i.e., a month is 30 days, half of which is 15, and half of that is taken to be 7. Of course the scribes had fun with "half" being written bà (i.e., 30), so "half (bà) of Sin (30) is half of a half (of sixty)." Also, 30 = Sin is half of 60 = Anu, which is why in the commentary the scribe multiplied 15 by 4 to get 60 (= 1), or Anu. Livingstone, *Mystical*, p. 45, says that the name "fruit" is the name of Sin which applies to him as the new moon, or first crescent. The phonic similarity of *inbu* and *imbu* (> *nabû* 'to name') are taken to signify the idea that Anu named Sin, therefore Sin is 'named,' i.e., *inbu*, otherwise 'fruit.'

The idea behind the association between moon and fruit has to do with the notion of cyclical renewal from oneself, i.e., the fruit is brought forth from the fruit, or the seed of the fruit, but nonetheless, the fruit is the engendering self. This is the idea expressed in the hymn to Sin (IVR 9:22f.; see Langdon, *Babylonian Penitential Psalms,* pp. 6–11): *enbu ša ina ramānišu ibbanû . . . ša ana naplusi asmu lalāšu la eššebū* "fruit, which is brought forth of its own self . . . , pleasing to look upon, whose beautiful appearance cannot be restrained." That the term "fruit" should be more specifically tied to the first crescent moon perhaps best conveys the notion of renewal, as the first visibility is the same as day 1 of the month and so by definition is indeed the renewed moon/month.

47. M. E. Cohen, *The Cultic Calendars of the Ancient Near East* (Bethesda, MD: CDL Press, 1993), p. 402. Cohen's argument about the significance of the equinoxes as dividing the year into two segments where "between the seventh and the first month the moon was visible longer in the skies" (pp. 401–2) is unclear. On one hand, the nights do not become progressively longer from month VII to I, but rather from month IV to XII, i.e., between the solstices. On the other, lunar visibility varies throughout each month, increasing until the day of opposition, when the lunar disk is visible all night long, and then decreasing until conjunction, when it is not visible at all.

Sin, the god as the moon was called upon in prayer and incantation to help make a haruspicy propitious. One such prayer opens with an invocation to Sin, the god, in his guise as the celestial body the moon:

> O Sin, shining, radiant god, luminary of [heaven], firstborn son of Enlil,
> [foremost one] of Ekur, You reign as king of the uni[verse], you s[et] your throne [in] the
> [shining] heavens,
> You set out a superb linen, you [don] the resplendent tiara of lordship whose waxing never fails! [lines 1–3]

The description of the god becomes a description of the moon as the prayer continues:

> O luminary Sin [. . .] . . . . At sight of Sin, the stars are jubilant, the night rejoices.
> Sin takes his place in the center of the shi[ning] heaven. [lines 7–9][48]

Equally clear is a prayer to Sin in his astral manifestation accompanying an offering made on the 30th day to bring absolution and favor and propitious days to the supplicant:

> O Sin, luminous and splendid one, foremost of the gods,
> O perpetually renewing Sin, illuminator of darkness . . . .
> Your day of disappearance is your day of splendor, a secret of the great gods.
> The thirtieth day is your festival, day of your divinity's splendor.
> O Brightly Rising God, strength without rival . . . .
> I make for you a pure night offering.[49]

And according to a prayer to Sin on a stela of Nabonidus from Harran, the moon-god as a celestial body is the one

> whom all gods and goddesses dwelling in the heaven watch for,
> whose utterance they carry out, (that being) the command of Nannaru, the father who begot them,
> who controls the responsibilities of heaven and netherworld,
> without whose sublime command, which he speaks in heaven daily, no land can rest secure.[50]

That these prayers are addressed to the god Sin is explicitly stated, but it is equally clear that the god is viewed as the celestial object in the sky, appearing, disappearing, and bringing light.

Sin's daughter (sometimes Anu's) is the goddess Inana/Ištar. Sumerian hymns reveal the fact that already in the third millennium, she was seen in astral form as

---

48. Perry, *Sin*, No. 5a, translated in Foster, *Muses* (2nd ed.), p. 665.
49. BMS 1:1–20, translated in Foster, *Muses* (2nd ed.), p. 667.
50. Foster, *Muses*, p. 757.

the planet Venus, called ^{mul}Dili-bad. She is hailed as "the great lady of the horizon and zenith of the heavens,"[51] and in a poem of praise to Inana and Iddin-Dagan, she is addressed as "the radiant star, Venus (^{mul}Dili-bad), the great light which fills the holy heavens."[52] The planetary aspect of Inana can also be read in the Sumerian mythological work *Inana's Descent*, as Heimpel has described. He argues further for the recognition of the morning and evening star as one and the same planet before its/their association with the anthropomorphic goddess Inana/Ištar, and argues as well for the association of Venus and Inana before the fusion of the Sumerian Inana with the Akkadian Ištar.[53]

In Akkadian texts, Ištar is also called "luminary of heaven and earth (*nannarat šamê u erṣetim*)."[54] Another hymn states that "her very first name, her great appellation which her father Anu, whom she adores, named her of old, is Ninanna 'Queen of Heaven', mistress of the inhabited world, who loves the peoples, companion to the sun."[55] *Tintir* Tablet IV 23 refers to a temple named "House which Rivals Heaven" belonging to the astral Ištar called *Ištar-kakkabi* (^{d}15-MUL).[56] A form of this same appellation occurs in ritual contexts, where offerings are made before "Ištar of the stars" (15.MUL.MEŠ).[57] The goddess is the "star of the battle-cry" in the *Great Prayer to Ištar* just mentioned, where she is described as a "strong lady of battles . . . who is draped in battle, clothed in chilling fear."[58] The warrior goddess of valor is here juxtaposed with the celestial goddess of light, "shining torch of heaven and earth, brilliance for all human habitations."[59]

It seems that Ištar's aspect as the goddess of war is given its own specific astral manifestation, embodied in the fixed star MUL.BAN/*Qaštu* 'Bow star' (δ, ε, σ, ω Canis minoris and κ Puppis).[60] This second astral manifestation of Ištar is symbolized as the bow that was part of the weaponry of Marduk as he prepared for battle against Tiamat (*Enuma Eliš* IV:35). In Tablet VI the identity of Marduk's

---

51. *Exaltation of Inana*, see ETCSL t.4.07.2:112. Of course Venus cannot be seen on the zenith, due to her being tied to the sun by a short (46°) leash.

52. Iddin-Dagan, ETCSL t.2.5.3.1:89.

53. Heimpel, "A Catalog of Near Eastern Venus Deities," pp. 11–12.

54. E. Reiner and H. G. Güterbock, "The Great Prayer to Ištar and Its Two Versions from Bogazköy," *JCS* 21:258 NB (5) and Bo (8b) and in the Hittite translations "celestial daughter of Sin" [*JCS* 21:258 Hi (5)]; also Foster, *Muses*, p. 508:5.

55. Foster, *Muses*, p. 503, lines 53–56.

56. A. R. George, *Babylonian Topographical Texts*, Orientalia Lovaniensia analecta 40 (Leuven: Departement Oriëntalistiek: Peeters, 1992), p. 60–61 and commentary p. 318; also mentioned on a late Babylonian Sippar school text, BM 75144 no. 30:7′, as being "adjacent to the Arahtu" (p. 356).

57. E. Reiner, *Astral Magic in Babylonia*, Transactions of the American Philosophical Society 85 (Philadelphia: American Philosophical Society, 1995), p. 23 and note 88. Further references to "Ištar of the stars" may be found in CAD s.v. *kakkabu*, meaning 1 c.

58. Reiner and Güterbock, "The Great Prayer to Ištar," p. 259, lines 11–12.

59. Reiner and Güterbock, "The Great Prayer to Ištar," p. 261, lines NB (35).

60. See MUL.APIN I ii 7, and ^{MUL}PAN ^{MUL} *Dilbat ina* ITI.NE "in the 5th month Venus is the Bow Star," T. G. Pinches and J. N. Strassmaier, *Late Babylonian Astronomical and Related Texts* (Providence, R.I.: Brown U. Press, 1955), no. 1564:3.

bow is made explicit when Anu raises it up, kisses it and calls it his daughter, and then finally dubs it "Bow Star," making it visible in heaven (*Enuma Eliš* VI:86–90). In instructions for performing a *namburbi* ritual, a kid is to be offered to the Bow star at the altar set up for Ištar.[61] The invocation of Ištar in a curse in the treaty of Aššur-nirari V and Mati'ilu of Arpad alludes to the association of the goddess and the bow, enjoining her to "take away their 'bow,'" and cause their sterility if Mati'ilu violates the treaty with the king of Assyria.[62]

Ritual texts from the cult of Ištar presuppose the identification between the goddess and the planet Venus, the two-gendered nature of the goddess sometimes appearing to be tied to the synodic behavior of the inner planet, dividing its appearances into morning (rising, station, and setting) and evening (rising, station, and setting) phenomena. Heimpel traces the dual gender of the Babylonian goddess to the amalgamation of the original female Sumerian goddess and male Semitic god Aštar/Ištar, citing evidence for the male deity from Ebla (Aštar), Ugarit (ʿttr), Moab (ʿštr) and Yemen (ʿttr), and from Mari (both the male Aštar and the female Ištar). On the basis of passages from *Lugalbanda and the Lord of Arata* and an Inana-Dumuzi text, he has suggested that Ištar in the south (Uruk) was identified principally with the evening star, while the Semitic male Venus deity was associated with the morning star.[63] The cuneiform evidence is not so clearly demarcated. As Reiner has pointed out, the Middle Babylonian name *Ina-nipḫiša-alsīš* 'I called to her at her rising' refers to a female Venus as the morning star.[64] Omen texts make explicit reference to the two genders of the planet, although the assignment of male or female gender to the appearances in the east or west is not consistent.[65] B. Groneberg found that the astral nature of the goddess determined that the ritual preserved in the "Ištar-Louvre" hymn occurred at the moment of the heliacal rising of the morning star.[66] In addition, the element of the inner planet's appearances as morning and evening star may have been expressed in metaphorical terms as the goddess's ability to change "her mind" at night by virtue of her appearance.[67] Her change of gender is also reflected in of-

---

61. Reiner, *Astral Magic,* p. 88 and note 367.
62. ANET, p. 533.
63. Heimpel, "A Catalog of Near Eastern Venus Deities," p. 12.
64. Reiner, *Astral Magic*, p. 23, note 84. See also the invocation to the female Ištar "in the midst of the sky," in a ritual for a woman whose husband is angry, ibid., notes 90–92.
65. See U. Koch-Westenholz, *Mesopotamian Astrology: An Introduction to Babylonian and Assyrian Celestial Divination* (Copenhagen: The Carsten Niebuhr Institute of Near Eastern Studies, Museum Tusculanum Press, U. of Copenhagen, 1995), pp. 125–6; E. Reiner and D. Pingree, *Babylonian Planetary Omens: Part 3* (Groningen: Styx, 1998), pp. 20, 218 and 223 for Group F, K. 3601, rev. 31–32, where Venus is female in the east and male in the west.
66. Brigitte R. M. Groneberg, *Lob der Ištar: Gebet und Ritual an die altbabylonische Venusgöttin*, Cuneiform Monographs 8 (Groningen: Styx, 1997), pp. 136–37.
67. *šubalkut* ᵍⁱˢAL-*ki išid kabtāti ṭūb libbi mušītu šunnû tēmi u nakrūṭu kûmma Ištar* "das Umkehren mit deiner Hacke die Fundamente des Gemätes, der Herzensfreude, des nachts das ändern der Meinung und das Mitleid, das ist dein, Ištar." See Groneberg, *Lob der Ištar*, p. 123, col. i, lines 17–18.

ferings to obtain a good haruspicy presented to "Lord Ninsianna," i.e., the male manifestation of Venus.[68]

The other important child of the moon-god was the sun-god Utu/Šamaš. Utu was a young man in Sumerian mythology, but in Akkadian, Šamaš was anthropomorphized as a king, this association being carried over into the logographic writing of the divine name with the sign MAN(20) = šarru 'king' (^{d}20/MAN = Šamaš and 20/MAN = šarru). A Neo-Assyrian report explicitly states that "the sun is the star of the king."[69] In the Sumerian hymn to the temple of Utu in Sippar, the rising and setting of the sun are clearly referred to in anthropomorphic terms because the god is the referent: "when he the lord reposes, the people repose (with him). When he arises, the people arise (with him)."[70] The god, identified with the most brilliant of all celestial bodies and considered above all to be the principal judge of the universe, was the frequent recipient of prayer and entreaty. The language used to address the sun-god is often descriptive of his solar nature, e.g., in the opening lines of one of his prayers:

> O most great, perfect, son of the Brightly Rising God (Sin),
> Perpetually renewing light, beacon of the people, discloser of light,
> O Shamash, who administers dead and living, who scrutinizes all there is,
> O Shamash, light of heaven and earth, splendor of the world.[71]

The prayer asks the sun-god for favors, including that he provide "good fortune in my days," "good repute," "acceptable speech in public" and that I "pass my days in pleasure and joy." As in other prayers to Šamaš, the speaker addresses the god in a fully anthropomorphic sense, asking Bunene his courier to speak to him and referring to his wife Aya,[72] but the solar aspect of Šamaš's nature and the fact that he is embodied in the physical appearances of the sun as a sign are also clearly depicted. For example, Nabonidus' inscription commemorating the rebuilding of the Ebabbar says, "Each day as you rise and set, make my signs favorable in sky and terrain."[73] The great hymn to the sun-god from the second millennium begins with twenty lines describing the god in terms of his solar aspect:

> Illuminator of all, the whole of heaven,
> Who makes light the d[arkness for mankind] above and below,
> Shamash, illuminator of all, the whole of heaven,

---

68. Reiner, *Astral Magic*, p. 6 and note 14; Reiner, "The Uses of Astrology," *JAOS* 105 (1985), p. 591; see further, Koch-Westenholz, *Mesopotamian Astrology*, p. 40, note 4.

69. Hermann Hunger, *Astrological Reports to Assyrian Kings*, SAA 8 (Helsinki: Helsinki University Press, 1992), No. 95, r.7: ^{d}UTU MUL šarri šû.

70. Sjöberg and Bergmann, *Sumerian Temple Hymns*, p. 45, lines 482–83.

71. BMS 6, 97–130, edited by W. Mayer, *Untersuchungen zur Formensprache der Babylonischen "Gebetsbeschwörungen,"* Studia Pohl Series Maior 5 (Rome: Biblical Institute Press, 1976), pp. 503–10, translated in Foster, *Muses*, pp. 665–66.

72. Foster, *Muses*, p. 753.

73. Foster, *Muses*, p. 755.

Who makes light the dark[ness for mankind a]bove and below.
Your radiance [spre]ads out like a net [over the world],
You brighten the g[loo]m of the distant mountains.
Gods and netherworld gods rejoiced when you appeared,
All the Igigi-gods rejoice in you.
Your beams are ever mastering secrets,
At the brightness of your light, humankind's footprints become vis[ible]
Your dazzle is always seeking out [. . .],
The four world regions [you set alight] like fire.[74]

That Šamaš sees all with his light makes him the "careful judge who gives just verdicts" (line 101), seeing human action for what it truly is and listening to all who appeal to him, "the meek, the weak, the oppressed, the submissive" (line 133). The sun-god is more than the sun, but is finally also the sun, as is stated at the conclusion of this prayer, where Šamaš is called

. . . brightener of gloom, illuminator of shadow, penetrator of darkness,
illuminator of the wide world, who makes daylight shine,
who sends down the heatglare of midday to the earth,
who makes the wild world glow like flame,
who can shorten the days and lengthen the nights (lines 176–180).

The Sippar cultic calendar prescribed festival days for the sun-god that also reflect the astral nature of Šamaš as well as that of his father Sin. S. Maul points to the recitation of certain songs on calendrically significant moments, such as on the morning of the twentieth day of the month when as the sun rises the moon culminates.[75] He further clarifies the especially sacred nature of the twentieth day for Šamaš, the day when the song (balag) ᵈUtu lugal-àm 'Utu is King' is sung, in terms of the numeral 20 being both the writing for the name of the sun(-god) as well as the logographic writing for the word "king."[76]

Another god conceived of as having an astral nature is Marduk, identified primarily with the planet Jupiter. The same deity was also identified, however, with the closest planet to the sun, i.e., Mercury, which perhaps explains the writing of Marduk's name as Amar.utu 'calf of the sun', assuming awareness that Mercury was never far from the sun, being visible only as an evening or morning star near

---

[74]. W. G. Lambert, *Babylonian Wisdom Literature* (Oxford: Clarendon Press, 1960), pp. 121–38, 318–23, 346, and Foster, *Muses*, p. 536–44.

[75]. See S. Maul, "Gottesdienst im Sonnenheiligtum zu Sippar," in B. Böck, E. Cancik-Kirschbaum, and T. Richter, eds., *Munuscula Mesopotamica: Festschrift für Johannes Renger*, AOAT 267 (Münster: Ugarit-Verlag, 1999), p. 310–11 [article on pp. 285–316].

[76]. *Ibid.*, pp. 303–4. See also in the compilation text on the topography of Nippur, in the section with theological correlations between days of the month and divine names, that the twentieth day belongs to Šamaš: A. R. George, *Topographical Texts*, pp. 152–3, The Nippur Compendium (No.18), Section 12: 9′.

the horizon around sunrise or sunset. The explicit identification of Marduk's star with Mercury is found in Neo-Assyrian reports: "The star of Marduk, Mercury, is going beyond its (normal) position and ascends," and " 'If the star of Marduk becomes visible at the beginning of the year: that year his furrow will prosper.' Mercury becomes visible in Nisan."[77] A commentary to *Enūma Anu Enlil* 56 explains " 'if a planet becomes visible in Nisannu' (this refers to) Jupiter, variant: Mercury."[78] Mercury was, however, more often associated with Ninurta, and being less luminous and more difficult to see, it was attached to unfortunate omens, portending flood and death, again perhaps because of the destructive character of its mythological divine identities as both Ninurta and Marduk.

The manifestations of Marduk in the various appearances of Jupiter took on other names besides the "Marduk Star," e.g., when on the eastern horizon he became d/mulšul.pa.è. The god Šulpae 'Brilliant Youth' is found in Sumerian texts as early as the Fara texts and as late as the Ur III and Old Babylonian periods, and his astral aspect is traceable to the Old Babylonian period (and perhaps earlier),[79] although his identification as Jupiter in these early references is not at all clear. Šulpae's epithets convey his attributes as a radiant god of awe-inspiring splendor (*ša puluḫtu melammī našû* 'who bears awe-inspiring splendor': 4R 27, No. 4:48) and as 'heroic' (*dāpinu*). Later references in omen texts to Šulpae, written with the determinatives DINGIR and MUL, all concern the planet Jupiter.[80]

When the planetary manifestation of Marduk appeared in the middle of the sky, he was called d/MUL*Nēberu* 'the Ford'. This name appears in the *Astrolabe* and in MUL.APIN (as well as in other texts[81]) explicitly identified with the god Marduk. It is conceivable that both planets associated with Marduk, i.e., Jupiter and Mercury, could assume the role of "crossing point" as a counterpart or extension of the mythological significance of Marduk as "the king who divided the gods,"[82] an epithet referring to his division of the 600 Anunna gods into heavenly and netherworld deities. This apportioning of the gods was the prelude to the construction of Esagila at the world-center and the final setting in order of the cosmic

---

77. Hunger, *Astrological Reports*, No. 93, rev. 3 and 503:1 ff.; cf. *Enūma Anu Enlil* 50 in E. Reiner and D. Pingree, *Babylonian Planetary Omens 2: Enūma Anu Enlil Tablets 50–51*, Bibliotheca Mesopotamica 2 (Malibu: Undena, 1981), p. 42, iii 29a.

78. H. Hunger, *Spätbabylonische Texte aus Uruk*, Ausgrabungen der Deutschen Forschungsgemeinschaft in Uruk-Warka 9 (Berlin: Gebr. Mann Verlag, 1976), No. 90:1; see CAD s.v. *šiḫṭu*, meaning 2.

79. A. Falkenstein, "Sumerische religiöse Texte," *ZA* 55 (1963), pp. 14–28, and p. 33 on the astral aspect of the deity.

80. Hunger, *Astrological Reports*, No. 114, r. 4; 147:7, r. 6; 214:3; 288, r. 4 (all dŠulpae) and 212:1, 3–4; 93:1; 398:3; 288, r .3; 438:4 (all MUL.dŠUL.PA.È.A).

81. Such as Hunger, *Astrological Reports*, No. 323:7; see also CAD s.v. *nēberu*, meaning 3a. For discussion of the identification of Nēberu, see J. Koch, "Der Mardukstern Nēberu," *Welt des Orients* 22 (1991), pp. 53–62.

82. *Enūma Eliš* VI 39.

designs (*uṣurātu*, in *Enūma Eliš* VI 78) and establishing of the places of all the gods. Marduk was the central deity, whose "place" lay at the central point of the cosmos where one crossed from heaven to earth. Carrying out the extension of this role in the visible heaven were points such as the midpoint on the horizon due east, where Mercury could be seen, or high on the meridian, where Jupiter could be seen. Such visual counterparts to the idea of the crossing point could have given rise to the star name Nēberu:

> Nēberu shall hold the passage of heaven and earth,
> So they shall not cross above and below without heeding him,
> Nēberu is his star which he made visible in the skies,
> It shall hold the point of turning around,
> they shall look upon him,
> Saying, "He who crossed back and forth,
> without resting, in the midst of Tiamat,
> Nēberu ('Crossing') shall be his name,
> who holds the position in its midst.[83]

The name "Nēberu" for the planetary embodiment of Marduk, usually as Jupiter, also occurs in celestial diviners' reports, such as one written when the moon was observed surrounded by a halo enclosing Jupiter and Scorpius within it.[84] The protases cited in the report are explained with a statement that defines the appearance of the planet as a manifestation of the god Marduk, but explains that the god's appearance in different positions has different names: "The star of Marduk at its appearance is (called) Šulpa'e; when it rises 1 'double-hour' it is (called) Sagmegar; when it stands in the middle of the sky, it is (called) Nēberu."[85]

The names of Jupiter, with the exception of Nēberu which refers to an inanimate object (if one can call a crossing-point an "object"), are appropriate to the anthropomorphic conception of a heroic god. The god's appearance as Jupiter on the western horizon has the name Dāpinu ($^{d/mul}$UD.AL.TAR) 'The Heroic One.' The name Dāpinu, also conjuring an anthropomorphic divine image, occurs in an omen: "if when the sun sets, Dāpinu stands in its place," meaning Jupiter in its appearance in the west.[86] Šulpae was also explicitly identified with Dāpinu in the

---

83. *Enūma Eliš* VII 124–129, translation Foster, *Muses*, p. 399, but note that Nēberu is written there with the divine determinative. On the basis of *Enūma Eliš* V 6, which introduces Nēberu as marking by virtue of its central position the relationships among stars, Koch (in "Der Mardukstern") argued Nēberu must be located on the horizon; for this reason he identifies Nēberu with the planet Mercury.

84. The following omen protases were cited in the report: "If the moon is surrounded by a halo and Sagmegar stands in it; If the moon is surrounded by a halo, and Nēberu stands in it" (Hunger, *Astrological Reports*, No. 147:3 and 5).

85. Hunger, *Astrological Reports*, No.147:7–rev. 1. For another Report making use of the various names of Jupiter, see ibid., No. 254.

86. C. Virolleaud, *L'Astrologie chaldéenne*, Šamaš (Paris: P. Geuthner, 1907 and 1905), 16:12.

lexical list *Antagal*,[87] and in another bilingual text is characterized by the phrase u d a l.t a r, interpreted as *ūmu dāpinu* 'overwhelming spirit'.[88]

Aššurbanipal's hymn to Marduk and his wife Zarpanītu praises the god's exalted position throughout the cosmos, in the heavens as well as on earth, including in the description of his capacities his manifestation as the planet:

> Your shining name is Jupiter (^dSAG.ME.GAR), the first-ranking god,
> the foremost of the foremost, the highest god, who [. . . . .],
> who at his rising makes manifest a sign, [. . .] the Ple[iades . . . . .].[89]

In a version of Marduk's theomachy different from that in *Enūma Eliš*, the god does battle against Anu. The scene of conflict with the sky-god is, of course, heaven, so Orion, the figure of the True Shepherd of Anu and therefore the enemy of Marduk, is spattered with the blood of Anu:

> When Marduk got up and ascended behind Orion, Ea stood behind him,
> and having g[irt] his loins and defeated Orion,
> Bēl recited the incantation of Ea and consigned him to the Anunnaki.[90]

A divine allegorical tale is told here, set in heaven, in which the characters are gods and constellations are personified in figures such as the constellation True Shepherd of Anu (Orion). This shows that divine stories through their cosmic mise-en-scène could be symbolized by celestial bodies. The references to Marduk's theomachy in the Assyrian cult were useful for their symbolism of kingly power. In a commentary to the Assyrian cultic calendar,[91] an oblique reference to *Enūma Eliš* can be read in the passage where Marduk vanquishes his enemies and casts Qingu and his sons from the roof in the form of a bull and rams, their blood being ritually represented in the act of casting oil and honey into the gutter (line 4). Mention is also made of Marduk's vanquishing of Anu and the evil Sibitti (Pleiades), sons of Enmešara. The nineteenth day is there assigned to "the day the king defeated Anu, the day King Marduk defeated Anu."

The existence of Marduk as a deity predates the astralization of that god as ruler of the cosmos, but of his origins not much is known. Marduk's astral nature seems to have stemmed from the later development of his cult that accompanied the ascendancy of the state of Babylonia. The association of Marduk with the already astral (= Jupiter?) Šulpae may rest on their shared feature as warriors.

---

87. *Antagal* G 305; see CAD s.v. *dāpinu*, meaning 2.
88. CAD s.v. *dāpinu*, lexical, and cf. in the *Song of the Hoe* (ETCSL c.5.5.4:47 ud al-tar "mighty(?) light."
89. Alasdair Livingstone, *Court Poetry and Literary Miscellanea*, SAA 3 (Helsinki: Helsinki University Press, 1989) [hereafter Livingstone, SAA 3], No. 2: 41–42.
90. Livingstone, SAA 3, No. 38, rites in the Ištar temple at Arbil where various objects are identified as gods. See lines 24–27.
91. Livingstone, SAA 3, No. 40.

Indeed, both bear relation to the ferocious and heroic figure of the god Ninurta.[92] While Šulpae seems to have held a relatively modest position in the Sumerian pantheon, it is tempting to view Marduk's identification with him as the conscious coopting of a herioc and astral figure to add to the sublime nature of the head of the Babylonian pantheon.

In addition to the major celestial deities, the moon, sun, Venus and Jupiter, other gods took on astral identities as well. Ninurta, the heroic god of war who defends cosmic order in the myth of Anzû, was identified in the heavens as the bright star Sirius in the constellation the Arrow (Canis Maior).[93] The association of the arrow with Ninurta is a consequence of that god's mythology, in particular his role as "king of battle," the heroic champion of the gods, who triumphed over the evil Asag/Anzû. The weapons of Ninurta were transposed to the sky in the form of the star Sirius as well as the planet Mercury ("if the moon rises . . . and the Arrow stands within it, the Arrow (is) Mercury").[94] A. Annus has drawn attention to the fact that both the mythological arrow of Ninurta (*šukūdu*) and that of Marduk (*mulmullu*) were given astral form as Sirius and the Pleiades respectively. The *Astrolabe*'s identification of the month of Ningirsu with the Pleiades[95] echoes the personification of these stars as gods of war carrying bow and arrow, as attested to in an inscription of Esarhaddon as well as in the *Epic of Erra*.[96] Hymn and prayer texts address Ninurta as the star Sirius, calling him "tireless arrow" and the god "who is Sirius (^mul^KAK.SI.SÁ) in heaven,"[97] and the identification of the star with the god gives rise to the following obvious anthropomorphism:

> When the stars rise, [your] features are shining [like] the sun,
> (When) you watch over the totality of habitations [in] your brightness [. . .]
> Mankind [looks to you] to do justice to the rejected and to the sleepless ones.[98]

Omen texts further attest to Ninurta's manifestation as a celestial object, as in the following omen protasis in which a planet is identified with Ninurta: *šumma* MUL.UDU.IDIM *bi-ib-bu ša Ninurta šumšu ina ṣīt šamši lu ina erēb šamši innamirma* "if a planet whose name is Ninurta is seen either at sunrise or at sunset."[99] A Neo-Assyrian report quotes the protasis "If the moon is surrounded by

---

92. Falkenstein, "Sumerishe religiöse Texte," p. 31.
93. See A. Annus, *The God Ninurta in the Mythology and Royal Ideology of Ancient Mesopotamia*, SAAS 14 (Helsinki: Helsinki University Press, 2002), pp. 133–38.
94. LBAT 1553 r. 22 f., cf. CAD s.v. *šukūdu*.
95. *Astrolabe B*, KAV 218, A I 12 f. and 19; see Annus, *The God Ninurta*, p. 135.
96. R. Borger, *Die Inschriften Asarhaddons, Königs von Assyrien*, Archiv für Orientforschung Beiheft 9 (Graz: Im Selbstverlage der Herausgebers, 1956), p. 79:12, for Pleiades, "the warlike gods, who carry bow and arrow, whose rising means war," and L. Cagni, *L'epopea di Erra*, Studi semitici 34 (Rome: Istituto di Studi del Vicino Oriente dell'Università, 1969), pp. 28–40.
97. Hymn to Ninurta; see Annus, *The God Ninurta*, Appendix, Text 2, p. 207:8 and 12.
98. *Ibid.*, lines 14–16.
99. ZA 52, 252:99, in CAD s.v. *bibbu*, meaning 1c.

a halo and Ninurta (written ᵈNIN.URTA) stands in it."¹⁰⁰ In this case, Ninurta means Saturn.¹⁰¹

Finally, Nergal, king of the netherworld and terrifying ruler over the dead, was seen in the heavens as the planet Mars. Despite the god's malefic character, Nergal's manifestation as a heavenly body was glorified in prayer. He was called the "star who rises again and again on the horizon, whose glow (stands) high," and was described as standing in lordly fashion in the height of heaven. The radiance (*melammu*) of his countenance was extolled as in other descriptions of astral deities.¹⁰² His astral manifestation is attested to in reports, such as "If Nergal is small and white at his appearance and twinkles like a fixed star."¹⁰³ Omens also underscore his malefic nature, by deriving negative portents when Mars is visible, as in "Gemini is for devouring by Nergal. 'If Mars approaches Gemini: the prince will die,'"¹⁰⁴ and positive portents if Mars is dim or not visible, as in "if Mars is dark: the people who saw hunger will eat abundant food; the heart of the land will be happy."¹⁰⁵ The astrological association of planets and parts of the body in the style of a melothesia also attests to Nergal's identity as the planet Mars, as in the omen "if a man's kidney hurts him, (the disease comes from the god) Nergal, as they say: 'the kidney-star is Mars.'"¹⁰⁶

The evidence collected in the present section situates divinity in heaven in the form of gods represented by planets or stars visible in the sky, and having the physical attributes of celestial bodies, such as shining and spreading light. The luminous quality of the celestial bodies seems to have been perceived as a manifestation of this divinity. The astral nature of the Mesopotamian deities in question, therefore, seems to be a function of this relation between god and star. Associating the anthropomorphic gods with the celestial bodies gave rise to particular ways of speaking of and describing the celestial bodies themselves. These modes

---

100. Hunger, *Astrological Reports*, No.154:5.

101. See S. Parpola, *Letters from Assyrian Scholars to the Kings Esarhaddon and Assurbanipal, Part II: Commentary and Appendices*, AOAT 5/2 (Neukirchen-Vluyn: Verlag Butzon & Bercker Kevelaer, 1983), p. 343, footnote 636.

102. E. Ebeling, *Die Akkadische Gebetsserie "Handerhebung"* (Berlin: Akademie-Verlag, 1953), p. 116: 9, translation in CAD vol. 21:121 s.v. *zīmu*, meaning 2, and *ibid.*, line 2 "(Nergal) who in the height of heaven stands lordly," line 3 "whose face continually lights up the heavens," and line 8 "whose sheen is high in heaven."

103. Hunger, *Astrological Reports*, No.502:11, 114:8, and Simo Parpola, *Letters from Assyrian Scholars to the Kings Esarhaddon and Assurbanipal. Part I: Texts*, AOAT 5/1 (Neukirchen-Vluyn: Butzon and Bercker Kevelaer, 1970) [hereafter LAS], no. 110+300:20 ff., cited in Koch-Westenholz, *Mesopotamian Astrology*, p. 129.

104. Reiner-Pingree, *Babylonian Planetary Omens 2*, Text III:12–12a.

105. Ch. Virolleaud, *L'Astrologie chaldéenne*, Ištar (Paris: P. Geuthner, 1908 and 1909), 20:95.

106. See F. Rochberg-Halton, "Elements of the Babylonian Contribution to Hellenistic Astrology," *JAOS* 108 (1987), pp. 51–62, and for the melothesia, see E. Reiner, "Two Babylonian Precursors of Astrology," *N.A.B.U.* 26 (1993), pp. 21–22.

of expression are taken up in the next sections, devoted to the second and third of the "perspectives" defined above.

IV.1 Perspective 2. Celestial Bodies as Gods: The Stars as Images and Manifestations of Gods

All celestial bodies, stars, constellations, and planets were designated as mul 'star.' The planets were further distinguished by the term *bibbu*, a sheep of some kind, on the analogy that their movements are not fixed in relation to one another as are those of the fixed stars because they "keep changing their positions."[107] However, their definition is not limited to this physical feature, as the fuller context shows:

> [These (Sagmegar, Dilibat, Šiḫṭu ša Ninurta, Ṣalbatānu, Kajamānu, also called the Scales or the stars of the sun) are the gods who] keep changing their positions and their glow [and] touch [the stars of the sky]; on the day their stars become visible, [their *risnus*[108] . . .] where they become visible, and the wind that blows; on the day they become visible, you present offerings to them.[109]

These celestial bodies, as specified in MUL.APIN, were not simply defined in terms of their movements but viewed as gods who should receive offerings when they "become visible." This aspect of the conception of the celestial bodies as visible gods to whom one prayed and made offerings will be discussed under the third perspective, below. The present section takes up the perspective, found primarily in celestial omen texts, in which celestial bodies are of interest for their visible appearances as images of gods, manifesting their agency in the physical world. This variant on the relation between gods and celestial bodies raises the question of whether the images of divine agency in the world represented by the observable luminaries belong to a category different in conception from the anthropomorphic gods offered in literary, pictorial, or sculptural representations.

Within the genre boundaries of mythological and hymnic texts, such as those quoted in the previous section, the identification between god and star points to a conception of the celestial bodies as manifestations of deities. Outside of these genres, in celestial omen texts, the very different idea that celestial bodies are vis-

---

107. MUL.APIN II, i 8; see Hermann Hunger and David Pingree, *MUL.APIN: An Astronomical Compendium in Cuneiform,* AfO Beiheft 24 (Horn, Austria; F. Berger, 1989). Reiner, *Astral Magic,* p. 7, note 22, notes that doubt has been cast (on semantic grounds) on the reading of UDU.BAD as UDU.IDIM 'wild sheep.' Horowitz argues for retaining the reading 'wild sheep'; see *Cosmic Geography,* p. 153, note 3.

108. The word *risnu* occurs here in a different sense from its meaning 'soaking, bathing.' In the commentary to MUL.APIN II i 27, Hunger suggests that it might be a synonym for some visible property, such as brilliance or luminosity.

109. MUL.APIN II, i 40–43, see Hunger-Pingree, *MUL.APIN,* pp. 80–81.

ible indicators of divine will derives from the principles of divination, i.e., that physical phenomena constitute signs (omens) that communicate divine will to humankind. As such, celestial objects, as in the case of all omens from natural signs, became physical mediators between human beings and gods. This would seem to be straightforward enough, however, in many cases in the scholastic literature the notion of the stars as both indicators of divine will and also embodiments of gods is conveyed, such as in the explanation of Jupiter's name Sagmegar in a scholastic list, where he is the "bearer of signs to the inhabited world."[110] This epithet can be interpreted to mean that the physical appearances of Jupiter are signs produced by the god Marduk to demonstrate his will, or, alternatively, that the planet embodied the god and as such made manifest Marduk's will by his appearances. While it is possible to make such a distinction for purposes of our own interpretations of the meaning of "Sagmegar is the bearer of signs, etc.," the dichotomy implied between "god" and "star" in such passages is probably artificial. This problem of interpretation will be addressed in section V. In order to clarify the terms of the present analysis, I will proceed on the assumption that it is legitimate to separate out as a second "perspective" the former approach, i.e., that stars physically represented divine agency by being images, or "likenesses" of gods, as exemplified in the opening lines of *Enūma Eliš* Tablet V:

> He (Marduk) created the stations for the great gods,
> setting up the stars, their (the great gods') likenesses, as constellations.[111]

The same idea is echoed in the opening lines of *Enūma Anu Enlil* 22 (although the relevant passage is restored):

> When Anu, Enlil, and Ea, the great gods, created heaven
> and earth
> and made manifest the celestial signs . . . [(and with) the
> stars as their (the gods')
> likenesses, they drew the constellations.]

The meaning of "the stars, their likenesses" seems to be that images of the gods are made visible in the stars. This conception has a parallel in Esarhaddon's inscription concerning his laying anew the foundation of the temple Esagila, the "palace of the gods," described as the (earthly) image (also expressed with the word *tamšīlu*) of the celestial plot $^{mul}ikû$ 'The Field'(= Pegasus).[112] The word *tamšīlu* 'image' or 'counterpart' in these passages conveys the idea that just as the temple represents a terrestrial counterpart to the celestial "field," so the stars

---

110. CAD s.v. *ṣaddu*, usage b2′.
111. *Enūma Eliš* V 1–2.
112. Borger, *Esarhaddon*, p. 21:51 and 94:33; see CAD s.v. *ikû*, meaning 2. Also cited in George, *Topographical Texts*, p. 297.

themselves represent physical counterparts to the gods.[113] The invocation of the constellation Ursa Major in the prayer for an ominous dream illustrates this idea in a manner reminiscent of the identification of the body parts of one god with other gods that are viewed as lesser powers.[114] The prayer describes features of the constellation as representations of a number of deities.

> O Wagon Star, heavenly wagon!
> Whose yoke is Ninurta, whose pole is Marduk,
> whose side-pieces are the two heavenly daughters of Anu.[115]

Behind such a graphic explication must be the notion of the personified divine heaven.

The astrological compilation known as the *"Great Star List"*[116] contains many such identifications of celestial bodies (mul) and gods (dingir). Among the more comprehensible entries are found the equations ^{mul}dil.bat (=) ^{d}ištar bēlet mātāti 'Venus is Ištar, queen of all lands,' and ^{mul}gír.tab (=) ^{d}išhara 'The constellation Scorpius is Išhara.' An entire section is devoted to the identifications of ^{d}Ṣalbatānu, i.e., Mars. Compiled there are a series of muls, including ^{mul}makrû 'The fiery red star,' ^{mul} sa$_5$ 'The red (star),' ^{mul} sig$_7$ 'The yellow (star),' ^{mul}šanumma (MAN-ma) 'The sinister star,' ^{mul}ahû 'The Strange star,' and ^{mul}nakaru 'The Hostile star.' While we think of Ṣalbatānu as the planet Mars, the star list correlates a surprising number of constellation names (for example ^{mul}apin 'The Plow star', ^{mul}šudun 'The Yoke star', ^{mul}šu.pa 'ŠU.PA', ^{mul}bat.téš.a 'Dignity', ^{mul}ug$_5$.ga 'The Raven star') with the divine name ^{d}Ṣalbatānu. In this list deities are correlated with many more than one star, planet, or constellation, but how such correlations figured in the interpretations of celestial omens by scholars is not evident. Despite the impenetrable nature of some of the list's content, what is important in the present context are the identifications of stars with gods that provide a systematic representation of the notion of the stars as likenesses of the gods.

The drawing of stars by the god Marduk (Bēl) is further specified in another scholastic religious commentary text.[117]

---

113. Note also the use of the word *tamšīlu* in the genealogy of the gods in *Enūma Eliš* I:16 to define the relation between Anu and Ea: (First Anšar made his child Anu his match), "then Anu generated Ea, his likeness (*tamšīlašu*)."

114. For example, in the hymn to Ninurta KAR 102; see Annus, *The God Ninurta*, Appendix 1, pp. 205–6 and parallels, KAR 328 rev. and STT 118.

115. STT 73:71–73; Reiner, *Astral Magic*, p. 71.

116. E. F. Weidner, *Handbuch der Astronomie*, Band I (Leipzig: J. C. Hinrichs, 1915, reprinted 1976), pp. 6–20, idem, "Ein astrologischer Sammeltext aus der Sargonidenzeit," *AfO* 19 (1959), pp. 105–13, and Koch-Westenholz, *Mesopotamian Astrology*, p. 93 and Appendix B, pp. 187–205.

117. Neo-Assyrian religious text VAT 8917, KAR 307, obv. 30–33; edition in Livingstone, SAA 3, p. 100; cf. the Late Babylonian parallel AO 8196, *AfO* 19 (1959), pls. 31–34, especially the lines rev. I 20–22.

The upper heaven of *luludanitu* stone is Anu's.
He settled the 300 Igigi gods there.
The middle heaven of *saggilmud* stone is of the Igigi gods.
Bēl sits there in a high temple on a dais of lapis lazuli and made a lamp of electrum shine there.
The lower heaven of jasper is of the stars.
He drew the constellations of the gods on it.

The cosmographical image here is of heavenly levels that house various gods, the lowest heaven being visible to human beings and displaying the "constellations of the gods" drawn on (*ina muḫḫi*) its surface of jasper stone. The heavens are described as being populated by gods and stars (in the Lower Heaven). The highest heaven belonged to Anu and was populated by 300 Igigi. Middle Heaven belonged to the Igigi, and Marduk (Bēl) had his throne dais there. This passage and the phraseology "constellations of the gods" seem to imply a conception of separate domains for gods and stars. The gods, from this point of view, inhabit a different realm from the stars, which in this context are not themselves fully gods because they exist on a different "level" from the gods, i.e., the material world. The parallel text states "The lower heavens are jasper. They belong to the stars."[118] The image of the lower heavens as a stony surface, albeit beautifully decorated, contrasts in this depiction with what must be a divine realm of agency and will beyond the sensory reach of mankind.

Another location sometimes given for the planetary deities is denoted by the term *šupuk šamê*, literally 'base of heaven,' or 'horizon,' where planetary phenomena such as risings and settings occur. The term has also been taken to mean 'firmament,' as in "they installed Sin, Šamaš, and Ištar to keep the firmament in order"[119] and "through her (Inana as the evening star) the firmament is made beautiful in the evening,"[120] although these passages could also (and probably should) refer to the horizon.[121] What is of importance in this context is that planets as physical images of deities are observed to appear in this place, whether on the horizon, or above in the sky as a whole.

---

118. AO 8196, iv 22.

119. CT 16 19:59–61; see Horowitz, *Cosmic Geography*, p. 239.

120. Sjöberg and Bergmann, *Sumerian Temple Hymns*, p. 36, TH No. 26:324, and see note on p. 115.

121. CAD s.v. *šupuk* 'base' does not include the meaning 'firmament' and indeed, most passages are better translated 'horizon' rather than 'firmament,' or 'vault of heaven.' One problematic context is found in *Gilgamesh* IX ii 4, where in describing the size of Mt. Mašu, *šupuk šamê* is set in relation to its top: *elušunu šupuk šamê k[ašdu]*, just as the netherworld is set in relation to its side: *šapliš Arallê iratsunu kašdat*. CAD translates "over which [extends only] the horizon," while Gallery Kovacs translates "above which only the dome of the heavens reaches" (The Epic of Gilgamesh [Stanford, CA: Stanford University Press, 1989], p. 76), and Horowitz takes it to mean "whose peak reaches up to *šupuk šamê*" (Horowitz, *Cosmic Geography*, p. 241).

Stars and constellations were also imagined as cuneiform signs inscribed upon the stone surface of the heavens. The metaphor of 'heavenly writing' (*šiṭir šamê*) clearly reflects the idea of the stars as signs written by gods for human beings to observe and from which to forecast the future. A similar reference to the drawing of stars is given in the conclusion to *Enūma Anu Enlil* Tablet 22, although instead of Marduk as creator, it is the great gods Anu, Enlil, and Ea who created the universe, established the ominous signs, divided the paths, drew the stars, and made day, night, month and year. According to this depiction, the stars are entities separate from gods. Because of the allusion to Marduk's drawing of constellations in *Enūma Eliš*, we interpret the "constellations of the gods" not so much in the sense of their being material possessions of, i.e., belonging to, the gods, than as being physical representations of them. Moreover, the god Marduk, who in this passage is anthropomorphized as drawing constellations on the sky in the images of gods, is of a different status and nature from his material handiwork, the heavenly stars. From this perspective it seems that we can separate two natures, material and divine, corporeal and incorporeal, that define the relation between celestial bodies and gods.

The beginning of *Enūma Eliš* Tablet V deals with the order and regularity of the appearance of heavenly bodies, describing features of the heavens as the work of Marduk. Marduk arranged the stars into constellations, the "images" of the gods themselves. By means of the fixed stars he organized the year into twelve months, marked by the (heliacal) risings of three stars in each month in their specified "paths."[122] These paths, named for Anu, Enlil, and Ea, were in fact used in early Babylonian astronomical texts such as MUL.APIN, the Astrolabes, and their derivatives as a reference system for positions of stars and constellations. The acrostic hymn to Marduk refers to the creation of the paths, saying that "in the east and west he (Marduk) set up constellations, gave them roads and passages [. . .].[123] The god created the zenith, the moon and the month from the lunar phases, designated as the new moon crescent, the half-moon on the seventh day, the full moon on the fifteenth day (opposition), and the second half of the moon as the reverse of the first. The relation between the moon and sun was duly noted: "At the day of di[sappeara]nce, approach the sun's course, on the [. . .] of the thirtieth day, you shall be in conjunction with the sun a second time."[124] Marduk was the creator of the heavenly domain and all that was visible in it, but he was also a member of it, shining as Jupiter (or Mercury).

The heavenly domain, whether it was viewed as the creation of Marduk or given some other mythological etiology, became the focus of observational attention. Because the phenomena were interpretable as signs of divine will, the obser-

---

122. Foster, *Muses*, p. 378, *Enūma Eliš*, V 3–4.
123. Livingstone, SAA 3, No. 2, rev. 9.
124. Foster, *Muses*, p. 379, *Enūma Eliš*, V 21–22.

vation of what occurred "above" was significant for what would happen "below." For this practice, an observational language developed to describe the phenomena empirically. The descriptions of the appearances of celestial bodies were compiled as omens in the series *Enūma Anu Enlil*, which together with a variety of commentaries and excerpts formed the basic reference work quoted by the Neo-Assyrian scholars in their letters and reports to the Sargonid kings. It must be noted that the language of the omen protases despite their empirical character is replete with metaphor. Many phenomena are in fact described by means of personifications (e.g., the sky shouts, planets confront each other, wear crowns and clothing, carry radiance, have anthropomorphic physical attributes, such as a head, eyes, a beard).

H. Hunger and D. Pingree list all the phenomena found in reports and letters indicating the empirical nature of the phenomena that interested the scribes and that were regarded as ominous,[125] such as "being with a particular constellation," "heliacal rising or setting," "conjunctions with other planets or the moon," "being in the halo of the moon," or "being visible during an eclipse." Many examples of such phenomena can be culled from the protases of lunar, solar, and planetary sections of *Enūma Anu Enlil*. In *Enūma Anu Enlil* Tablet 1:2, the moon at its appearance is seen on the twenty-eighth day as on the first day (i.e., "on the day of first visibility");[126] in *Enūma Anu Enlil* Tablet 4, rev. 7, two stars "[stand by bo]th cusps of the moon"[127]; in *Enūma Anu Enlil* 23(24), I 2, the sun at its appearance on the first of Nisannu is yellow[128]; in *Enūma Anu Enlil* 23(24), V 8, the sun at its appearance on the first day of Ulūlu appears in a black cloud, and at its setting it sets in a black cloud and the east wind blows[129]; in *Enūma Anu Enlil* 28(29):27 on the first day the light is red and the day is gloomy[130]; in *Enūma Anu Enlil* 59(60) K. 148:8, Venus at her appearance goes progressively higher[131]; in *Enūma Anu Enlil* 59(60) K. 35:3, Venus flashes and goes around the Yoke star, an observer observes her, and someone sees it.[132] On the surface, such passages do not clue us into the conception of the stars as images of deities, but a strong correla-

---

125. Hermann Hunger and David Pingree, *Astral Sciences in Mesopotamia* (Leiden, Boston, and Köln: Brill, 1999), pp. 122–37.

126. Cf. the commentary tablet *Sin ina tāmartišu* I, line 97, U. Koch-Westenholz, "The Astrological Commentary *Sin ina tāmartišu* Tablet 1," in Rika Gyselen, ed., *La Sciences des Cieux: Sages, Mages, Astrologues*, Res Orientales XII (Bures-sur-Yvette: Groupe pour l'Étude de la Civilisation du Moyen-Orient, 1999), p. 160.

127. L. Verderame, *Le Tavole I-VI della serie astrologica Enūma Anu Enlil*, Nisaba 2 (Messina: Dipartimento di scienze dellantichità, 2002), p. 132.

128. W. H. van Soldt, *Solar Omens of Enuma Anu Enlil: Tablets 23 (24)–29 (30)* (Leiden: Nederlands Historisch-Archaeologisch Instituut Te Istanbul, 1995), p. 5.

129. Van Soldt, *Solar Omens*, pp. 8–9.

130. Van Soldt, *Solar Omens*, p. 98.

131. Reiner-Pingree, *Babylonian Planetary Omens 3*, pp. 56–7.

132. Reiner-Pingree, *Babylonian Planetary Omens 3*, pp. 100–101.

tion between the stars and the gods emerges in the way the omen texts denote each celestial body.

In the case of the lunar omens, the word "moon"*sīnu* (*suēnu*), derived from the Sumerian divine name ᵈEN.ZU (=ᵈSin, also ᵈZU.EN) is not used. The word *suēnu* could be used to refer to crescent-shaped objects,[133] but when referring to the moon itself, the name of the celestial object was synonymous with the divine name of the moon-god. Divination texts favor the symbolic writing as the numeral 30, referring to the schematic or ideal length of the lunar cycle, but this was frequently written with the divine determinative, i.e., ᵈ30, denoting the moon/the month as the embodiment of the moon-god. Yet the moon is not of interest for its behavior as a god *per se*, but for its appearances on various days of the month, whether it appears "early" or "late," the description of the crescent, the full moon at opposition, and eclipses, using the sort of "empirical" language previously illustrated.

Similarly, the word "sun" in omen or astronomical texts is indistinguishable from the name of the sun-god Šamaš. In such contexts, the word "sun" also has the meanings "sunlight," "day" or "sun disk." Sun-disk objects, such as those made from gold, silver, or lapis lazuli as votive offerings, and representations of sun disks such as those drawn on a clay tablet as part of a ritual were either called *šamšat* or *šamšu*.[134] The apodosis of an Old Babylonian omen refers to both the sun-god and the solar disk object: "the sun will request a votive sun from the man (in return) for his life."[135] References to appearances of the sun(-god) in omens focus mainly on the appearance of the solar disk when it rises (its color, brightness/dimness) and when it sets, whether various types of clouds or stars are seen with it, and whether it is surrounded by a halo. The solar omens contain very few anthropomorphic descriptions, with some notable exceptions, such as: "If the sun weeps because of the decision of the Anunnaki" (*Enūma Anu Enlil* 24[25] III), explained in a commentary as a solar eclipse.[136]

Another personification of sun and moon that occurs in omen texts is in the expression for lunar and solar opposition, i.e., when "one god is seen with the other," as in the omen "If the moon and sun are in opposition: . . . . It means that on the 14th day one god is seen with the other."[137] This expression occurs as well in early, i.e., seventh and sixth century, astronomical diary texts, e.g., No. 651, col.

---

133. see CAD vol. 15:294 s.v. *sīnu*, meaning 2a.
134. CAD vol.17/I:333-334 s.v. *šamšatu*, meaning 1a and c; see also Beaulieu, *Pantheon*, App 3, p. 387 s.v. *šamšu/šanšu*.
135. CAD vol.17/I:338 s.v. *šamšu*, meaning 4.
136. See van Soldt, *Solar Omens*, p. 36, notes 3 and 4 and p. 42 for the commentary text, line 3′ and p. 47, line 5.
137. Hunger, *Astrological Reports*, No.110:8-9. This expression also occurs in the active voice, ᵈ30 *u* ᵈUTU *ahēiš ētamrū* "the moon and sun saw each other"; see Hunger, *Astrological Reports*, No.134:4; 135:7-8; 137:3-4, written ᵈ30 ᵈ*šá-maš a-ḫe-iš e-tam-ru*; 138:3-4.

i 6: 14 DINGIR KI DINGIR {x} IGI "The 14th, one god was seen with the other."[138] By the fourth century, however, the statement that the moon and sun were in opposition was replaced by references to the intervals between sunrise/set and moonrise/set around opposition, termed the "lunar four." Diary No. 384, obv. 8′, for example, instead of stating that the gods were seen with each other, provides the interval (GE_6) between sunset and moonrise in degrees. This represents the time in mid-month when the moon rose for the last time after sunset. No. 382, obv. 8′ gives the interval from sunrise to moonset (na) on the fifteenth day of month II, and line 16′ gives moonset to sunrise (ŠÚ) for the fourteenth of Month III and moonrise to sunset on the fifteenth day. The sun and moon may have been referred to as "gods" in the early diaries, but the observation of the luminaries on the day of opposition was a matter of astronomical interest in the same way as the later observations of the four mid-month intervals between their risings and settings.

For Venus, a plurality of divine associations is reflected in the names used to designate the planet, i.e., Dilbat, Ninsianna, and Ištar (written ^{d}EŠ$_4$.DAR or ^{d}15) as well as Ištar of the Stars (^{d}15 MUL.MEŠ[139]). In the Ur III period, the planet Venus was called Ninsianna 'Lady (who is) the Light of Heaven.'[140] In addition, she was associated with Šamaš at sunrise and Ninurta at sunset.[141] Her dual gender shows up in omens as well, e.g., "If Venus rises in the East, she is female, favorable; if she is seen in the West she is male, unfavorable."[142] Omens in *Enūma Anu Enlil* 59–60 for the male Venus planet, the evening star, include references to his having a beard, an image also represented in some cylinder seals.[143] Other traces of anthropomorphic language occur in the Venus omens, when the planet wears a crown,[144] or "has a head" or "a rear," all of which have astronomical explanations.[145]

Jupiter's name in celestial omen texts or astronomical sources outside those of the late Babylonian astronomy is primarily $^{d/mul}$Sag.me.gar, whose meaning and even pronunciation are unknown. Late astronomical texts use the name ^{MUL}BABBAR, which is not attested earlier. Jupiter omens in *Enūma Anu Enlil*

---

138. See A. J. Sachs and H. Hunger, *Astronomical Diaries and Related Texts from Babylonia*, Vol. 1 (Vienna: Verlag der Österreichischen Akademie der Wissenschaften, 1988), No. 651 col.i 6, also *ibid.*, col. iv 13′, No. 567, obv. 4.

139. See Reiner-Pingree, *Babylonian Planetary Omens 3*, K. 3384, obv.? 12′.

140. References collected in Heimpel, "A Catalog of Near Eastern Venus Deities," pp. 10–11, also mentioned in Beaulieu, *Pantheon*, p. 106 and note 25.

141. Virolleaud, *L'Astrologie chaldéenne*, 8:10–11.

142. Reiner-Pingree, *Babylonian Planetary Omens 3*, pp. 82–3 K. 800:7–9, pp. 213 and 223, K. 3601+, rev. 31–32, pp. 237 and 241, ND 4362:27; cf. pp. 248–49, line 57, said of Mercury, and see Pingree's notes on p. 20.

143. See Reiner, *Astral Magic*, p. 6, notes 14 and 15.

144. Reiner-Pingree, *Babylonian Planetary Omens 3*, p. 43 and 65; 222.

145. See Pingree's commentary in Reiner-Pingree, *Babylonian Planetary Omens 3*, pp. 11 and 16.

make use of a number of other names, namely Nēberu and Šulpae, 'the Marduk star' (mulAmar.utu) as noted above.

Koch-Westenholz suggested that the variant names may be differentiated by the various appearances of the planet through its synodic cycle, Šulpae being the planet in its heliacal rising, Sagmegar when in the east, Nēberu when on (or near) the meridian, and Dāpinu when in the west.[146] In the poetic context of Aššurbanipal's acrostic hymn to Marduk and Zarpanītu, the god's name Engišgalanna 'lord of the heavenly station' occurs in broken context, but has to do with the positions of the Anunnaki (manzāzi ^{d}600).[147] The term manzāzu has a specific celestial connotation,[148] and perhaps this relates to Marduk's division of the Anunna gods in Enūma Eliš VI 39, mentioned above. This name also appears in a Neo-Assyrian scholar's report explaining the omen protasis "If Engišgalanna becomes bright" as referring to Jupiter. Jupiter was one of the principal benefic planets. A Late Babylonian astrological text enumerates the planets and their signs, beginning with Jupiter, calling its sign "favorable" (šalāmu). Where Jupiter is the object of astronomical consideration, the attribution of a benefic character is reflected in the order in which Jupiter (designated either as ^{MUL}Sagmegar or ^{MUL}BABBAR) is listed among other planets, i.e., as the first benefic with Venus and Mercury.[149] The name ^{MUL}BABBAR, whether it stemmed from an abbreviated form of UD.AL.TAR, or simply meant "shining/bright/white star," could have denoted the planet's appearance as well as the divine radiance of Marduk, of which the planet was a "likeness."

Saturn, the slowest moving of the planets, was named Kajamānu 'the constant,' or 'the steady.' Although Saturn's primary appellation was descriptive, he was associated with the god Šamaš and also with Ninurta. Because of his association with both of these gods, each of whom had close identification with the king, Saturn's phenomena could be interpreted as significant royal signs. The practical result can be seen in the scholars' response to Saturn's approaching the moon; omens for the sun in proximity to the moon were collected for the interpretation of the sign.[150] In another report referring to the appearance of Saturn in the lunar halo, the planet is identified with Ninurta. Again, an omen for the sun

---

146. In his discussion of the planetary names, D. Brown brings out the valid point that consideration should be given to the period and the genre in which a name occurs, so as to avoid giving the impression that the texts are simply inconsistent. This is particularly apt in the case of the name *Nēberu*. See David Brown, *Mesopotamian Planetary Astronomy-Astrology*, Cuneiform Monographs 18 (Groningen: Styx, 2000), p. 58, note 168.

147. See Livingstone, SAA3, No. 2:43.

148. See CAD s.v. *manzāzu*, meaning 5.

149. See F. Rochberg-Halton, "Benefic and Malefic Planets in Babylonian Astronomy," in E. Leichty, R. Ellis, and P. Gerardi, eds., *A Scientific Humanist: Studies in Memory of Abraham Sachs*, Occasional Publications of the Samuel Noah Kramer Fund 9 (Philadelphia: The University Museum, 1988), pp. 323–28.

150. Hunger, *Astrological Reports*, Nos. 95 and 297.

standing in the halo of the moon is adduced for its apodosis. The construction of these reports demonstrates the technique of correlating an observed sign with a "prediction" on the basis of associations with roots in mythology and other systems of symbols. For this purpose, the correlation of planets (and fixed stars) with gods was easily manipulated and therefore well adapted to the goals of divination.

Another planet with a descriptive Akkadian name was Mercury, or *šiḫṭu* 'the jumping one.' This name has been understood to refer to the planet's fast motion and perhaps to the fact that it was not often or easily visible (CAD s.v. *šiḫṭu*). But by etymology, the logographic spelling of the name *šiḫṭu*, ^dGUD.UD 'bull of Utu/the sun,' illustrates the bovine metaphor commonly used of celestial bodies associated with gods. As expected, Mercury had divine identifications. He was associated with the gods Ninurta (Hunger-Pingree 1989:71, MUL.APIN II i 5) and Nabû,[151] symbolizing the crown prince or son of Marduk. The dual association of Mercury with these gods may relate to the appearances of the planet as a morning and evening star. Like the other inner planet, Venus, Mercury was assigned two genders (^dGUD.UD NITA SAL[152]), although its identification with a goddess is not known. The planet was also sometimes referred to as an arrow of the heroic warrior god Ninurta.[153] The use of the 'Arrow' (^{MUL}KAK.SI.SÁ) to mean Mercury is attested in a late Babylonian astrological omen text.[154] Here the Arrow star must represent a planet, as it occurs in the context of omens dealing with cases in which only planets are correlated with whether business will rise or fall. In keeping with the planet's dual associations, the theory of benefic and malefic planetary influence assigns both qualities to Mercury, illustrated here by the fact that Mercury (the 'Arrow') being bright predicts both prosperous business and the attack of the enemy.

The planet Mars was called Ṣalbatānu. This name was interpreted as 'the one who reveals deaths,' and indeed in the omens and reports from *Enūma Anu Enlil*, the planet Mars portended plague and other evils because the planet was considered to be the image of Nergal, god of pestilence and fearsome king of the dead.[155] Some omens refer to the planet as ^dU.GUR (Nergal).

---

151. P. Gössmann, *Planetarium Babylonicum* (Rome: Biblical Institute Press, 1950), p. 113, No. 290.

152. See Reiner-Pingree, *Babylonian Planetary Omens 3*, pp. 248–49 (K. 2346+:57).

153. Annus, *The God Ninurta*, pp. 134–35.

154. H. Hunger, "Stars, Cities, and Predictions," in C. Burnett, J. P. Gegendijk, K. Plofker and M. Yano, eds., *Studies in the History of the Exact Sciences in Honour of David Pingree* (Leiden and Boston: Brill, 2004), pp. 19 and 23. It seems worth mentioning that in the practice of planet worship in Sanskrit texts, the image of Mercury was (and still is in modern India!) the arrow; see Michio Yano, "Planet Worship in Ancient India," in Burnett et al., eds., *Studies in the History of the Exact Sciences*, p. 342. Pingree has established Babylonian origins for many elements of Indian astrology. Perhaps we can count this symbolic representation of the planet Mercury among them.

155. CAD vol.10/II:296 s.v. *mūtānu*, lexical section.

This is clear in reports which group together omens for a particular phenomenon. One such report juxtaposes the omen "If Mars (Ṣalbatānu) rises scintillating and its radiance is yellow" with "If Nergal in his appearance is very small and white, and scintillates very much like the fixed stars."[156] Another report includes a section with five omens concerning Mars in Scorpius, the first one of which is "If Nergal stands in Scorpius."[157] As previously mentioned, omens from the appearance of Mars when it was dim were positive, as in one of the reports from the astrologers to the Neo-Assyrian court: "If Mars becomes faint, it is good; if it becomes bright, misfortune."[158] The names given for Mars in the *"Great Star List"* cited above carry maleficent overtones, "The Liar star," "The False star," "The enemy star."[159] Not surprisingly, Ṣalbatānu counted among the malefics, together with Saturn and the eclipsed moon and sun.[160]

In addition to the planets, constellations too had divine identities, as has already been noted on the basis of the *"Great Star List."* From *Enūma Anu Enlil* such correlations are also known, for example the Pleiades as the 'Seven gods' (^{d}7.BI= *Sibitti*), as in the protasis "In month II the Bristle, the Seven gods (the great gods); if it rises heliacally at its specified time,"[161] or "The Seven gods are for (predicting) the devouring of cattle."[162] The designation of the Pleiades as "the gods" is also found in the section for the month Ajaru in *Astrolabe B*, in which the Pleiades have their heliacal rising in that month.[163] Other identifications between stars or constellations and deities occur in commentary texts, but the sense of many of these equivalences escapes us. For example: "Jupiter is the star of Sin and Sin is Aššur; the MÚL.MÚL-star is Aššur; the Yoke-star is Aššur ... the *ikû*-constellation is the seat of Aššur; ... Mercury is the star of Adad; the SAG.DU-star is the star of Šamaš."[164] Perhaps in the case of the Field star being "the seat of Aššur," a parallel is made to the description of Marduk's temple Esagila as being the earthly replica of the constellation that was imagined as a celestial field or plot.

---

156. Hunger, *Astrological Reports*, No.114:6–8.
157. Hunger, *Astrological Reports*, No.502:11.
158. Hunger, *Astrological Reports*, No.114, rev. 3.
159. Koch-Westenholz, *Mesopotamian Astrology*, pp. 190–91.
160. TCL 6 13 ii 2–4; see Rochberg-Halton, "Benefic and Malefic Planets," pp. 324–25.
161. *Enūma Anu Enlil* 50 IX 13; see Reiner-Pingree, *Babylonian Planetary Omens 2*, pp. 58–59. See also Hunger, *Astrological Reports*, 275:6 "If in Iyyar (II) the Pleiades, [the Seven], the great [gods, rise] at [their] appropriate time."
162. *Enūma Anu Enlil* 50 IV 4; see Reiner-Pingree, *Babylonian Planetary Omens 2*, pp. 44–45. See also K. 10756+ ii 8; W. Horowitz, "A Join to Enuma Anu Enlil 50," *JCS* 46 (1994), p. 129.
163. Reiner-Pingree, *Babylonian Planetary Omens 2*, Appendix, p. 81, KAV 218 ii 19.
164. G. van Driel, *The Cult of Aššur* (Assen: Van Gorcum, 1969), p. 97, BM 121206 lines 53–60; cf. B. Menzel, *Assyrische Tempel*, Band II, Studia Pohl, Series Maior 10/II (Rome: Biblical Institute Press, 1981), No. 35.

It was mentioned above that the luminous aspect of the heavenly divine manifestations was important in texts referring to the gods in their astral form. In omen texts, the luminosity of the celestial bodies is also a prominent element in descriptions of the appearance of the planets that focus on whether they are bright or dim, or of various colors. Brightness or dimness was interpreted in accordance with the quality of the planet, either benefic or malefic; accordingly it was favorable if a benefic was bright, but unfavorable if a malefic was bright. It is tempting to see the roots of this astrological theory in the symbolism of the planets as gods. Whether the planet was bright or faint can be imagined as a variable which functioned to communicate the decision of a god, indicating by that sign the coming of propitious or unpropitious events.

Although ostensibly aimed at physical descriptions of phenomena, the omen texts and related material contribute to the evidence for the idea that celestial bodies were regarded as divine. From this point of view they are entirely consistent with the perspective of the mythological and hymnic texts that make clear that some gods had astral aspects and could be referred to as heavenly bodies. Thus Marduk could be spoken of as ^{MUL}Nēbiru, in which form he could be "the bearer of signs to the inhabited world" or "show a sign at his rising."[165] These lines do not support the idea that the gods are removed from the phenomena and that the phenomena simply move to demonstrate the god's will, as though the cosmos were a physical realm controlled by but separate from the divine. Indeed, in some contexts the heavenly bodies seem to be more than mere mediators. They are not only personified, but are also referred to and sometimes addressed as gods. I turn now to the third and final variant in the discourse about gods and stars, the third "perspective," in which celestial bodies are not merely images or emblems, but material embodiments of gods.

IV.2 Perspective 3. Celestial Bodies as Gods: Personifications of Stars as Gods

The third perspective is encapsulated in the Akkadian phrase 'gods of the night' (*ilāni mušīti*), attested in a number of prayers from Old to Standard Babylonian, as well as in epistolary Neo-Assyrian. In the prayers to the 'gods of the night' the stars and planets are conjured and offered sacrifice so that 'I may obtain what I want!'[166] The practice is not without Sumerian antecedents, as illustrated in Dumuzi's formulaic entreaty to Utu to enable him to escape 'his demons':

The lad raised his hands towards heaven to Utu:
O Utu, you are my brother-in-law, I am your sister's husband!

---

165. See Livingstone, SAA 3, No. 2: 42 (*ina nipḫišu ukallamu ṣaddu*).
166. *Prayer to the Gods of Night*, line 53, A. Leo Oppenheim, "A New Prayer to the 'Gods of the Night,'" *Analecta Biblica* 12 (1959), p. 284.

... Utu received his tears
.... He escaped all the demons.¹⁶⁷

In the Akkadian prayers to the "gods of the night," the stars and constellations are addressed as agents with "power" to produce signs from which the future can be divined.¹⁶⁸ Two Old Babylonian copies of the "nocturnal prayer" say that the "gods and goddesses of the country," here Šamaš, Sin, Adad and Ištar, have "gone home to heaven to sleep" (Lines 5–7), in which case they give no verdicts, i.e., do not send signs, whereas the visible constellations invoked at the poem's conclusion, the Fire-star, Irra, Bow-star, Yoke-star, Orion, Dragon-star, Wagon, Goat-star, Bison-star and Serpent-star, are asked to "put a propitious sign in the lamb I am blessing now." To ensure that the extispicy of the next morning will go well, the speaker in the prayer addresses the constellations as gods who have power to be, using Reiner's expression, "harnessed."¹⁶⁹ The prayer to the gods of night invokes the stars, constellations and planets (Jupiter and Venus) to accept the speech of the supplicant, just as though the celestial objects were themselves divinities with the power to hear and act in response to human entreaty. In a similar prayer not addressed to the "gods of the night" but rather to the "divine judges in the pure heavens," the stars are again asked to provide a good omen to ensure the success of an extispicy.¹⁷⁰

The invocation of stars as gods, according to Reiner, serves to define astral magic, and is closely connected, in her view, to the practice of celestial divination to determine divine will from the appearances of heavenly bodies (astral omens).¹⁷¹ As the various prayers to the gods of night show, the divinities in heaven accessible to human appeal are identified with planets, constellations and stars. Some of these heavenly divine agents take their shapes from animals (the lion star, snake star, goat star, pig star, horse star), others from gods (Standing gods of Ekur, Sitting gods of Ekur, Šullat, Haniš), human figures (True Shepherd of Anu, Hired Man, Old Man), or even inanimate objects (bow, arrow, field, wagon, plow, furrow, frond, yoke), yet all are personified, irrespective of their form, for the purpose of being asked to act upon various manipulations made by the diviner or magician. It is therefore less in the conceptualization of the form of the celestial deities and more in the expectation of a response from them as gods that the essence of anthropomorphism lies. The opening invocation of the ritual

---

167. B. Alster, *Dumuzi's Dream: Aspects of Oral Poetry in a Sumerian Myth*, Mesopotamia, Copenhagen Studies in Assyriology 1 (Copenhagen: Akademisk Forlag, 1972), pp. 72–79 (lines 164 = 191 = 226), and parallels in *Inana's Descent, Lugalbanda in Hurrumkurra*, and *Gilgameš and Huwawa;* see commentary, pp. 114–17.
168. Reiner, *Astral Magic*, pp. 1–2.
169. Reiner, *Astral Magic*, p. 2.
170. STT 73:110–117, Reiner, *Astral Magic*, p. 73 and note 301.
171. Reiner, *Astral Magic*, p. 2.

text against sorcery, *Maqlû* 'Burning,' not only calls upon the "gods of the night," but also on the personified watches and on night itself, "night, veiled bride."[172] A Neo-Assyrian letter further specifies the celestial bodies (called "stars") Jupiter, Venus, Saturn, Mercury, the moon, the sun, Bēl mātāti, the Arrow-star (Sirius), Lisi (Antares), Bēlet balāṭi (Vega), Sebettu (the Pleiades) and Išum, before whom *maqlû*-rituals are to be performed.[173] While the letter begins "[concern]ing the stars," it specifies that the burnt offerings be made "before these gods."[174] The gods of the night are also invoked in the *mīs pî* ritual for the purpose of, as it were, infusing spirit into flesh, or sanctifying the divine statue. In the Babylonian version of the ritual, twenty-four altars are set up to the gods of the night, which are enumerated as being the seven planets, six named stars of the path of Enlil, four of the path of Anu, four of the path of Ea, and three stars of Anu, Enlil and Ea, left unnamed and presumably meaning all the rest of them.[175]

The planets are referred to as gods in the astronomical compilation MUL.APIN. This text is interested in the positions of the planetary gods, and so defines them as "the six gods who have the same positions (i.e., in the Moon's path) (and) who touch the stars of the sky (which the moon touches) and keep changing their positions (relative to the stars)."[176] Another passage in MUL.APIN, cited above, defines the planets as gods to whom one made offerings. Similar personification is also expressed in a passage concerning Antares (α Scorpii), the Lisi-star: "On the day the Lisi-star (written with the divine determinative, as $^{d}Li_9$-si_4) becomes visible, a man should wake up at night all that is around his house, people, cattle, sheep, donkeys, and he must not sleep; he should pray to the Lisi god ($^{d}Li_9$-si_4), and then he and all that is around his house will experience success."[177] Therefore,

---

172. Knut Tallqvist, *Die assyrische Beschwörungsserie Maqlu* I, Acta Societatis Scientiarum Fennicae 20/VI (Leipzig: 1895), 1f. Cf. "I invoke you (stars), divine judges in the vast heavens," STT 73:110, cited in CAD s.v. *šasû*, meaning 4b2'. The personification of night occurs in *namburbi* texts; see S. M. Maul, *Zukunftsbewältigung: Eine Untersuchung altorientalischen Denkens anhand der babylonisch-assyrischen Löserituale (Namburbi)*, (Mainz am Rhein: Verlag Philipp von Zabern, 1994), p. 422:13 and p. 427:61.

173. Steven W. Cole and Peter Machinist, *Letters from Priests to the Kings Esarhaddon and Assurbanipal*, SAA 13 (Helsinki: Helsinki U. Press, 1998), No. 72. See also Marc J. H. Linssen, *The Cults of Uruk and Babylon: The Temple Ritual Texts as Evidence For Hellenistic Cult Practice*, Cuneiform Monographs 25 (Leiden: Styx, 2004), p. 32: DINGIR.DIDLI MI.GAR 'gods of night' in a text listing lamentations for "intercessions (*taqribtu*)," on days 1/2, 7, 14/15, and 20 of every month. For performance of *maqlû* in the month Abu at the ominous time of the disappearance of the moon, see Cohen, *The Cultic Calendar*, p. 464.

174. Cole and Machinist, *Letters*, No. 72, rev. 4.

175. Reiner, *Astral Magic*, p. 141, and now see C. Walker and M. Dick, *The Induction of the Cult Image in Ancient Mesopotamia*, State Archives of Assyria Literary Texts 1 (Helsinki: University of Helsinki Press, 2001), pp. 75 and 79. Note also the nine censers to the gods of the night that are set up in the Nineveh version, line 107: Walker-Dick, *Induction*, pp. 45 and 60.

176. MUL.APIN II, i 7–8, Hunger-Pingree, *MUL.APIN*, p. 148.

177. MUL.APIN II, iii 35–37.

the star Lisi is referred to as the god Lisi, who receives the prayer of the man, but who must be present in the visible form of the star (^{d}Lisi).

Such offerings and invocations imply a personification of the stars, who are expected to transmit their divine power to an object. But an even more basic and general personification of divine heaven is rooted in the mythology of creation. An essential element in Mesopotamian cosmogonic mythology is that the world came to be as a result of the separation of heaven and earth. The motif is preserved in the etiological introduction to the Sumerian myth *Gilgamesh, Enkidu and the Netherworld,*[178] in which the region "heaven" (or "above") was separated from earth and "carried off" by the god An ('sky'), and "earth" became the possession of Enlil 'Lord Wind'. The cosmic deities in this myth, seemingly existent before the separation of cosmic regions, were, according to divine genealogy, the issue of the goddess Nammu, who represented an eternal watery state. A tablet from the Early Dynastic period containing a myth of beginnings introduces heaven and earth before any gods came into being and before sunlight or moonlight existed.[179] There, however, An 'heaven' and Ki 'earth' are already personified, 'heaven' as "a youthful man."[180] The cosmic realms of heaven and earth were also personified as father and mother in the composition *Lugale*, which accounts for the birth of Azag, the demonic opponent of the warrior god Ninurta, as resulting from the union of An and Ki.[181] A chief attribute of the divine sky was its generative powers, often expressed metaphorically in terms of the sky's rains as semen engendering the vegetation on earth.[182] Yet in the theology disseminated from Nippur, An was not the creator god. This role was taken by Enlil, who in the *Song of the Hoe* effected the separation of An and Ki and took Ki, the earth, as his province.

Sky was also derived theologically through divine descent. This idea was developed in the form of the list of gods entitled "An = *Anum*," which gives the genealogy of the sky god An (*Anu*) as being descended from Uraš and Ninuraš 'Earth and Lady Earth.'[183] In what seems to echo the genealogy of the sky god An, the earth god Enlil is descended from Enki (and Ninki) 'Lord (and Lady) Earth' (a god not to be confused with Enki Nudimmud, the god of sweet waters). The original unified whole of heaven and earth was later separated by the god

---

178. Aaron Shaffer, "Sumerian Sources of Tablet XII of the Epic of Gilgamesh" (Philadelphia: University of Pennsylvania dissertation, 1963), pp. 48–49, 99, lines 8–9, 10–11.

179. Å. Sjöberg, "In the Beginning," in T. Abusch, ed., *Riches Hidden in Secret Places: Ancient Near Eastern Studies in Memory of Thorkild Jacobsen* (Winona Lake, IN: Eisenbrauns, 2002), pp. 229–39.

180. Sjöberg, "In the Beginning," p. 231, AO 4153, ii 1.

181. Jacobsen, *Treasures*, p. 95, note 85.

182. Cagni, *L'epopea di Erra*, p. 61, line 28, and CAD vol.14:252–253 s.v. *reḫû*, lexical section and meaning 2.

183. W. G. Lambert, "The Cosmology of Sumer and Babylon," in C. Blacker and M. Loewe, eds., *Ancient Cosmologies* (London: Allen and Unwin, 1975), pp. 51–54.

Enlil, who then introduced into the celestial region a body, the god Nanna (moon). The moon-god produced children in the form of the sun, the god Utu, and of Venus, the goddess Inana. The deified celestial bodies thereby took their place as gods in the divine genealogies and in the generational hierarchy that took shape within the pantheon, i.e., An, Enlil, and Enki (in Akkadian, Anu, Enlil, and Ea) as the senior great gods, and Nanna, Utu, and Inana as their children/ grandchildren.

Another, albeit different, strain of cosmogony also presents the god Anu 'heaven' as being the offspring of ancestor divinities rather than the result of a cosmogonic separation. The best-known account of this version of creation is found in the Akkadian epic poem *Enūma Eliš*. Here the origins of all the gods are traced to the commingled waters of the male Apsû and the female Tiamat, who in time engendered gods within themselves. From Anšar 'the totality of sky' and Kišar 'the totality of earth' came An, the sky god, who produced Ea Nudimmud, Marduk's father. The principal revision of the older Sumerian cosmogonic tradition here lies in the identity of the creator, who is no longer Enlil but Marduk, grandson of Anu and son of Ea. Once in power, Marduk repeats, or revises, the act of creation, this time following a grand theomachy, establishing "heaven" by splitting into two parts the body of the slain Tiamat. Heaven is the physical remains, so to speak, of the watery carcass of the salt-sea mother, and, like every other part of the world, is under the authority of Marduk (*Enūma Eliš* V 133–235), who is no longer simply "beloved son," but now "king" (*Enūma Eliš* V 109–10 and 151–52).[184]

The appearances of the heavenly bodies that are conceived of as signs of divine agency or embodiments of divine agents are further illustrated in the principle of celestial divination that defines the meaning of the appearances (what we would call "predictions") as divine verdicts (*purussû*). Šamaš, of course, is well known as "supreme judge" and "decider of decisions of the great gods." In a prayer to this deity, he is addressed as "lofty judge," "creator of the above and below," the god "who never wearies of divination" and who renders "daily verdicts for heaven and earth." The connection between judgments and divine oracles is

---

184. Not only was the celestial part of the universe a locus of divine activity, the terrestrial part was as well. The oldest attested Near Eastern storm god, Enlil 'Lord Wind', brought both the spring winds holding the good rains that made plants flourish, as well as the destructive storm cloud with its accompanying flood waters. The clouds that produce rains and allow the crops to grow are understood as acting through Enlil's agency, but he is also immanent in the storm itself: "The mighty one, Enlil . . . , he is the storm" (Jacobsen, *Treasures*, p. 101) and "his word, a storm cloud lying on the horizon, its heart inscrutable" (Jacobsen, *Treasures*, p. 102). His hymns attest to his benevolent nature as a fertility god, but lamentation texts reveal him as the destroyer of farmlands, animals, and people. Enlil's influence, both positive and negative, is therefore seen as working through the natural forces of the atmosphere, which embody the god but are also transcended by him; see A. R. W. Green, *The Storm-God in the Ancient Near East*, Biblical and Judaic Studies 8 (Winona Lake, Indiana: Eisenbrauns, 2003).

apparent from the use of the words *dīnu* 'verdict' and *dajānu* 'judge' in legal contexts as well as in reference to gods and divination.[185] The parallel between lists of omens and collections of legal precedents ("laws") and their "judgments" or "verdicts" is further suggested by prayers and incantations referring to the gods as "deciders of decisions" (*pārisū purussî*), often said of Sin, and of Sin and Šamaš together.[186] The late theological and "astrological" commentary series entitled I.NAM.GIŠ.ḪUR.AN.KI.A states "Sin and Šamaš, the two gods, are present and decide the decisions of the land (*purussê māti iparras*) [. . .], they give signs to the land."[187] But Sin and Šamaš were not the only heavenly judges. The collective designation of the stars as "divine judges" in the prayer to the gods of night invokes the same principle, making explicit the personification of the stars as gods who by their behavior displayed each night against the sky make their decisions evident to the trained eye. In a prayer to Ninurta as Sirius, the supplicant, the son of the haruspice, as he awaits the appearance of the celestial manifestation of the god, i.e., Sirius at night, calls upon Ninurta to give judgment: "I have my hands raised, take your station in the middle of the sky and hear what I say."[188] The prayer closes with the rubric "prayer to Sirius when it stands at sunrise," demonstrating that the prayer addresses the god as star and the star as god at the same time.

Even in the reports from scholars to the Sargonids, when blessings to the king are offered and the names of celestial bodies are given, these latter are referred to explicitly as gods: "Aššur, Sin, Šamaš, Adad, Nusku, Jupiter (called Sagmegar), Venus (called Dilbat), Marduk, [Zarpanītu], Nabû, Tašmetum, Saturn (called ᵈUDU.IDIM.GUD.UD), Lady [of Nineveh], . . . the great gods of heaven and earth,

---

185. See CAD s.v. *dīnu*, meaning 1 3′b, and *dajānu*, usage m.

186. See F. Rochberg-Halton, "Fate and Divination in Mesopotamia,"in H. Hirsch and H. Hunger, eds., *Vorträge gehalten auf der 28. Rencontre Assyriologique Internationale in Wien, 6.-10. Juli 1981*, AfO Beiheft 19 (Horn, Austria: Verlag Ferdinand Berger und Söhne, 1982), p. 367, and F. Rochberg, *The Heavenly Writing: Divination, Horoscopy, and Astronomy in Mesopotamian Culture* (Cambridge and New York: Cambridge University Press, 2004), p. 258.

187. A. Livingstone, *Mystical and Mythological Explanatory Works of Assyrian and Babylonian Scholars* (Oxford: Clarendon Press, 1986), pp. 24–25. See also A. Falkenstein, *Literarische Keilschrifttexte aus Uruk* (Berlin: Staatliche Museen zu Berlin, Vorderasiatische Abteilung, 1931), 32:3 (Sin), and cf. ᵈSin ᵈSin *ša purussê* "Sin is (the equivalent of) Sin of the decision." L. W. King, *Cuneiform Texts from Babylonian Texts in the British Museum*, 24 (London: British Museum, 1908) T 24 39:15; for Sin and Šamaš, KAR 18, r. 44. The literary stylists of Aššurbanipal's royal inscriptions also made reference to the god Sin's making cosmic "decisions," as in "the Fruit (i.e., the new moon) revealed to me his decisions, which cannot be revoked": M. Streck, *Assurbanipal und die letzen assyrischen Könige bis zum untergange Nineveh's*, Vorderasiatische Bibliothek 7 (Leipzig: J. C. Hinrichs, 1916), p. 110, v 10. This seems to be a clear metaphor for the idea that only the appearances of the heavenly bodies, i.e., while they are above the horizon, are capable of providing omens. See also E. Reiner, *Astral Magic*, pp. 66–67.

188. Annus, *The God Ninurta*, Appendix A, Text 2, p. 207:25. I might translate "I raise my hands; be present in the midst of the pure heaven and hear my words."

the gods dwelling in Assyria, [the gods] dwelling in Akkad, and all the gods of the world . . . ."[189] The same mode of expression is used in another letter that mentions rituals for Venus when the planet has risen, showing that when the planet is present (visible), so is the goddess.[190] *Šuilla* prayers recited before Sin, Pleiades, Sirius, Mars, Vega and other stars are reported to the king with the assurance that these "hand-lifting" prayers are recited only on propitious days. Despite these measures, the exorcist Marduk-šakin-šumi suggests that additional "hand-lifting" prayers be performed "before the moon-god" and expresses concern about "this observation of the moon," again showing the moon-god and the moon to be one and the same.[191] Similarly in a letter from Nabu-nadin-šumi to the king, the performance of a *šuilla* prayer for ^{د}Sin and the watching of the moon for an omen are made together. Seven days of performing *šuilla* prayers before the "gods of the night" are followed by *namburbi*s against evil of any kind.[192] Such actions presuppose an anthropomorphic conception of the stars as divine agents ready to hear the prayer and act favorably on behalf of human beings; the invocations to personified celestial bodies, however, suggest that in these instances the god and the celestial body are united in one divine nature. In a report concerning the day of opposition, the scholar Issar-šumu-ereš quotes the king's question to him: "How did you observe that the gods saw each other?" and the answer is "before daybreak, when he whom the king, my lord, knows revealed himself."[193] The language used here is clearly anthropomorphic, metaphorical, and arguably metaphysical; yet the next statement, "we saw where the moon was standing—it was an observation,"[194] shows that the omen phenomenon was not a strictly metaphysical experience, but, perhaps above all, an empirical one. It is certain that the fact that the moon represented the moon-god did not affect consideration of the moon's appearance as a phenomenon. Another report begins with the statement that Ištar (^{d}15) loves the king and sends him the very best. Then the observation of Ištar/Venus as a sign is given: "Venus (^{d}Dilbat) made her position perfect."[195] And in another instance, the moon in conjunction with the Pleiades is interpreted as the moon-god (^{d}30) interceding on behalf of the king to the other gods so that "the king is safe."[196] Perhaps because the reports include such reassurances to the king of his safety, the language personifies, i.e., the stars are spoken of as gods.

---

189. Simo Parpola, *Letters from Assyrian and Babylonian Scholars*, SAA 10 (Helsinki: Helsinki University Press, 1993), No. 197: 7–19, p. 160.
190. Parpola, *Letters*, SAA 10, No. 31 (LAS 11).
191. Parpola, *Letters*, SAA 10, No. 240:3–12 and rev. 9–13 and 14–16.
192. Parpola, *Letters*, SAA 10, No. 277, rev. 1–7.
193. Hunger, *Astrological Reports*, No. 21:3–5.
194. Hunger, *Astrological Reports*, No. 21 r.1–4.
195. Hunger, *Astrological Reports*, No. 27:6.
196. Hunger, *Astrological Reports*, No. 72:6.

Cultic texts reflect the same practice of regarding the stars as gods who may receive offerings and prayers of appeasement. A cultic text from Assur (BM 121206) provides a section specifying what offerings certain gods are to receive (X:13′–39′). Here, among the divine recipients of offerings are Sin, Šamaš and Ištar of Heaven (^{d}15 ša šamê).[197] Reiner discussed the *ikribu*-prayers as "a special category of prayer accompanying a nocturnal consultation by the diviner," in which the planets are addressed as gods, as in "Šulpae (Jupiter), holy god, foremost of the gods, more majestic (?) than the stars in the sky."[198] The Seleucid period ritual text for the *Akītu* festival in Uruk (?) also invokes stars, constellations and planets as though they are gods, although without referring to them collectively as the gods of night. On the fifth day of Nisannu, during the final four hours of the night, immediately preceding the purification of the temple and the *āšipu*'s handling of the ritually sacrificed sheep (much as in the prayer to the gods of night prior to the extispicy of the next morning), prayers to calm Bēl and Bēltiya begin with the invocation of Bēl himself and continue with the invocation of "Boötes, Eridanus, Asari, Jupiter, Mercury, Saturn, Mars, Sirius, ŠU.PA, NE/IZI.GAR, Numušda, Star, sting of the scorpion, Sun, light of the universe, Moon who illuminates the darkness," and following Bēltiya, the feminine names "Damkina, Venus, Bow-star, She-goat star, Star of Abundance, Star of Dignity, Wagon Star, Star Aru, Star of Ninmaḫ," all explained as names "for my lady (that is, Bēltiya)."[199] A Hellenistic ritual text for daily offerings to the deities of the Uruk pantheon, i.e., the gods who lived in Uruk[200], specifies that "every day during the whole year: 10 fat, pure sheep, whose horns and hooves are perfect, will be slaughtered for Anu and Antu of the Heaven, (for) Jupiter, Venus, Mercury, Saturn (and) Mars, (at?) sunrise and the appearance of the moon, to be offered as voluntary (?) offering in the *bīt maḫazzat*."[201] And in addition, "on day 16, monthly, (the priest) will offer 10 first-quality sheep, fat (and) pure, whose horns and hooves are perfect, for Anu and Antu of Heaven and the 7 planets (written ^{d}UDU.IDIM.MEŠ 7-*šú-nu*), as cooked meat, on occasion of the cleansing of the hands ceremony, in the Baramaḫ on the temple tower of Anu, just as on day 16 of Ṭebētu."[202]

Another source for divine celestial personifications is found in the names of diseases, such as "Semen of Jupiter," "hand of Sin," "hand of Šamaš, "hand of Ve-

---

197. Van Driel, *Cult of Assur*, pp. 100–03; see also B. Menzel, *Assyrische Tempel*, Band II, no. 35.
198. Reiner, *Astral Magic*, pp. 73–4 and note 306.
199. See Cohen, *Cultic Calendars*, pp. 444–45.
200. F. Thureau-Dangin, *Tablettes d'Uruk à l'usage des prêtres du temple d'Anu au temps des Séleucides* (Paris: P. Geuthner, 1922), TCL 6, 38:24 [hereafter cited as TU; see Linssen, *Cults*, p. 173, and for text transliteration and discussion, pp. 132 ff.
201. TU 38 rev. 29–31, Linssen, *Cults*, p. 175.
202. TU 38 rev. 32–34, Linssen, *Cults*, p. 175.

nus,"²⁰³ and "hand of Dāpinu (UD.AL.TAR = Jupiter)."²⁰⁴ Because the etiology of disease was thought to be divine (or demonic), the attribution of this power to celestial bodies implies their divinity and agency. Divine agency, as it comes into play in mythology, divination, or cult, seems to entail the anthropomorphic, and it seems likely that the "likenesses" of gods in the stars and planets referred principally to anthropomorphic gods, conceived of as heroes and lords (or as a lady, as in the figure of Ištar) who both transcended and acted in the world.²⁰⁵

V. Contemplation of the Divine Heaven: The Unification of Perspectives

Unifying the three perspectives so far discussed are aspects of a Mesopotamian conceptualization of gods and celestial bodies, such as personification, anthropomorphism, transcendence and immanence, all of which have been illustrated in the discussion thus far.²⁰⁶ The personification of heavenly bodies implies that a relation was made between the stars and the personae and mythologies of certain gods. This relation enabled the development and elaboration of a system of symbols and associations evident in the contents of hymns and prayers to stars, as well as in omen texts, which made further use of these symbols and associations by creating metaphorical descriptions of celestial phenomena in terms of gods. In addition to shedding some light on the nature of the particular gods associated with stars, the evidence further clarifies the establishment of heaven as a locus for the divine, and what constituted the contemplation of that divine heaven. It remains to consider whether the three perspectives outlined above represent separate conceptions of the star-god relation, or are merely different manners of speaking of one and the same idea.

Essential to the formation of correspondences between stars and gods seems to have been the idea that natural phenomena made manifest the attributes and the agency of certain deities. Because the particular character of divine will and the attributes of particular gods were understood in human terms, i.e., the gods'

---

203. Reiner, *Astral Magic,* pp. 102 and 107, and Simo Parpola, "The Neo-Assyrian Word for 'Queen'," *State Archives of Assyria Bulletin* 2/2 (1988), p. 74, n. 4.

204. R. Labat, *Traité akkadien de diagnostics et pronostics médicaux* (Paris: Académie internationale d'histoire des sciences, 1951), 76:59.

205. See LAS 2 67; Koch-Westenholz, *Mesopotamian Astrology,* p. 122 on omens for *asakku*-disease from the appearance of Jupiter and/or Mercury; LAS 268 in which the *galmaḫu* of the king reports that the kettle drum will be set up that night.

206. It may well be that our language of transcendence and immanence is inadequate to an analysis of Mesopotamian religion, not only because of unfortunate Christian theological overtones, but because the Mesopotamian conception of divinity seems to require greater differentiation than the simple duality of immanent vs. transcendent. Indeed it seems advisable to come away from such potentially misleading terminology to forge new analytic categories for the study of Mesopotamian religion. Meanwhile, however, I will reluctantly use these terms for convenience.

capacities for action in various arenas such as in warfare, justice, or sovereignty, the conceptualization of the gods was fundamentally anthropomorphic. Irrespective of the gods' manifested forms, as star, animal, object, or indeed as human, they were spoken of in human terms. Anthropomorphism has loomed large in modern scholarly interpretations of Mesopotamian religion. M. Linssen's recent discussion of the cults of late Babylonian Uruk and Babylon is based on the premise that

> although the gods were thought to reside in heaven and the underworld, in every Mesopotamian city many gods also lived in their own temples. Furthermore, each city also had its own main god, a city patron, who resided in the major temple, where he or she was represented by an anthropomorphic statue. The statues were considered to be manifestations of the gods on earth; rather than being mere images they were regarded as extensions of the personality of the gods. The statues were identified with the gods in question and were considered to be like living beings, who, just like humans, had to eat, sleep, wake and be dressed, and were therefore in the center of ceremonies and presented with regular and special offerings.[207]

Linssen further refers to the close correspondence between Mesopotamian cultic rituals and the mythological stories about the gods for whom the rituals were created, admitting that "it is often difficult for us to assess how the Mesopotamians conceived a ritual to be connected with a particular myth."[208] He appeals to A. Livingstone's idea that "there is no fundamental difference between myth and ritual," in which case "the statues and symbols which are used in the temple rituals *are in fact the deities which they represent*,"[209] and adds that the "official cult maintained up to the end of Mesopotamian civilization the fiction that the divine meal was consumed by the gods, or rather their statues" (p. 129).

The relation of the god(s) to their representations in statuary is relevant to the present consideration of the relation of the gods to their representations as celestial objects, because both functioned as images and divine embodiments of particular gods. Although the anthropomorphism inherent in each case is certainly a significant part of how we must understand the divine element in the relation, here with respect especially to the heavenly bodies, the issue is also a question of the relation between a physical object and the metaphysical notion of the divine. In the case of the divine image in its statue, Linssen's view is consistent with that of P.-A. Beaulieu, who understands the cult statues as "literally brought to life," adducing Jacobsen's claim that the statue mystically became the god by a process of transubstantiation.[210] Beaulieu also says, however, that the statues "became re-

---

207. Linssen, *Cults*, p. 12.
208. *Ibid.*, p. 23.
209. Linssen, *Cults*, p. 23; the emphasis here is mine.
210. Beaulieu, *Pantheon*, p. 5 and note 6.

positories of the divine presence," which is perhaps a better way to express the vivification of the divine statue than the claim of *conversio substantialis*, a Latin Christian invention, the applicability of whose particular theological implications has yet to be convincingly argued for ancient Mesopotamian religious texts.[211] The statue, as a representation and embodiment of the divine, functioned as the focus of cult and worship, as a result of which it held a status on the edge of the physical and metaphysical, participating in both. There is no question whether a Mesopotamian priest ever saw a divine statue consume the *naptanu* 'sacred meal,' as these foods were distributed to temple prebendaries *après-rituel*.[212] Because cultic activities are ceremonial and symbolic in nature, the discourse of the cultic texts is equally so. Indeed, by exercising such symbolic language the *mīs pî* 'washing of the mouth' ritual effected the transformation of the material (statue) into the divine (god), who would then receive offerings and ensure the stability of the temple and its domain.[213]

The idea that the physical heavenly bodies are images of the gods seems somewhat similar to the idea of the divine representation in the cult statue. In both cases, a distinction between matter (star, statue) and the immaterial (god) is made but can be overcome through ritual, such as *mīs pî*, or invocation, as in prayers to stars. If we take into account those instances where the divine recipients of offerings are planets, i.e., gods embodied or represented in astral form, the relation between the gods and their physical counterparts becomes difficult to understand if the role of symbolism and metaphor is not given its due. We have no trouble understanding the references to celestial bodies as sheep and cattle moving about in their 'cattle pen' *tarbaṣu* (which is our horizon) as metaphorical, although this too refers to gods.[214] For us not to grant the metaphorical force of the references to stars as gods would be to claim that the ancients confused the stars with gods, saw no difference and made no distinction between the realm of the phenomena and

---

211. Walker and Dick, *Induction*, pp. 6–7, appeal to the idea of the "Eucharistic Presence." Interestingly, however, their conclusion that the *mīs pî* was "essentially a purificatory rite which prepared the object/person for contact with the divine," being therefore necessary for the statue to function as a representation of the god, together with their compilation of examples of other sacred objects on which *mīs pî* could be performed, constitute an excellent argument against parallels with the doctrine of transubstantiation and go further to define the particular Mesopotamian theology inherent in the practice.

212. Beaulieu, *Pantheon*, pp. 25–27.

213. In view of the fact, as Linssen points out (see *Cults*, p. 154), that the *mīs pî* ritual was performed on other cultic objects (e.g., the bull whose hide will cover the ritual kettledrum and the drum itself) it seems worth considering whether the effect of the *mīs pî* ritual with respect to the divine statue was less vivification and more sanctification.

214. E.g., *Enūma Eliš* VII 131: "Let him (Marduk) assign the regular motions of the stars of heaven; let him herd all the gods like sheep." Note also that star names were commonly written with the determinative ÁB (= *littu* 'cow') in the Seleucid period, read MUL_x, see F. Rochberg-Halton, *Aspects of Babylonian Celestial Divination*, Archiv für Orientforschung Beiheft 22 (Horn: Ferdinand Berger & Söhne, 1988), p. 289.

the conceptual domain of the divine. This is untenable in light of *Enūma Eliš* V 2, where clearly the stars are not the gods, but 'likenesses' of the gods (*kakkabī tamšīlšunu*).

Of course, other aspects make the relation between the gods and their images in statues quite different from that of their relation to the stars. The stars were not fashioned by human beings and were not in fact in human form. In addition, the statue was the focus of cultic activity exclusively, whereas presumably the observation of the heavenly bodies had a meaning apart from religious practices. At the level of empirical and theoretical work on celestial phenomena, it seems to me reasonable to separate the belief that the celestial bodies were divine from the interest in their behavior as phenomena that is evident in celestial divination and astronomy. By this I do not mean that for empirical work the stars were "downgraded" to mere physical objects, but only that such work is possible within a conceptual framework in which the celestial phenomena are associated with or even embody the divine. That these forms of engagement with the celestial phenomena can be seen to coexist, i.e., the cultic as well as the observational, argues for the symbolic manner of speaking employed in the religious texts.

The plurality of ways of speaking about the divine, e.g., anthropomorphic, transcendent (which does not preclude anthropomorphism), or immanent (which also does not preclude anthropomorphism), adds to the complexity and difficulty of the problem of understanding the relation between god(s) and physical entities, such as stars (or the divine statue). In the context of her investigation of the meaning of Akkadian *ilu* 'god,' B. Porter has discussed the anthropomorphic character of the Mesopotamian gods as one part of a complex notion of the divine, without subsuming all other divine aspects under a primarily anthropomorphic identity. She has interpreted the identification between god and celestial body as an independent aspect of the god so identified, parallel to its anthropomorphic aspect or its aspect as a kind of force or essence. Accordingly, Ištar can be understood as a divine lady, as (the essence of) love or of war, or, indeed, as the planet Venus or the Bow Star. The plurality of divine aspects, in Porter's view, functioned independently, while relating to a single deity.[215] Her analysis removes the hierarchy of other conceptions, e.g., that of Bottéro, that subsume multiple aspects of a deity under one principal anthropomorphic identification. Where Bottéro, for example, would preserve a marked ontological separation between god and star, Porter seems to allow for an ontologically unified conception of the god *as* star, at least in contexts in which the power of the god has an astral function, e.g., Venus *is* Ištar in contexts where the goddess Ištar is spoken of as the planet Venus. At the same time, her notion of the astral nature of a deity does not preclude its

---

215. See Barbara N. Porter, "The Anxiety of Multiplicity: Concepts of Divinity as One and Many in Ancient Assyria," in Barbara Nevling Porter, ed., *One God or Many? Concepts of Divinity in the Ancient World*, Transactions of the Casco Bay Assyriological Institute I (Chebeague Island, Maine: The Casco Bay Assyriological Institute, 2000), pp. 243–48.

other natures or powers, thus avoiding a kind of animism in Mesopotamian religion. In my view, however, to recognize the identification between a god (Ištar) and a celestial body (Venus) does not necessarily support the ontological claim that the goddess is the planet, i.e., that no distinction as to their order of "being" can be made between them.

Another interpretation of the relationship between god and star sees the celestial bodies as representations of deities whose existence is understood as metaphysical or "conceptual" (even when anthropomorphically imagined) and therefore not (physically) real. This interpretation is implied rather strongly by Bottéro, when he says that "the stars, while participating somewhat through 'contagion' in divine nature, were not in themselves gods."[216] That is, by their physical closeness to the gods, who dwelled "above the stellar," the stars were nearly (that is "somewhat") divine, but because they were not entirely transcendent of the physical world, they could not be divine. To more clearly differentiate celestial bodies and gods, Bottéro puts it that the gods "constituted a sort of ontological 'third order' above the stellar as the stellar was above the terrestrial."[217] Bottéro constructs a cosmology, and an accompanying ontology, that sets the "real" gods in the realm of the immaterial and incorporeal, albeit imagined in human form and existing in their special sublime order of being. To explain the numerous instances where identities are made between gods and celestial bodies, and because material objects in the world could not be gods themselves, he reasons, they could only be emblems (or images) of them. In Bottéro's analysis the observable sun, moon and planets would be iconic representations of deities, serving as emblems, much as the barge was the emblem of Sin himself.[218] Statements such as "the great gods who dwell in the city of the king, my lord, covered the sky and did not show the eclipse"[219] or "as soon as the moon clears up the eclipse"[220] certainly argue for Bottéro's view of the gods having an existence apart from the phenomena. The implication is that divine agents controlled the phenomena but were themselves removed from the phenomena, thus creating a gap between transcendent gods and worldly phenomena, much as Bottéro describes. Intimations of a Platonic universe can unfortunately be perceived in this analysis, imposing what

---

216. Bottéro, *Religion*, p. 70.
217. Ibid.
218. má-gur$_8$-^{d}Suen ʼsù-sùʼ -[x] "The barge of Suen which moves (across the sky)": Hall, *Moon-God*, p. 517. The emblem of a god is known to have substituted for the divine statue on occasion, as did the solar disk for Šamaš in Middle Babylonian evidence; see Wm. W. Hallo, "Cult Statue and Divine Image: A Preliminary Study," in Wm. W. Hallo, J. C. Moyer, and L. G. Perdue, eds., *Scripture in Context II: More Essays on the Comparative Method* (Winona Lake, IN: Eisenbrauns, 1983), p. 12 and note 89, and also Walker-Dick, *Induction*, p. 8.
219. Parpola, *Letters*, SAA 10, 114, rev. 6–7.
220. Albert T. Clay, *Epics, Hymns, Omens, and Other Texts*, Babylonian Records in the Library of J. Pierpont Morgan 4 (New Haven: Yale U. Press, 1923), 6:28′ and rev. 54′; see Linssen, *Cults*, pp. 307–8.

seems to me too radical a split between the visible heavens and an alleged "realm" of deities, whose powerful effect on the world of our experience thereby emanated somehow from "without." Too many examples of divine immanence in physical phenomena counter such a reconstruction.

Explicit expressions of divine transcendence are indeed attested to in religious cuneiform texts. Such passages are concerned to describe a god as surpassing in size or greatness anything known in the world, yet these descriptions are without exception drawn in terms of the world. Thus Ningirsu appears to Gudea in a dream as a figure "like heaven and earth in extent,"[221] and in *Lugale*, Ninurta "arose, touching the sky, with one step (?) he covered a league."[222] One such elaborately developed description of the enormity of a god is found in the hymn to Ninurta in which Ninurta's face is the Sun, his eyes are Enlil and Ninlil, his mouth is Ištar of the stars, Anu and Antu are his lips, and other parts of his head, neck, chest and shoulders are other astral figures.[223] In this way, the heavens become a mere portion of the transcendent "body" of the god Ninurta. Similarly, in the hymn to the sun god, Šamaš is said to see into the heavens as one would into a bowl, but the eyesight of the god is greater than the physical limits of both the heavens and the entire earth.[224] The scale of the world as something dwarfed by the imagined greatness of Ninurta is also shown in a hymn to Gula in its description of the god wearing "the heavens on his head, like a tiara" and wearing the netherworld on his feet like sandals![225] In *Ludlul Bēl Nēmeqi*, Marduk is much greater in size than even the heavenly cosmos: "Marduk! The skies cannot sustain the weight of his hand."[226] Marduk's transcendence is equally well expressed in a prayer recited to that god during the Babylonian New Year's festival, in which the priest states "the expanse of heaven is (but) your insides."[227] And Nanna/Sin is said to fill "the wide sea" and "the distant heavens" with his divinity.[228] Accordingly, a natural phenomenon, such as storms, the sky, the sun or the moon, might become the embodiment of a divine power or the manifestation of a deity envisioned in anthropomorphic terms, but such a conceptualization of divine power cannot be contained within the limit of a single natural phenomenon.[229]

---

221. Gudea Cylinder A, v 13; see D. O. Edzard, *Gudea and His Dynasty*, The Royal Inscriptions of Mesopotamia Early Periods 3/1 (Toronto/Buffalo/London: University of Toronto Press, 1997), p. 72.
222. *Lugale*, 75 ff., *apud* Annus, *The God Ninurta*, p. 159.
223. KAR 102: see Annus, *The God Ninurta*, Appendix 1, pp. 205–6.
224. W. G. Lambert, *Babylonian Wisdom Literature*, p. 134, lines 154–55.
225. Foster, *Muses*, p. 497, Gula Hymn of Bullutsa-rabi, xiv, 133–34.
226. *Ludlul* I 9 and 11, in Foster, *Muses*, p. 310.
227. Cohen, *The Cultic Calendar*, p. 441.
228. Langdon, *Babylonian Penitential Psalms*, translated in ANET, pp. 385–86, line 14.
229. An argument against animism was presented in the review of H. Frankfort, Mrs. H. A. Frankfort, J. A. Wilson, and T. Jacobsen, *Before Philosophy: The Intellectual Adventure of Ancient Man* (Chicago and London: The University of Chicago Press, Pelican reprint 1961) by Samuel Noah

Although the gods were sometimes described as being beyond the limits of perception, they were also thought capable of inhabiting the world, for example, in their temples or in ominous phenomena. Sin, in this sense, was the moon and the moon-god. The transcendence of the god precludes any animistic interpretation of the divinity of the moon, yet the immanence of the god in the physical world mitigates any dualistic Platonic overtones. The moon cannot represent the totality of, but only a manifestation or image of, the god Sin, who was conceived of as transcending the limits of the physical world, yet was manifested in lunar phenomena. Both notions, the transcendent and the immanent, were expressible. Thus, Sin, as divine agent removed from the visible lunar disk, could be said to "show" the eclipse, just as the eclipse could be described in terms of its being the despondent moon-god in mourning.

The tension between the metaphysical and physical aspects of the heavenly bodies is reflected in the metaphorical and empirical (or literal) description of stars. Quite obviously, neither the identifications and associations made between heavenly bodies and gods, nor the belief that the stars were representations/manifestations/embodiments of gods, were the result of the stars "looking like" particular gods to the ancients. Descriptions of stars as gods have no bearing on any intrinsic facts about stars. Jupiter was not the star of Marduk because that planet "looked like" Marduk, and Marduk had no "appearance" apart from the imagined characteristics of that deity which stemmed from Babylonian religion. The creation of a system of divine identities introduced the basis for the perceiver/believer to assert the identity of star and god, i.e., to "see" the star as a god. Given the establishment of these identifications, what was "seen" came to be determined and described by that conceptual framework. Hence the coexistence in omen texts and astronomy of metaphorical (referring to gods) and empirical (referring to the appearance of physical phenomena) language. As a result, the description of what was "seen" in the heavens reflects the same set of associations characteristic of "religious" texts that talk about gods. The descriptive metaphorical and anthropomorphic language of omen protases shows how entwined were the "perceptual" and the "conceptual" dimensions of the practice of omen taking, but need not lead to the conflation of these dimensions in our interpretation of the texts. The diviners expressed their relationship to the heavenly phenomena in terms of their "seeing" the divine in the world and "experiencing" the gods' agency through the observation of phenomena (signs) and their consequences. The talk of the stars as gods must therefore be metaphorical, and therefore not to be read as evidence that the ancients did not differentiate between physical objects and gods.

Kramer in *JCS* 2 (1948), pp. 39–70, especially pp. 40–44, reprinted in Robert A. Segal, ed., *Theories of Myth: From Ancient Israel and Greece to Freud, Jung, Campbell and Lévi-Strauss*, Vol. 3 (New York and London: Garland Publishing, Inc., 1996), pp. 213–44.

Finally, the question was raised whether the three ways of referring to the relation between heavenly bodies and gods reflect distinct conceptualizations, or simply different manners of speaking about one and the same idea. How we understand this can have far-reaching implications for the relation of the astral dimension of Mesopotamian religion to Greek and Greco-Roman religion and philosophy, within which the planets as "visible gods" in their own right held quite different meanings. Indeed, the significant point seems to hang on whether the planets (or other stars) were divinities with direct and determinative power to affect the world and human life. Of course this idea of the planets as divine determiners of fate formed the premise of Hellenistic astrology. Interestingly, the gods (not the planets) as divine determiners of fate was a fundamental conception in Mesopotamian religion. But these are not at all the same idea.

It is with respect to the meaning of the celestial bodies as indicators of the future, reflected in celestial divination and supported by other evidence adduced in the present discussion, that I strongly suspect no such notion of the stars as autonomous divine determiners was formulated in the Mesopotamian cultural-historical context. Put another way, despite undeniable evidence of an astral component to Mesopotamian religion, there seems to be no evidence of "astral religion," complete with stellar or planetary worship. The discourse about stars and gods, however, does reflect some fundamental aspects of Mesopotamian "theology," i.e., the motif of the stars "as likenesses" of gods reflects the transcendent nature of deities, yet the personified stars point towards the idea of divine immanence. If there is a notional difference between the stars as divine images (likenesses) and the stars as divine embodiments, it seems not to have posed any problem within Mesopotamian theology. It makes no difference whether a prayer was addressed, say, to Ninurta or to Sirius, because the prayer in fact addressed the god represented by the star and was therefore to be recited in the physical presence of the star as the representation/embodiment of the god. In omen texts as well, stars and planets represented gods and so could be described metaphorically in terms appropriate to a description of anthropomorphic figures who display human capacities such as crying, seeing, showing, etc. This was possible because of these particular gods' astral nature and because of the power of symbolic language to bring the attributes of the gods to bear on the appearance and behavior of the celestial bodies.

With respect to the idea and function of autonomous astral gods in later antiquity, which generated many questions as to the life, intelligence, and soul of the stars for philosophers and theologians of the Greco-Roman and early Christian world, the distance from the Sumero-Assyro-Babylonian conceptualization is great and remains a function of differences in cosmologies. But, as we have seen, the cuneiform evidence does not present a unified picture either. Although the three "perspectives" did not seem to introduce irreconcilable disunities in the mythology, religion, divination or astronomy of ancient Mesopotamia, they may indeed be more than an artifact of language or a mere manner of speaking, revealing subtle tensions between immanence and transcendence in the conceptualization of the relation between celestial bodies and gods.

In the Likeness of Man

Reflections on the Anthropocentric Perception of the Divine in Mesopotamian Art

Tallay Ornan
The Hebrew University, Jerusalem

> L'essentiel est invisible pour les yeux.
> (Antoine de Saint-Exupéry, *Le petit prince*)

The aim of this contribution is to shed light, via some examples from the rich resources of Mesopotamian imagery, on the human form and properties of Mesopotamian gods and goddesses. I will argue that despite a preponderance of non-anthropomorphic representations of the divine in certain periods of Mesopotamian imagery, conceptualization of the divine remained anthropocentric throughout Mesopotamian history—in other words, that the concept of the essence of the divine was primarily based on a human model, even though the divine was not always represented by, or referred to, the human form. The question posed here is not whether there were other possible ways of alluding to the divine in addition to the human-like construct, but rather, which kind of metaphor—human or non-human—governed the Mesopotamian concept.

A case that underscores the complexity of the issue of the concretization of the divine form in Mesopotamia is the virtual absence of Anu, father of the gods, and Enlil, his son, from visual display.[1] That these two gods (and many other gods

---

Author's note: I wish to express my deep gratitude to Irene J. Winter, Boston, Joan Westenholz, Jerusalem, and Barbara Nevling Porter, Chebeague Island, for reading the first draft of this paper and for their insightful and helpful remarks. I am most thankful to Francesca Rochberg and Herman Vanstiphout for the stimulating and enjoyable discussions we had during the workshop. All the drawings prepared especially for this volume were made by Pnina Arad.

1. It is not only that we lack clear anthropomorphic representations of these two gods; even their specific attributes are unknown (U. Seidl, *Die babylonischen Kudurru-Reliefs*, OBO 87 [Fribourg and Göttingen: Vandenhoeck and Ruprecht, 1989]). In this regard, however, see Szarzyńska's suggestion that one of the Uruk reed symbols (see below)—a pole terminating in a volute—may have stood for Anu (K. Szarzyńska, "Some of the Oldest Cult Symbols in Archaic Uruk," *Jaarbericht Ex Oriente Lux* 30 [1987–1988], p. 11, symbol II). There are some textual references to emblems linked to Anu and Enlil, although here again, these are not necessarily their specific emblematic signifiers, as in an inscription of Nazi-Maruttaš, for example: " ... the socle and divine headdress of Anu, king of the heavens; the *gergīlu*-bird courier of Enlil ... " (K. E. Slanski, *The Babylonian Entitlement Narûs (Kudurrus): A Study in their Form and Function* [Boston: American Schools of Oriental Research, 2003], p. 129).

and goddesses, all of them members of the Mesopotamian pantheon) were envisioned as having human-like characteristics and form can be inferred from myth and ritual, according to which deities were fathered, born, nurtured, and raised in a manner similar to that of humans.[2] The use of the verb *walādu* (tud) 'to give birth, to fashion a cult image' in regard to the making of the gods' cultic images lends further credence to the notion that the Mesopotamian deity was based on the human model.[3]

If this was indeed the case, why are anthropomorphic portrayals of both Anu and Enlil, the supreme deities of the Mesopotamian pantheon, missing from the pictorial records? Such an absence may indicate an inherent difficulty for Mesopotamians to giving concrete form through visual images to the conceptual image of a human-shaped god. It may, in addition, signal a profound ambiguity in regard to the divine: that while deities were conceived of as personified entities, they were not always thus represented. It is this tension—that on the one hand, conceptually the divine was modeled on human characteristics and hence is to be regarded as an anthropocentric construct, and that on the other hand, the Mesopotamians found it difficult to give this mental construct concrete form in pictorial renderings—that first triggered my interest in the issue of the anthropomorphic and non-anthropomorphic depiction of gods and its possible bearing on the question of what a god was in ancient Mesopotamia.[4]

The subject of deified cult objects in Sumerian texts has been thoroughly treated in a study by G. J. Selz, which begins by considering the definition of "cult

---

2. V. A. Hurowitz, "The Mesopotamian God Image, From Womb to Tomb," *Journal of the American Oriental Society* 123 (2003), pp. 147–57.

3. R. M. Boehmer, "Götterdarstellungen in der Bildkunst," RLA 3 (1957–1971), pp. 466–69. U. Seidl "Kultbild, B," RLA 6 (1980–1983), pp. 317–18. J. T. Jacobsen, "God or Worshipper ?" in A. Leonard and B. Beyer Williams, eds., *Essays in Ancient Civilization Presented to Helene J. Kantor*, Studies in Ancient Oriental Civilization 47 (Chicago: The Oriental Institute of the University of Chicago, 1989), p. 126. W. G. Lambert, "Ancient Mesopotamian Gods: Superstition, Philosophy, Theology," *Revue de l'Histoire des Religions* 207 (1990), pp. 122–23. K. van der Toorn, B. Becking and P. W. van der Horst, eds., *Dictionary of Deities and Demons in the Bible (DDD)*, (Leiden, Boston, Köln: Eerdmans and Grand Rapids, 1999, 2nd edition), p. 357. J. Bottéro, *Religion in Ancient Mesopotamia*, trans. Teresa Lavender Fagan (Chicago and London: The University of Chicago, 2001), pp. 58–59 and 64–69. It should be noted, however, that *walādu* is not the only verb used to refer to the making of cult images; at times *epēšu* 'to make' is used: J. Renger, "Kultbild, A," RLA 6 (1980–1983), pp. 309 and 312–13, and Slanski, *Entitlement* narûs, pp. 2284–85, note 3. For the anthropomorphic behavior and form of Egyptian deities, see D. P. Silverman, "Divinity and Deities in Ancient Egypt," in B. E. Shafer, ed., *Religion in Ancient Egypt: Gods, Myths, and Personal Practice* (Ithaca and London: Routledge, 1995), pp. 13–23 and 28–30.

4. For the bearing of this issue on the biblical approach, see T. Ornan, "Idols and Symbols—Divine Representation in First Millennium Mesopotamian Art and its Bearing on the Second Commandment," *Tel Aviv* 31 (2004), pp. 90–121, and idem, *The Triumph of the Symbol: Pictorial Representation of Deities in Mesopotamia and the Biblical Image Ban*, OBO 213 (Fribourg: Academic Press, and Göttingen: Vandenhoeck and Ruprecht, 2005), chapter 7.

object" and how to distinguish between a holy object used in a religious ceremony and an object actually worshipped in a religious cult.[5] Selz then asks, "were these objects *themselves* thought of as deities, or was the divine being an anthropomorphic god or goddess equipped with the *characteristics* or the essence of the object?" (p. 172). The non-anthropomorphic cult objects Selz deals with are designated as divinities by the use of the DINGIR determinative as well as by the contexts in which they appear, including lists of gods, offering and ritual texts, inscribed votive donations, "name-giving" legends for cultic objects, and mouth-opening and -washing rituals (*pīt pî* and *mīs pî*). Selz classifies the deified cult objects into several categories, including professions and offices, cultural achievements and cultural properties, musical instruments, cultic paraphernalia, images, divine emblems and animals.[6] Although these deified objects often seem to represent non-anthropomorphic entities, the nature of the divinity attributed to them is not self-evident, since many of them demonstrate inherent associations with personified divine entities.[7] Hence, the appearance of non-anthropomorphic deified cult objects in texts, pictures and archeological finds can hardly be used to argue for a non-human concept of the divine in Mesopotamia. The only way to comprehend the significance of inanimate deified objects such as thrones, chariots, daggers, music instruments[8] or beds,[9] for example, is to acknowledge that they imply the existence of a human-like entity imagined as able to sit, ride, stab, play music or lie down.

That deified objects were regarded as the equals of deities represented by human-like images is apparent, for example, from a first-millennium Babylonian text describing a ritual carried out in the month of *Šabāṭu*, in which various gods accompanied Marduk in a procession from Babylon to Kiš.[10] Alongside the many human-shaped deities who took part in this ceremony were several inanimate

---

5. G. J. Selz, "The Holy Drum, the Spear, and the Harp': Towards an Understanding of the Problems of Deification in Third Millennium Mesopotamia," in I. L. Finkel and M. J. Geller, eds., *Sumerian Gods and Their Representations*, Cuneiform Monographs 7 (Groningen: Styx, 1997), pp. 167–213.

6. *Idem*, p. 172.

7. Lambert, "Ancient Mesopotamian Gods," pp. 128–29.

8. R. M. Sigrist, *Les* sattukku *dans l'Ešumeša durant la période d'Isin et Larsa*, Bibliotheca Mesopotamica 11 (Malibu: Undena, 1984), pp. 149–51 (for deified objects such as thrones, weapons, gates and chariots in the Isin-Larsa period). Lambert, "Ancient Mesopotamian Gods," pp. 128–29. Selz, "The Holy Drum," pp. 170–74 and 178. For pictorial and textual evidence referring to the chariot of Ningirsu as mentioned and depicted by Gudea, see C. E. Suter, *Gudea's Temple Buildings: The Representations of an Early Mesopotamian Ruler in Text and Image* (Groningen: Styx, 2000), p. 187.

9. For a rare appearance of beds as recipients of offering and probably of cult offerings in Neo-Assyrian inscriptions, see B. N. Porter in this volume.

10. A. R. George, "Four Temple Rituals from Babylon," in A. R. George and I. L. Finkel, eds., *Wisdom, Gods and Literature: Studies in Assyriology in Honour of W. G. Lambert* (Winona Lake: Eisenbrauns, 2000), pp. 289–99.

objects, such as a divine scepter, divine weapons and standards, whose divinity is clearly conveyed through the use of the divine determinative as well as by the fact that they appear alongside personified gods and goddesses. As all of these items can only be "used" by personified figures it is, again, conceivable that they stand for (and reflect a specific facet of) anthropomorphic deities. The relationship of these deified objects to personified gods is in particular demonstrated in this text by the identification of some of the weapons, the *muštēšir-ḫabli*, the $^{d.giš}$tukul and the ^{d}sa.zu, as belonging to Marduk.[11] In the same way, non-anthropomorphic deified objects mentioned in Neo-Babylonian texts from Uruk,[12] such as the divine staff (*ḫuṭāru*), the divine quiver (*išpatu*), the divine star-shaped branding iron (*kakkabtu*) of Ishtar and the divine standards (*urigallu*) of Ishtar and the goddess Uṣur-amāssu are also to be seen as cultic paraphernalia which could only "operate" and have "meaning" by being part of and "belonging" to the personified image of Ishtar, or of Uṣur-amāssu. That the latter cult objects were not deified on their own merit and that they "needed" the "background" image of the goddess is supported here by the very use of the quiver and the star-form of the branding iron (as well as its name, *kakkabtu*), as the star and the quiver are the goddess Ishtar's most frequent symbols and attributes. The idea that these deified non-anthropomorphic objects indeed "received" their divinity from Ishtar is strengthened, in this case, by P.-A. Beaulieu's suggestion that they were housed in the goddess's temple at Uruk.[13] Similarly, cult objects classified by Selz as cultural achievements, cultural properties or professions[14] were conceptually modeled on human social institutions and, hence, could only "function" and be meaningful in constructs that duplicated human existence. In the same way, deified objects such as man-made shrines, or city and temple gates[15] are to be seen as objects whose divinity was obtained from the major personified deity who was the patron of the given city and was the main deity worshipped in its temple.[16]

---

11. George, "Four Temple Rituals," line 20 and p. 298.

12. P.-A. Beaulieu, *The Pantheon of Uruk during the Neo-Babylonian Period*, Cuneiform Monographs 7 (Leiden and Boston: Brill and Styx, 2003), pp. 351–54. For the identification of Uṣur-amāssu as a goddess who dwelled in the Eanna temple and possibly shared a shrine with the goddess Urkayītu, see *ibid.*, pp. 229 and 255–56.

13. Beaulieu, *The Pantheon of Uruk*, p. 351. When looking at various deified cult objects as manifesting one facet of a multivalent personified god and receiving their divinity from this divinity, it is hard to accept Beaulieu's division between the inanimate emblems of Marduk and Nabu and other non-anthropomorphic deified cult objects and hybrids, ibid., p. 351, note 1.

14. Selz, "The Holy Drum," pp. 171–74.

15. For deified temples and city gates found, for example, in first-millennium *tākultu* ritual texts see the discussion of B. N. Porter, "The Anxiety of Multiplicity," in B. Nevling Porter, ed., *One God or Many? Concepts of Divinity in the Ancient World*, Transactions of the Casco Bay Assyriological Institute 1 (Chebeague Island, Maine: The Casco Bay Assyriological Institute, 2000), pp. 231–32.

16. Lambert, "Ancient Mesopotamian Gods," p. 129. See also *idem*, "The God Aššur," *Iraq* 45 (1983), p. 83: " . . . however, there is never confusion between god and temple or god and city, and

When animals, fantastic creatures, natural phenomena and celestial bodies appear as deified objects, however, their associations with divine metaphors of the human type are not as easy to comprehend as with the inanimate cult objects discussed above. But, as Lambert and Wiggermann have proposed, fantastic hybrids and animals are strongly linked to personified deities, since they are considered to be rivals defeated by a personified deity in the remote mythological past which had consequently become his or her servants and emblems.[17] First-millennium deified fantastic creatures, which appear with a divine determinative and are recipients of offerings, are mentioned, for example, in the Neo-Babylonian archive of the Eanna temple at Uruk, discussed above.[18] At first sight it seems that the two hybrids in question—the *urdimmu* 'the lion-man' and the *urmaḫlûlu* 'the lion centaur'—represent independent non-anthropomorphic deities because their images, as rendered in pictorial compositions, reveal clear theriomorphic affinities. However, the human elements combined with the nonhuman features of these hybrids and, in particular, the human-like stance of the *urdimmu* may indicate that a human conceptual model governed their fashioning. In addition, their placement as protective hybrids at gateways hints at their mythological past, when they were among the defeated foes of Marduk, and implies that they might have been perceived as deified emanations of the god who had defeated them. The symbolization process illustrated here by the role of the *urdimmu* and the *urmaḫlûlu* accords well with age-old patterns of Mesopotamian cultic behavior in which a lesser divinity, an animated object or a former divine rival could be substituted for an imagined (human-shaped) deity and receive his or her deification. Nevertheless, it should be stressed that this process of divine symbolization became particularly intense in first-millennium Babylonia, when hybrids, animals, or demons that hitherto had appeared mainly as attributes became divine symbols and foci of a cult.[19] Among the factors that inspired this increasingly metaphorical world view was perhaps the Aramaization of southern Mesopotamia and its inevitable consequence, the increasing separation of spoken Aramaic from the written Sumerian and Akkadian languages.[20]

The anthropomorphized character of deified natural entities such as rivers or mountains, which according to Lambert were typical of northern Mesopotamia

---

the impression is received that as far as numinous quality attaches to temple or city, it is simply the reflected glory of the divine occupant."

17. *Ibid*. Wiggermann, "Mischwesen A," RLA 8 (1994), pp. 225–29.

18. Beaulieu, *The Pantheon of Uruk*, pp. 355–68 (with references to visual descriptions of the hybrids).

19. *Ibid*., p. 357. Ornan, *The Triumph*, chapter 5 (2.2).

20. P. Michalowski, "Presence at the Creation," in T. Abusch, J. Huehnergard and P. Steinkeller, eds., *Lingering Over Words: Studies in Ancient Near Eastern Literature in Honor of William L. Moran* (Atlanta: Scholars Press, 1990), p. 395.

and Syria,[21] can also, at times, be demonstrated. That the divine was perceived as a personified entity in these instances is supported, for example, by the reconstructed history of the god Aššur offered by Lambert, according to which the name of the natural hill of the city of Ashur became the name of its major, personified god.[22] Ascribing a body organ in the shape of a natural force to a major god imagined in human form also occurs in Gudea's dream, where Ningirsu is seen by Gudea as having a lower body in the shape of a flood storm.[23] The incorporation of a natural phenomenon into the image of a personified deity, exemplified here by the constructed image of Aššur and by the envisioned figure of Ningirsu, is in accord with some pictorial compositions, dealt with below, that represent fused icons in which a natural phenomenon is combined with a divine human body.[24] Similarly, that human-like form, properties and character were attributed to deified celestial bodies can be assumed from the plethora of textual equations of celestial bodies with prominent personified deities. As demonstrated by Francesca Rochberg in this volume, major deities such as Sin, Ishtar, and Šamaš, as well as Marduk, Ninurta and Nergal, were all envisioned as anthropomorphized divinities manifested, *inter alia*, in particular heavenly bodies. Pictorial associations of the star, the moon crescent and the solar disc with anthropomorphic representations of Ishtar, Sin and Šamaš,[25] respectively, support the supposition that deified celestial bodies were basically envisaged as manifesting only one aspect of multi-faceted, personified divine images. A rare first-millennium pictorial depiction of the *sebetti*, the Pleiades, from the North Palace of Ashurbanipal[26] underscores the personified character of celestial luminaries. The *sebetti*, otherwise visually rendered non-anthropomorphically as the seven-circles emblem,[27] are represented on a doorway relief of the North Palace by figures in human form whose belligerent portrayal befits the nature of the Pleiades as warrior gods (fig. 1).[28]

---

21. Lambert, "Ancient Mesopotamian Gods," p. 127. *Idem,* "The God Aššur," p. 84.

22. *Ibid.,* pp. 85–86.

23. D. O. Edzard, *Gudea and His Dynasty,* RIMA 3:1 (Toronto, Buffalo and London: University of Toronto, 1997), p. 71, iv: 18.

24. Wiggermann, "Mischwesen," p. 236.

25. For the identification of the moon, star and sun disc with Sin, Ishtar and Šamaš respectively on the Sippar Tablet, the Bel-Harran-bel-uṣur stele and Sargon's Larnaka stele, and on the rock relief of Sennacherib at Bavian, see Seidl, *Kudurru,* pp. 97–101 (with bibliography).

26. R. D. Barnett, *Sculptures from the North Palace of Ashurbanipal at Nineveh, 668–627 B.C.* (London: The British Museum Publications, 1976), p. 48, pl. 38.

27. E. D. van Buren, *Symbols of the Gods in Mesopotamian Art,* Analecta Orientalia 23 (Rome: Pontificium Institutum Biblicum, 1945), pp. 78ff. Seidl, *Kudurru,* p. 103. J. Black and A. Green, *Gods, Demons and Symbols of Ancient Mesopotamia: An Illustrated Dictionary* (London: The British Museum, 1992), p. 162. S. Herbordt, *Neuassyrische Glyptik des 8.–7. Jh. v. Chr. unter besonderer Berücksichtigung der Siegelungen auf Tafeln und Tonverschlüssen* (Helsinki: The Neo-Assyrian Text Corpus Project, 1992), p. 103.

28. F. Rochberg, "The Stars Their Likeness," notes 95 and 96 (in this volume).

Although Mesopotamian theological thinking is manifest in diverse traditions that were probably, at least in their initial phases, independent of one another,[29] it nevertheless betrays a systematic approach, as Lambert postulates. This approach is typified, among other factors, by a theological concept in which no distinction is made between cosmic and natural phenomena and man-made achievements: "The distinction we make between phenomena of nature, such as rivers, and human products, such as canals, was not part of their thinking."[30] In this kind of world-view a separation between a divine entity and its natural or man-made emanations is rather improbable. Consequently, the idea of the classification of deified stars, plants or constellations into a special category not included within the personified divine realm, as postulated by Bottéro,[31] is hardly convincing. Moreover, looking at the systematic religious thinking of Mesopotamia as a holistic world-view, one may suggest that in cases of a deification of objects upon which the human imprint cannot be traced, the conceptual paradigm for such non-anthropomorphic divine agents was also centered in, and fitted to, a human model.

Fig. 1. A personified *sebettu*, North Palace, Nineveh (after R. D. Barnett, *Palace of Ashurbanipal*, pl. 38).

The notions discussed above place in the foreground the "dependence" of deified cult objects on personified deities and on a divine structure that mirrors human properties, forms and existence. This conclusion strongly suggests that deified objects and non-anthropomorphic entities should be regarded as emanations of divinities perceived as having human form.[32] The issue at stake here is not whether the various non-anthropomorphic manifestations of the divine could have been worshiped as independent cult objects but, rather, the hierarchical

---

29. Bottéro, *Religion*, p. 60.
30. Lambert, "Ancient Mesopotamian Gods," pp. 119, 125, 127.
31. Bottéro, *Religion*, p. 70. See on this matter F. Rochberg, "The Stars Their Liknesses," in this volume.
32. Lambert, "Ancient Mesopotamian Gods," p. 128.

relationship that was envisioned between non-anthropomorphized cult objects and anthropomorphic divine images. The following survey of pictorial representations will, I hope, sustain the notion that the overall cognitive understanding of divinities in Mesopotamia was governed by human-like images and is to be reconstructed as focusing on the human model and, hence, can be regarded as an example of anthropocentric religious thinking.

In order to illuminate the complex relationship between the cognitive concept of the divine and its visual expressions, this paper will first survey non-anthropomorphic representations of the divine from the mid-second to the mid-first millennium, when the removal of human-shaped deities became a dominant characteristic of the pictorial message (Part I. 1–3). That an anthropocentric perception of deity continued to govern Mesopotamian thinking even in these periods will be demonstrated by the presentation of anthropomorphic renderings of divinities dating from those same periods (Part II. 1–4). This will be demonstrated by the presence of human features woven into non-anthropomorphic divine representations (Part II. 2), by depictions of lesser divinities in human shape (Part II. 3), and by some exceptional anthropomorphic renderings of major deities (II. 4).

I. Non-anthropomorphic representations of Mesopotamian gods and goddesses

I.1 Preliminary Remarks

Before elaborating on the non-anthropomorphic representation of the divine in Mesopotamia, some general remarks concerning the typical characteristics of such representations are in order. A non-anthropomorphic divine depiction can take the form of an inanimate object, such as the wedge-like reed stylus of Nabu (*qan ṭuppi*); of an animal, such as the lion of Ishtar; of a composite fantastic creature, such as the *mušḫuššu* of Marduk; of the stylized image of a natural phenomenon, such as the crescent moon of Sin (*uskaru*) and the star of Ishtar; or of a floral motif, like Šala's ear of corn. At times, a composite icon made up of several elements, such as a tree flanked by ibexes, constitutes a divine symbol. Such objects, animals, hybrids and floral motifs have a dual role in Mesopotamian art. When they are shown carried by a (human-shaped) deity or depicted in his or her immediate proximity, they are to be understood as identifying attributes; when shown without a godly figure in human form, they are to be understood as emblems standing for their signified divine entity.[33] The role of a symbol as a substitute for a cult image of human shape can be determined from compositions where the symbol is accompanied by a mortal worshipper and its role as substi-

---

33. Seidl, *Kudurru*, pp. 120, 121, 125.

tute for the cult image is indicated by the cultic hand gesture of the mortal (e.g., fig. 2). By extension, we may also identify symbols depicted on their own, with no accompanying worshipper, as representing gods or goddesses. The conclusion that such symbols indeed replaced deities in pictorial compositions is reinforced by instances in which inscribed verbal labels accompany a symbolic visual representation and specifically identify it as a deity, as is exemplified by a few *kudurru* stone monuments (lately termed "Entitlement *narûs*"; see below) on which small labels accompany the emblems (see below, fig. 7).[34] Divine symbols also functioned as amuletic jewels, as is conveyed, for example, by the *dumāqu* ceremonial necklaces worn by the Neo-Assyrian kings. These necklaces are composed of emblems of the major Assyrian deities, Aššur, Šamaš, Sin, Ishtar and Adad, and mark the king who wears them as taking his traditional role as a *šangû* 'high priest' (fig. 3).[35] The diversity of pictorial contexts in which divine symbols appear highlights their varying roles as attributes, as protective images and also as objects of cult that were the focus of religious veneration.[36]

A divine symbol may refer to more than one deity. For example, the winged disc in Neo-Assyrian art

Fig. 2. Worshipper gesturing before the emblems of Marduk and Nabu, seal impression, Uruk (after E. Ehrenberg, *Eanna-Tablets*, pl. 5:44).

---

34. G. Contenau, "Fragments de kudurru (monuments divers)," in R. de Mecquenem, G. Contenau, R. Pfister and N. Belaiew, eds., *Archéologie susienne, Memoires de la mission archéologique en Iran 29, Mission de Susiane* (Paris: Universitaires de France, 1943), pp. 162–71. Seidl, *Kudurru*, pp. 28–30 (nos. 29, 34, 35, 36, 38), 35–36 (no. 50), 37–38 (no. 59). Slanski, *Entitlement narûs*, pp. 127–28.

35. U. Magen, *Assyrische Königsdarstellungen—Aspekte der Herrschaft, eine Typologie* (Mainz: Philip von Zabern, 1986), pp. 54–55. CAD 3, s.v. *dumāqu* b, 179. J. Börker-Klähn, *Altvorderasiatische Bildstelen und vergleichbare Felsreliefs* (Mainz: Philip von Zabern, 1982), nos. 136, 137, 148, 164. A. H. Layard, *Monuments of Nineveh* I (London: John Murray, 1849), pl. 25. E. Strommenger, *Die Neuassyrische Rundskulptur* (Berlin: Mann, 1970), pp. 16–17, figs. 4, 5, pls. 4a, 6a. A ceremonial necklace with divine emblems, which specifically signifies the king trampling his enemy, is also worn by Tiglath-pileser III (R. D. Barnett and M. Falkner, *The Sculptures of Aššur-nasir-apli II (883–859 B.C.), Tiglath-Pileser III (745–727 B.C.), Esarhaddon (681–669 B.C.) from the Central and South-West Palaces at Nimrud* [London: The Trustees of the British Museum, 1962], pl. XCV–XCVI). On the steles of Šamši-Adad V and Adad-nirari III a large Maltese cross replaces the five-emblem *dumāqu* necklace.

36. For the protective role of the divine symbols (complemented on *kudurru* monuments [*narûs*] by inscribed curses) in safeguarding both the monument and its content, see Slanski, *Entitlement narûs*, pp. 133, 144–45.

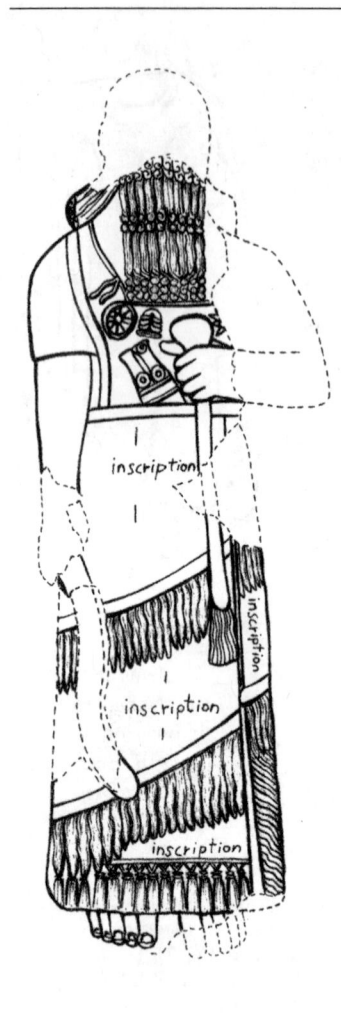

may stand for the god Aššur as well as Šamaš.[37] In first-millennium Syrian imagery, in particular, it can also refer to the moon god when a crescent is depicted with it, or allude to a goddess when a rosette is embedded in it.[38] The bull and its calf are other divine emblems which can refer to and symbolize two separate deities: Adad or Sin.[39] Similarly the composite icon of the suckling cow can be depicted in first-millennium glyptic art as a focus of cult (fig. 4) and concurrently as a mount-animal of both male and female deities (fig. 5).[40]

I.2 Divine Symbols in Babylonian Art

Inanimate symbols standing for deities

Although the replacement of human-shaped portrayals of deities by non-anthropomorphic symbols is best documented from the middle of the second millennium onwards, some forerunners of inanimate emblems standing for (presumably human-shaped) gods and goddesses are attested already in the late fourth millennium. This is illustrated on

Fig. 3. Basalt statue of Shalmaneser III, Ashur (after A. Pasinli, *Istanbul Archaeological Museums: The Ancient Orient*, Istanbul: Aturizm Yayinlari, 2001, p. 195).

---

37. W. G. Lambert, "Trees, Snakes and Gods in Ancient Syria and Anatolia," *Bulletin of the School of Oriental and African Studies* 48 (1985), p. 439 and n. 27.

38. T. Ornan, "A Complex System of Religious Symbols: The Case of the Winged-disc in First-Millennium Near Eastern Imagery," in C. E. Suter and Ch. Uehlinger, eds., *Crafts and Images in Contact: Studies on Eastern Mediterranean Minor Art of the 1st Millennium BCE*, OBO (Fribourg: Academic Press and Paulusverlag, 2005), pp. 221–27.

39. T. Ornan, "The Bull and its Two Masters: Moon and Storm Deities in Relation to the Bull in Ancient Near Eastern Art," *Israel Exploration Journal* 51 (2001), pp. 1–26.

40. D. Collon, *Catalogue of the Western Asiatic Seals in the British Museum, Cylinder Seals V: Neo-Assyrian and Neo-Babylonian Periods* (London: The British Museum Press, 2001), nos. 218, 219. B. Teissier, *Ancient Near Eastern Cylinder Seals from the Marcopoli Collection* (Berkeley: Suma and University of California Press, 1984), no. 236. O. Keel, *Das Böcklein in der Milch seiner Mutter und Verwandtes*, OBO 33 (Fribourg and Göttingen: Vandenhoeck and Ruprecht, 1980), fig. 99.

Fig. 4. A suckling cow as the focus of cultic veneration, unprovenanced seventh-century cylinder seal. WA 8950. ©Copyright The Trustees of the British Museum.

Fig. 5. Goddess on suckling cow, unprovenanced cylinder seal of *el'mr* (P. Bordreuil, "Le répertoire iconographique des sceaux araméens inscrits et son évolution," in B. Sass and Ch. Uehlinger, eds., *Studies in the Iconography of Northwest Semitic Inscribed Seals*, OBO 125 [Fribourg and Göttingen: Vandenhoeck and Ruprecht, 1993], p. 77, fig. 6).

some Uruk-type cylinder seals on which tall standards, usually considered to represent actual reed posts and identified with URI, are surmounted by crescents standing for the moon god or by a small disk representing a solar disk.[41] This manner of divine representation is best exemplified by a particular type of reed

---

41. Szarzyńska, *Cult Symbols in Archaic Uruk*, pp. 4 (table 1, symbol VI), 10. K. Szarzyńska, "Archaic Sumerian Standards," *JCS* 48 (1996), p. 6 (and fig. 3), 13–14 (Table 1, emblem V).

standard surmounted by a volute-like finial, common in cultic and ceremonial contexts, that is depicted on various artifacts from the Late Uruk period. In these cases the volute-like standard may appear on its own, symbolizing Inanna,[42] or in proximity to a human-shaped feminine figure, presumably that of the goddess as rendered on the Uruk Vase,[43] where it is to be understood as her specific signifier.

A later example of the role of a divine symbol is the lion-headed bird Anzu that symbolizes Ningirsu on Early Dynastic artifacts.[44] Although human-shaped deities became the norm in Akkadian glyptic art,[45] non-anthropomorphic emblems—astral symbols—appear above the deified ruler Naram-Sin on the Victory Stele.[46] Representations of divine emblems as the foci of veneration, such as a crescent moon placed on a standard, are found in Neo-Sumerian glyptic art.[47] And, despite the fact that human-shaped deities became more common in Old Babylonian imagery, the depiction of the crescent standard in place of human-shaped Sin was well known in Old Babylonian art.[48] The lightning bolt and the bull symbolizing Adad,[49] as well as the curved staff (*gamlu*) of Amurru,[50] are

---

42. U. Seidl, "Göttersymbole und -attribute," RLA 3 (1971), p. 490. Szarzyńska, *Cult Symbols in Archaic Uruk*, pp. 4 (Table 1, symbol I), 10. P. Steinkeller, "Inanna's Archaic Symbol," in J. Braun, K. Łyczkowska, M. Popko and P. Steinkeller, eds., *Written On Clay and Stone: Ancient Near Eastern Studies Presented to Krystyna Szarzyńska on the Occasion of her 80th Birthday* (Warsaw: AGADE, 1998), p. 87 (with earlier bibliography). On the basis of Early Dynastic texts, Steinkeller interprets the volute-like symbol of Inanna as an item made of fabric and lapis lazuli, probably a sort of a diadem (suh).

43. A. Moortgat, *The Art of Ancient Mesopotamia: The Classical Art of the Near East* (London and New York: Phaidon, 1969), pp. 11–12, pls. 19–21.

44. PKG, pls. 88, 97, 120 and compare pl. 90 (the Stele of the Vultures, where Anzu appears as an attribute held by the god). Suter, *Gudea*, pp. 187–88.

45. D. Collon, "The Near Eastern Moon God," in D. J.W. Meijer, ed., *Natural Phenomena, Their Meaning, Depiction and Description in the Ancient Near East* (Amsterdam: Royal Netherlands Academy of Arts and Sciences, 1992), p. 21.

46. H. A. Groenewegen-Frankfort, *Arrest and Movement: Space and Time in the Art of the Ancient Near East*, (Cambridge and London: Harvard University Press, 1987), pp. 163–64. D. Bänder, *Die Siegesstele des Naramsîn und ihre Stellung in Kunst- und Kulturgeschichte*, Beiträge zur Kulturgeschichte 103, (Idstein: Schulz-Kirchner, 1995), pp. 171–72.

47. G. Colbow, "More Insights into Representations of the Moon God in the Third and Second Millennium," in I. L. Finkel and M. J. Geller, eds., *Sumerian Gods and their Representations*, Cuneiform Monographs 7 (Groningen: Styx, 1997), pp. 22–24.

48. Ornan, "The Bull," pp. 9–11.

49. The replacement of the storm god by a bull was well known in Anatolia during the third millennium as evidenced by bronze standards from Alaca Höyük. It appears in local glyptics from Kanesh level II, as well as on the Old Hittite relief vase from Inandik and on wall decoration from Alaca Höyük. See T. Özgûç, *Inandiktepe, An Important Cult Center in the Old Hittite Period* (Ankara: Turk Tarih Kurumu, 1988), p. 100; N. Leinwand, "Regional Characteristics in the Styles and Iconography of the Seal Impressions of Level II at Kültepe," *The Journal of the Ancient Near Eastern Society of Columbia University* 21 (1992), pp. 145–53.

50. CAD 5 s.v. *gamlu*, 35. F. A. M. Wiggermann, "The Staff of Ninšubura: Studies in Babylonian Demonology, II," *Jaarbericht Ex Oriente Lux* 29 (1985–6), p. 5 and note 6. D. Collon, *Catalogue of*

other common divine emblems depicted in Old Babylonian glyptics as attributes, as secondary elements, or as objects of cultic veneration.[51]

Non-anthropomorphic renderings became the most common form of divine representation on Babylonian stone monuments dating from the mid-fourteenth to the seventh centuries, where they are accompanied by written inscriptions engraved alongside the pictorial renderings (e.g., fig. 6). These stone monuments are termed in the modern scholarly literature *kudurru*s, or Entitlement *narû*s ('stone monuments') as suggested by Slanski, who sees the pictorial renderings and their written mode as commemorating the acquisition of the entitlements described in the text and assuring their transfer to future generations.[52] As a rule on these monuments, non-anthropomorphic emblems represent the deities whose role was to ensure and ratify the inscribed entitlements. Indeed, as pointed out by Seidl, the portrayal of the divine in human form was pushed aside by other means of representation—symbolic representation—in Middle Babylonian art in general, and on *kudurru*s in particular.[53] This process of non-anthropomorphic symbolization, which typifies the imagery of the *kudurru*s, is illustrated by the visual rendering of Gula. Whereas the

Fig. 6. Kudurru of Nebuchadnezzar I. WA 90858. ©Copyright The Trustees of the British Museum.

---

the Western Asiatic Seals in the British Museum, Cylinder Seals III: Isin-Larsa and Old Babylonian Periods (London: British Museum Publications, 1986), p. 27, nos. 225–34. G. Colbow, "Eine Abbildung des Gottes Amurru in Einem Mari-Brief," in D. Charpin and J-M. Durand. eds., *Florilegium marianum III,* Mémoires de N.A.B.U. 4 (Paris: Société pour l'étude du Proche-Orient ancien, 1997), pp. 85–90.

51. E.g., Collon, *Cylinder Seals* III, p. 53, no. 95. E. Porada, *Corpus of Near Eastern Seals in North American Collections* I: *The Pierpont Morgan Library* (Washington: Pantheon Books, 1948), no. 503.

52. Slanski, *Entitlement* narûs, pp. 19–55, 59–62, 143.

53. Seidl, *Kudurru,* p. 195. PKG, p. 299.

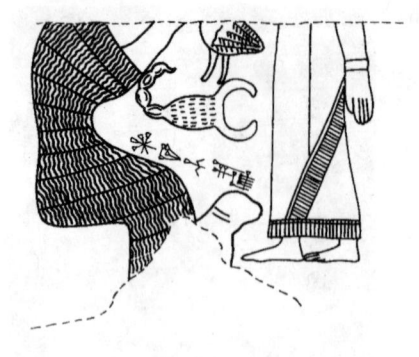

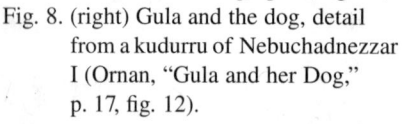

Fig. 7. (above) Gula with the dog and an identifying inscription on a mid-twelfth century kudurru (Ornan, "Gula and her Dog," p. 17, fig. 11).

Fig. 8. (right) Gula and the dog, detail from a kudurru of Nebuchadnezzar I (Ornan, "Gula and her Dog," p. 17, fig. 12).

goddess is depicted anthropomorphically in the twelfth and the first half of the eleventh century (e.g., figs 7, 8; see below), these representations decrease in number during the latter part of the eleventh century and disappear in the course of the first millennium.[54]

The propensity to favor divine non-anthropomorphic representations is also reflected, though to a lesser degree, in Middle Babylonian glyptics. It is illustrated by the depictions of a tree as an independent symbol on some seals classified as belonging to the Second Kassite glyptic group, dating from the mid-fourteenth century and continuing into the twelfth century.[55] In particular it is evident on twelfth-century Babylonian cylinder seals belonging to the Third Kassite group that reveal a resemblance to "mature" Middle Assyrian cylinder seals, where non-anthropomorphic divine representations were common.[56] The tendency to avoid human-shaped portrayals of the divine is also apparent in the twelfth-century Babylonian sub-group of cylinder seals belonging to the Pseudo-Kassite group,

---

54. Seidl, *Kudurru*, p. 28, no. 29, pp. 143, 196.

55. D. M. Matthews, *Principles of Composition in Near Eastern Glyptic of the Later Second Millennium B.C.*, OBO.SA 8 (Fribourg and Göttingen: Vandenhoeck and Ruprecht, 1990), pp. 60–63, especially nos. 157–73.

56. Matthews, *Principles*, pp. 64–66, 83. See, however, the reservations raised by Stein for the chronological correspondence of Third Kassite Babylonian seals and the mature Middle Assyrian style: D. Stein, "Principles of Composition?: Review Article of Matthews 1990," *Wiener Zeitschrift für die Kunde des Morgenlandes* 84 (1994), p. 165. See also B. Wittmann, "Babylonische Rollsiegel des 11.-7. Jahrhunderts v. Chr.," *BaM* 23 (1992), pp. 183–90.

also dating to the twelfth century and regarded by Matthews as a derivative of the First Kassite glyptic group.[57] These two latter glyptic groups include many seals that are made of soft stones or composite material, in contrast to the other Kassite cylinder seals, which are usually made of brightly colored hard stones, such as chalcedonies and agates.[58] The compositions most commonly rendered on these seals (trees flanked by animals, fantastic creatures and combat scenes) highlight the preference of late second-millennium Babylonian glyptic for non-anthropomorphic representations of the divine. The abstention of Middle Babylonian cylinder seals from representing human-shaped deities is underscored by seals showing only a worshipper, and by seals engraved with inscriptions only, with a divine image entirely missing (e.g., fig. 9).[59]

Fig. 9. Lapis lazuli cylinder seal of Kadašman-Enlil II, unprovenanced. IAA 65–210. Courtesy of The Israel Museum, Jerusalem.

Divine symbols are also represented on ninth- to eighth-century Babylonian modeled-style cylinder seals. On these seals, however, they do not appear as the foci of cult, but as secondary elements, often accompanying combat scenes.[60] The most numerous representations of divine symbols in Mesopotamia are attested on Babylonian cylinder and stamp seals dating from the seventh to fifth centuries.[61] The symbols shown on these seals, in front of which a gesturing worshipper

---

57. Matthews, *Principles*, pp. 66–69.

58. D. Collon, *First Impressions: Cylinder Seals in the Ancient Near East* (London: British Museum Press, 1987), p. 61.

59. Ornan, "Idols and Symbols," pp. 101, 103 (with bibliography). For the cylinder seal of Kadašman-Enlil II illustrated here in fig. 9, see E. Herzfeld, "Drei Inschriften aus persischem Gebiet," *Mitteilungen der altorientalische Gesellschaft* 4 (1928–1929), pp. 81–82, fig. 1. G. Stiehler-Alegria Delgado, *Die Kassitischen Glyptic* (Munich and Vienna: Profil, 1996), p. 211, no. 249.

60. E.g. Wittmann, "Rollsiegel," nos. 29, 30, 32, 34, 35.

61. The seventh to fifth centuries in the history of Babylonia are usually considered by art historians and archaeologists to be part of the Neo-Babylonian Period, which pertains to first-millennium Babylonia and includes both the time span parallel to the Neo-Assyrian Empire and the period of the Chaldean Dynasty founded by Nabopolassar (625–605 BCE). Assyriologists include these two centuries under the term "Late-Babylonian," the period which begins with Nabopolassar (E. Ehrenberg, *Uruk, Late Babylonian Seal Impressions on Eanna-Tablets:* Ausgrabungen in Uruk-Warka Endberichte 18 (Mainz am Rhein: Philipp von Zabern, 1999), p. 2.

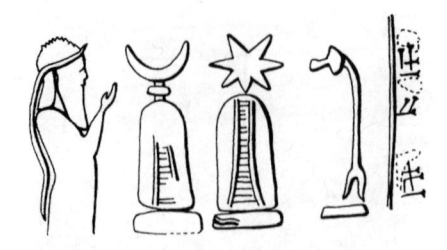

Fig. 10. Worshipper gesturing before a moon crescent, a star and a ram-headed staff, seal impression, Uruk (after E. Ehrenberg, *Eanna-Tablets*, pl. 13: 104).

stands, appear as the foci of cult.[62] The theme was especially common on conical or pyramidal stamp seals cut in the late drilled style, and on cylinder seals, mainly those worked in the modeled style (e.g., figs. 2, 10). The repertoire of emblems selected for these seals is diverse. It usually includes: a crescent or a star placed on a mountain-like rise, a ram-headed scepter and a goat-fish, a scorpion man, or some type of fowl, perhaps a rooster. Divine symbols on seventh- to fifth-century Babylonian glyptics also often appear as the only element on a seal, with no worshipper.[63] Based on the homology of the symbols depicted on their own with those shown accompanied by worshippers we can, as suggested above, identify the former as standing for divine entities and probably representing cult objects.

A few seventh- to fifth-century Babylonian seals depicting the veneration of divine symbols were revealed in a hoard of jewelry in the Enunmah temple at Ur, above a pavement attributed to Nebuchadnezzar II and below Persian buildings. The same theme is found on sealed tablets dating from the time of Nabonidus to Xerxes I that were uncovered at the Ebabbar temple at Sippar. The seals used for these impressions probably belonged to the *šangû* priests, personnel of the temple. The same theme also appears on more than half of the sealed tablets in the temple archive at Uruk, dating from the reign of Nabopolassar to the early years of Darius I.[64] Babylonian seals engraved with divine symbols were found in the *perlendepot* hoard, uncovered in a house found under a Parthian building at Babylon. The hoard included many luxury items and seals dating to various periods that were apparently collected and interred during the Parthian period. Among the precious objects found in this hoard were two huge, inscribed lapis lazuli cylinders depicting the human-shaped images of Marduk and Adad, which

---

62. E. Ehrenberg, "Sixth-Century Urukaean Seal Impressions," in W. W. Hallo and I. J. Winter, eds., *Seals and Seals Impressions,* Proceedings of the 45th Rencontre Assyriologique Internationale II (Bethesda: CDL, 2001), pp.188–90.

63. Cf. Porada, *Corpus*, pp. 95, 98–100. B. Buchanan and P. R. S. Moorey, *Catalogue of Ancient Near Eastern Seals in the Ashmolean Museum III: The Iron Age Stamp Seals* (Oxford: Clarendon, 1988). pp. 56–57, 66. Collon, *Cylinder Seals* V, p. 193.

64. C. L. Woolley, *Ur Excavations IX: The Neo-Babylonian and Persian Periods* (London: The British Museum, 1962), p. 29, pl. 30 (U. 487–8). J. MacGinnis, *Letter Orders From Sippar and the Administration of the Ebabbara in the Late-Babylonian Period* (Poznan: Bonami, 1995), pp. 170–73. Ehrenberg, *Eanna-Tablets*, pp. 15–25, 43, nos. 20–153. Idem, "Urukaean Seal Impressions," pp. 185, 188–90. Buchanan and Moorey, *Stamp Seals*, p. 57.

Fig. 11. Fish-*apkallu* as the recipient of cultic veneration, seal impression, Uruk (after E. Ehrenberg, *Eanna-Tablets*, pl. 9:68).

originally belonged to the Esagila temple (discussed below, figs. 37–39).[65]

The tendency of seventh- to fifth-century Babylonian glyptic toward non-anthropomorphic divine symbolization, clearly demonstrated by the Babylonian Šabāṭu ritual discussed earlier and by the documents from the archive of the Eanna temple at Uruk, is also apparent in the use of newly designed symbols. This is illustrated, for example, by the introduction of the star-topped, lion-headed emblem found on sealings from the archive of the temple of Eanna at Uruk. The emblem, inspired by Old Babylonian pictorial prototypes such as the portrayals of Nergal or Ishtar carrying a double-headed mace, was selected to fit the specific requirements of the shrine of Ishtar, patron goddess of Uruk, and reflects a pattern of archaisms typical of the period.[66] Another contemporary glyptic phenomenon, noted above, in which previously apotropaic hybrids of lesser divine rank become the foci of cult, further underlines the strong Babylonian tendency towards symbolization. The change in the role of hybrid creatures such as the merman-like fish-*kulullû*, the lion-dragon, the griffin, the scorpion-bird-man, or the fish-*apkallu* (fig. 11) from that of a protective entity into that of a deified image, is demonstrated by their representation as the foci of cult, standing in front of a gesturing worshipper.[67]

The Babylonian propensity for representing the divine in symbolic form is also well documented by first-millennium *kudurru*s. With some modification, they continue the pictorial traditions of the second millennium and represent the divine by emblems. The divine emblems of first-millennium *kudurru*s are usually arranged in one row at the upper part of the monument above two images of humans: the king and an official. Divine emblems—usually three astral symbols—appear on a few steles of Nabonidus,[68] where they are shown above the image of

---

65. F. Wetzel, E. Schmidt and A. Mallwitz, *Das Babylon der Spätzeit*, WVDOG 62, Berlin: Mann, 1957), pp. 36–38, pls. 43–44.

66. Ehrenberg, *Eanna-Tablets*, pp. 14, 41, nos. 1–19. See P.-A. Beaulieu, "Nabopolassar and the Antiquity of Babylon," *Eretz-Israel* 27 (2003), pp. 1*-9* for other aspects of Neo-Babylonian archaism.

67. Porada, *Corpus*, no. 785 (a *kulullu*). P. de Miroschedjide, "Notes sur la glyptique de la fin de l'Elam," *Revue d'Assyriologie* 76 (1982), p. 58, figs. 2, 3 (a lion-dragon). R. A. S. Macalister, *The Excavations of Gezer 1902–1905 and 1907–1909* I (London: John Murray, 1912), p. 293, fig. 154:14 (a griffin). Israel Museum IAA 65–322A (a scorpion-bird-man, unpublished). Ehrenberg, *Eanna-Tablets*, pl. 9:68 (a fish *apkallu*). See also Beaulieu, *The Pantheon of Uruk*, p. 367, note 49.

68. Börker-Klähn, *Felsreliefs*, nos. 263–266.

Fig. 12. Nabonidus before divine emblems, rock relief, Petra.
Courtesy of Eli Raz, Ein Gedi.

the king as, for example, on a rock relief from the vicinity of Petra, Jordan,[69] where, however a winged disc replaces the traditional Babylonian solar emblem of a star within a disc (fig. 12). These monuments accord very well with the molded brick decoration of Nebuchadnezzar II adorning various buildings in Babylon, for which only non-anthropomorphic divine symbols and highly charged pictorial elements were selected. These architectural embellishments are comprised of stylized volutes, "frames" of volutes and palmettes, rows of marching lions with upright or downward-pointing tails and rosettes, depicted on the façade of the throne hall in the Southern Palace and on the walls of the Processional Way leading from the North Palace to the Esagila temple. Rows of bulls alternating with rows of *mušḫuššu*s adorn the *Ištar-sakipat-tebiša* double gate, which stands at the end of the Processional Way.[70]

The Babylonian tendency to avoid the representation of anthropomorphic deities is further indicated by a unique stele, revealed in 1917 at Babylon, depicting Nebuchadnezzar II in front of a seven-staged, stepped building, identified by an inscription as the Etemenanki and its ground plan (fig. 13).[71] The portrayal of a

---

69. E. and T. Raz, A. Uchitel, "Selaʿ: The Rock of Edom," *Cathedra* 101 (2001), pp. 20–38 (Hebrew). F. Zayadine, "Le Néo-Babylonien à Selaʿ près de Tafileh: interpretation historique," *Syria* (1999), pp. 83–90. S. Dalley and A. Goguel, "The Selaʿ Sculpture: A Neo-Babylonian Rock Relief in Southern Jordan," *Annual of the Department of Antiquities of Jordan* 51 (1997), pp. 169–76.

70. J. Marzahn, *The Ishtar Gate, The Processional Way, The New Year Festival of Babylon*, Staatliche Museen zu Berlin (Mainz am Rhine: Philip von Zabern, 1992).

71. H. Shanks, "Scrolls, Scripts and Stelae," *Biblical Archaeology Review* 28 (2002), p. 33. M. van de Mieroop, "Reading Babylon," *AJA* 107 (2003), p. 264. Cf. http://www.nb.no/baser/schoyen/4/4.2/422.html.

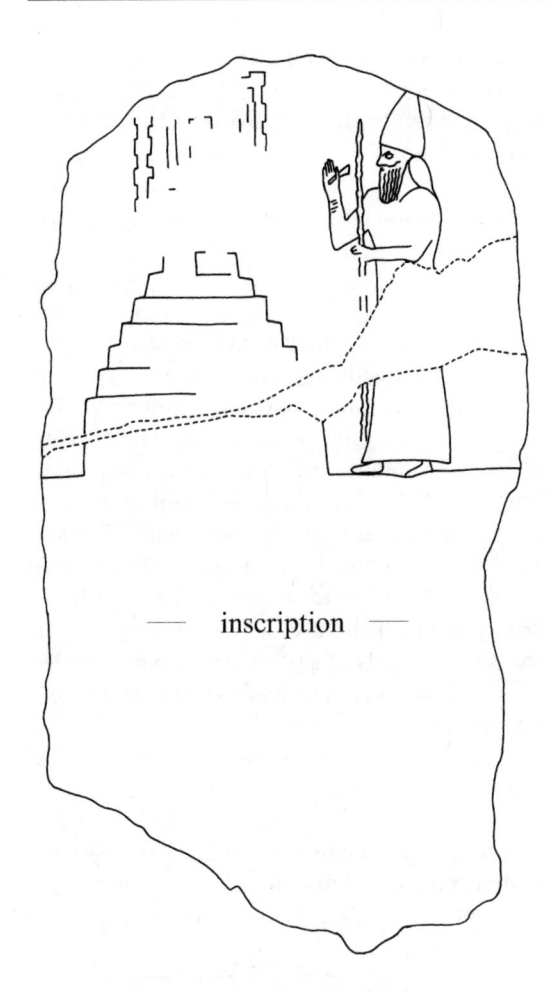

Fig. 13. Nebuchadnezzar II in front of a ziggurat and its ground plan (after H. Shanks, "Scrolls, Scripts and Stelae," *Biblical Archaeology Review* 28 [2002], p. 33).

Babylonian king in front of a temple's plan recalls much older south Mesopotamian imagery, that of enthroned Gudea holding the plan of the Eninnu temple, and it may also echo older themes such as those depicted on the disc of Enheduanna[72]—an association that is not inconceivable considering the strong archaism typical of the Chaldean dynasty, as noted above.[73] Another example of the theme

---

72. A. Parrot, *Tello, Vingt campagnes de fouilles (1877–1933)*, (Paris: A. Michel, 1958), p. 61, pl. 14b. Suter, *Gudea*, p. 58. J. Aruz, ed., *Art of the First Cities: The Third Millennium* B.C. *from the Mediterranean to the Indus*, The Metropolitan Museum of Art (New Haven and London: Yale University Press, 2003), pp. 200–201 (with bibliography).

73. Cf. E. Porada, "Suggestions for the Classification of Neo-Babylonian Cylinder Seals," *Orientalia* 16 (1947), pp. 154ff, 162–63. Idem, *Corpus*, p. 145 and n. 1. H. Frankfort, *Art and Architecture of the Ancient Orient* (5th ed.), (New Haven and London: Yale University, 1996), pp. 201–5.

of a worshipper standing in front of a stepped high building appears on an agate cylinder seal found in a thirteenth- to twelfth-century tomb at Babylon,[74] further evidence of the continuation of late second-millennium Babylonian traditions, including artistic ones, in the first millennium. The theme of a high structure, at times accompanied by a mortal worshipper, also occurs in Middle Assyrian glyptics and leads us now to consider non-anthropomorphic divine representations in Middle Assyrian art.

I.3 Non-anthropomorphic Assyria

The Middle Assyrian tendency to avoid anthropomorphic portrayals of deities is evident in the depictions of a high building, with or without a human figure, on several Assyrian glyptic items dating from the thirteenth century onwards. The motif is rendered on a seal impression from the time of Shalmaneser I from Dūr-katlimmu, on cylinder seals from Tell Mohammad Arab and from the Ishtar-din-itu temple at Ashur, on two seal impressions from the archive of Tiglath-pileser I (fig. 14) at Ashur, and on an unprovenanced lapis lazuli cylinder seal.[75] The tendency to avoid depictions of major deities in human form in Middle Assyrian glyptics is illustrated by the fact that the most common subject shown on Middle Assyrian cylinder seals is a combat scene in which figures in human shape are either absent altogether, or if present, are not clearly identifiable as (prominent) deities.[76] Supporting evidence for the Middle Assyrian tendency to prefer non-anthropomorphic divine representation can be found in the role of the stylized tree as a central motif, and at times as the focus of veneration, in Middle Assyrian art, a motif that was later transmitted into first-millennium iconography.[77] A related case of replacing anthropomorphic divinities by symbols occurs also in Mitannian glyptics, as Porada has observed: " . . . due to the change in iconography of most of the seal designs in the Mitannian period from the Old Babylonian subject of gods with or without worshippers to worshippers alone, often with a sacred

---

E. Ehrenberg, "Archaism and Individualism in the Late Babylonian Period," in J. Prosecky, ed., *Intellectual Life of the Ancient Near East, CRRAI 43rd, Prague July 1–5, 1996* (Prague: Oriental Institute, 1998), pp. 125–40. U. Seidl, "Das Ringen um das richtige Bild des Šamaš von Sippar," *ZA* 91 (2001), pp. 120–32 (for archaisms in the Sippar Tablet).

74. Matthews, *Principles*, no. 527. G. Stiehler-Alegria, "Das 'mittelassyrische' Rollsiegel VA 7736: Bemerkungen zur Klassifizierung eines Rollsiegels aus dem Vorderasiatischen Museum Berlin," *MDOG* 132 (2000), pp. 113–21.

75. H. Kühne and W. Röllig, "Das Siegel des Königs Salmanassar I. von Assyrien," in K. Emre, B. Hrouda, M. Mellink and N. Özgüç, eds., *Anatolia and the Ancient Near East, Studies in Honor of Tahsin Özgüç* (Ankara: Tasin Oezguece Armagan, 1989), pp. 295–99. Matthews, *Principles*, nos. 528–30. D. Collon, "Some Cylinder Seals from Tell Mohammed Arab," *Iraq* 50 (1988), no. 9. Idem, *First Impressions*, no. 562.

76. Matthews, *Principles*, p. 106. D. L. Stein, "Mittelassyrische kunstperiode," RLA 8 (1994), pp. 306–7.

77. Frankfort, *Art*, p. 137. Matthews, *Principles*, pp. 91–94, 106–7.

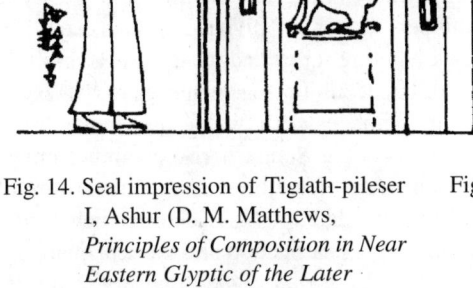

Fig. 14. Seal impression of Tiglath-pileser I, Ashur (D. M. Matthews, *Principles of Composition in Near Eastern Glyptic of the Later Second Millennium* B.C., OBO.SA 8 [Fribourg and Göttingen: Vandenhoeck and Ruprecht, 1990], no. 530).

Fig. 15. Veneration of the symbols of Marduk and Nabu, seal impression, Nimrud (S. Herbordt, *Neuassyrische Glyptik des 8/-7/ Jh. v. Chr. unter besonderer Berücksichtigung der Siegelungen auf Tafeln und Tonverschlüssen* [Helsinki: The Neo-Assyrian Text Corpus Project, 1992], pl. 14:6).

tree or with a sacred tree flanked only by animals or composite creatures."[78] The likelihood that the tree functions as a divine emblem is also suggested by the fact that the tree is often substituted for the image of a male deity, perhaps in Mitannian glyptics, that of the storm god.[79] Worship of non-anthropomorphic emblems in Mitannian glyptics is also apparent in the images of caprids, which are understood to represent Shawshaka-Ishtar.[80]

Although depictions of major deities in human shape are common on ninth- to eighth-century Neo-Assyrian cylinder seals (in contrast to their absence from

---

78. E. Porada, "A Cylinder with a Storm God and Problems," in D. J. W. Meijer, ed., *Natural Phenomena: Their Meaning, Depiction and Description in the Ancient Near East* (Amsterdam: Royal Netherlands Academy of Arts and Sciences, 1992), p. 228.

79. W. G. Lambert, "Trees, Snakes and Gods in Ancient Syria and Anatolia," *Bulletin of the School of Oriental and African Studies* 48 (1985), p. 435. For the representation and roles of the tree in ancient Near Eastern art, see C. Kepinski, *L'arbre stylisée en Asie Occidentale au 2ᵉ millenaire avant J.-C.*, Editions recherches sur les civilisations 7, vols. 1–3 (Paris: Editions recherches sur les civilisations, 1982).

80. D. L. Stein, "Mythologische Inhalte der Nuzi-Glyptik," in V. Haas, ed., *Hurriter und Hurritisch: Konstanzer Altorientalische Symposien II*, Xenia, Konstanzer Althistorische Vorträge und Forschungen 21 (Konstanz: Universitätverlag, 1988), pp. 177–78, fig. 11.

monumental palatial art, discussed below), the replacement of anthropomorphic deities by their surrogate symbols became most widespread in seventh century Assyrian glyptic, as is evident on dated sealed tablets from Nimrud (e.g., fig. 15), Nineveh, Ashur, Khorsabad and sites beyond the borders of Assyria's heartland, such as Carchemish.[81] These items confirm that a change in the Assyrian manner of representing deities and a shift towards the worship of symbols was already apparent in glyptic art as early as the last quarter of the eighth century. Although the theme is rightly considered to be typically Babylonian, late eighth-century Assyrian seals and sealings depicting worshippers in front of divine emblems establish that it was already in active use in Assyria before it reached its apex in seventh to fifth century Babylonia. As we are about to see, ninth- to seventh-century Assyrian monumental art (with the exception of images such as that of Ninurta from Nimrud, and the deities depicted on monuments of Sennacherib) exhibits a gradual but undeniable abstention from the depiction of major gods in human form. It seems, then, that apart from a few glyptic items dated to Sennacherib (such as the seal impression found on the Vassal Treaties of Esarhaddon and the seals with an enthroned goddess that are discussed below), Assyrian glyptic imagery as a rule followed monumental art in its tendency to reject the use of images of prominent gods in human shape. In other words, during the last century of the Assyrian Empire, monumental and small-scale art grew closer together in their approach to divine representation: both artistic genres rejected, albeit in varying degrees, the anthropomorphic rendering of prominent gods and goddess.

A notable non-glyptic example of the Middle Assyrian tendency to represent the divine non-anthropomorphically is a cult pedestal from the temple of Ishtar at Ashur that was inscribed and dedicated by Tukulti-Ninurta I (fig. 16).[82] The scene on the front of the pedestal shows the repeated figure of the gesturing king once standing, once kneeling before what seems to be a large vertical stylus and a tablet. Since these two emblems were most common on Babylonian *kudurrus* (though often positioned horizontally), it is conceivable that their unique display on this pedestal was the result of Babylonian influence. Babylonian inspiration is also reflected in the figure of the dog (a divine emblem associated with the goddess Gula[83] that is commonly shown on *kudurrus*) that appears on the Assyrian

---

81. B. Parker, "Excavations at Nimrud 1949–1953: Seals and Impressions," *Iraq* 17 (1955), pp. 111–12. Herbordt, *Neuassyrische Glyptik*, pp. 83–84, 110, pl. 14: 8, 12. Porada, *Corpus*, p. 97, nos. 704–23.

82. Seidl, *Kudurru*, pp. 124–125, 130, no. 18, pl. 9d, nos. 31–32, pl. 15a–b. For an alternative identification of the "stylus" as the staff associated with Nusku, who is invoked in the inscription engraved on the pedestal, see Wiggermann, "The Staff of Ninšubura," pp. 10–11 and Z. Bahrani, *The Graven Image: Representation in Babylonia and Assyria* (Philadelphia: University of Pennsylvania, 2003), pp. 185–201.

83. T. Ornan, "The Goddess Gula and her Dog," *Israel Museum Studies in Archaeology* 3 (2004), pp. 13–30 (with earlier bibliography). For Babylonian inspiration of thirteenth-century Assyrian

Fig. 16. Cult pedestal of Tukulti-Ninurta I, Ashur. VA 8146. Courtesy of the Staatliche Museen zu Berlin, Vorderasiatisches Museum.

sealed tablet from the archive of Tiglath-pileser I mentioned above, where the animal is represented as the focus of cultic veneration (fig. 14).

A further step in the Assyrian tendency to avoid the portrayal of major deities is evident on a second cultic pedestal from Ashur, found outside the Ishtar temple and also attributed to Tukulti-Ninurta I (fig. 17). Here only lesser divinities, two *laḫmu*s flanking an entrance to a shrine, are represented. The innovative feature introduced in this composition is its complete elimination of any major deity from the scene, whether represented by an anthropomorphic image or a divine

---

iconography, cf. C. Fischer, "A Goddess with Two Faces, A Story of Two Cultures," *Orient-Express* 4 (2004), pp. 102–5.

Fig. 17. Cult pedestal of Tukulti-Ninurta I, Ashur. Istanbul 7802. Courtesy of the Istanbul Archaeological Museum, Istanbul.

symbol.[84] Instead of the missing deity, the beholder is faced here with the figure of the king, who occupies the central position in the scene. The removal of the image of a major deity in favor of the royal image foreshadows the practice of Neo-Assyrian monumental art, which typically either minimizes the major divinities—

---

84. The identification of these as *laḫmus,* indicated by their six curls of hair, as well as by their lower status (which is implied by their role in the composition: as holding what appear to be door jambs: see below, II.3), precludes understanding them as major divinities. Similarly, the symbols depicted on the curved tips of the pedestal and on the two standards cannot be regarded as the focus of this shrine's cultic veneration.

Fig. 18. The Broken Obelisk, Nineveh. WA 118898. ©Copyright The Trustees of the British Museum.

whether anthropomorphic or non-anthropomorphic—or dismisses every major deity from the picture in order to leave the king as the sole pictorial protagonist.

A connection between the Assyrian tendency to remove deities in human shape from pictorial renderings and the agenda of focusing attention on the royal figure in official monuments is noticeable on the Broken Obelisk of Ashur-bel-kala from Nineveh (fig. 18).[85] As in the second pedestal of Tukulti-Ninurta, here too, the protagonist is the king, holding four prisoners with a rope. The godly

---

85. Moortgat, *The Art of Mesopotamia*, pp. 122–23, pl. 252. T. Ornan, "Who Is Holding the Lead Rope? The Relief of the Broken Obelisk," *Iraq* 69 (2007), pp. 59–72.

presence is restricted here to a row of five schematized symbols. The gods in their non-anthropomorphic renderings still dominate the scene, yet do not compete with the royal figure in the eye of the beholder. The very choice of emblematic representations of the divine suggests Babylonian influence, particularly when we consider the military campaigns carried out by Ashur-bel-kala in Babylonia.[86] However, the placement of the symbols, a little above the king but facing him, heralds the appearance of the Neo-Assyrian ṣalam šarrūtiya ('image of my kingship') steles and rock reliefs in which the large royal image is shown gesturing toward divine emblems. The four pleading enemy figures facing Ashur-bel-kala recall in particular the later steles of Esarhaddon from Til Barsip and Zinjirli.[87] The selection of the symbols—a horned headdress, a crescent, a bident, a star(?), and a winged disc—also foreshadows Assyrian imagery. The position of the winged disc at the center underlines the resemblance to Neo-Assyrian monuments and particularly accentuates the high rank of the deity it signifies. Its major role is further emphasized by its "holding" a bow, signaling its martial character and its identification with Aššur.

Moving on to Assyria in the first millennium, we may, indeed, epitomize the Neo-Assyrian approach to divine representation as characterized by two phenomena: first, the frequent abandonment of large-scale portrayals of major deities as a subject for palatial wall reliefs, as is evident in the extant collection of palatial wall reliefs at our disposal; and second, the substitution of symbols for anthropomorphic images of major divinities on steles and rock reliefs. The employment of these conventions in Assyrian monumental art probably represents a continuation of second-millennium Babylonian traditions but, at the same time, Assyrian art diverges from the Babylonian model by combining the depiction of gods in pictorial renderings with an explicit policy of exalting the king. The abandonment of the depiction of major gods in palace decoration, and the physical gap between the king and the divine emblems on steles and rock reliefs emphasize that, in Assyrian art, the needs of the monarch had subverted those of the divine. The new supremacy of royal requirements over those of the divine resulted in the stronger visibility of the king. That there was indeed a tendency to avoid large-scale anthropomorphic images of gods and goddesses in Assyrian palaces is corroborated by the fact that an absence of anthropomorphic divine images is evident even in the surviving wall reliefs found in the Southwest Palace of Sennacherib at Nineveh.[88] This elimination of anthropomorphic major gods and goddesses from

---

86. A. K. Grayson, *Assyrian Rulers of the Early First Millennium I (1114–859)*, The Royal Inscriptions of Mesopotamia, Assyrian Periods 2 (Toronto, Buffalo and London: University of Toronto, 1991), pp. 86, 99–105.

87. Börker-Klähn, *Felsreliefs*, p. 178, and compare no. 219.

88. R. D. Barnett, G. Turner, E. Bleibtreu, *Sculptures from the Southwest Palace of Sennacherib at Nineveh* (London: British Museum Press, 1998). The absence of major portrayals of deities from the sculptured palatial decoration of Sennacherib can be demonstrated by the empty chariot positioned

Fig. 19. Aššur in the winged disk and the king, Assyrian wall relief, North West Palace, Nimrud. WA 124555. ©Copyright The Trustees of the British Museum.

Sennacherib's palace decoration indeed underscores the strong tendency of Assyrian palatial imagery to depart from the anthropomorphic pictorial representation of deities because it stands in contrast to the tendency (typical of Sennacherib and unique to him) to depict major deities in human form on works of art other than palatial reliefs, such as the steles and rock reliefs discussed below (figs. 29–30, 34).

That the Assyrians were deliberately refraining from showing major gods and goddesses in palace decoration is even clearer when one examines the few

---

behind the enthroned Sennacherib on slab 14 of the Lachish siege scenes, possibly representing the chariot of the god Aššur; see Ch. Uehlinger, "Clio in a World of Pictures: Another Look at the Lachish Reliefs from Sennacherib's Southwest Palace at Nineveh," in L. L. Grabbe, ed., *'Like a Bird in a Cage': The Invasion of Sennacherib in 701 BCE*, JSOTS 363 (Sheffield: Sheffield Academic Press, 2003), pp. 290–91. For a much earlier possible parallel in which a divine chariot is shown without its godly owner, in this case Ningirsu, see the stele fragments of Gudea: Suter, *Gudea*, p. 187.

Fig. 20. Foreign statues of gods carried away by Assyrian soldiers, South West Palace, Nineveh (after Barnett et al., *Palace of Sennacherib*, pl. 451).

renderings that *do* show major deities. The depictions of such deities, which occur only in small scale, can be divided into three groups. The first includes depictions of the god Aššur rising from, or standing within, a winged disc, which are associated especially with the Northwest Palace at Nimrud.[89] In these representations, the human-shaped deity—fused with the non-anthropomorphic emblem of the winged disc—is shown hovering above the large figure of the king (fig. 19). The portrayal of the god in these cases with a partially human-shaped body—his head and torso being anthropomorphic, and his lower body concealed by a tail-like design—reveals, indeed, some concession to visual anthropomorphism (see below). The small scale of Aššur within the winged disc, however, stresses the "diminishing" representation of the divine icon, despite the fact that it retains the uppermost position in these scenes, an indication of importance in Mesopotamian art. It is the larger royal figure that catches the attention of the spectator. The decline in the anthropomorphizing tendency that is hinted at by these portrayals is further implied by later monumental depictions of the winged disc in which human traits are missing.[90]

---

89. Layard, *Nineveh* I, pls. 13, 21, 25. For the identification of the personified winged disc with Aššur, see Ornan, "A Complex System" (with bibliography).

90. E.g., The Black Obelisk, PKG, pl. 207.

Fig. 21. Removal of the statue of Marduk and an eagle-shaped emblem from Babylonia, Central Palace, Nimrud (O. Keel, *The Symbolism of the Biblical World: Ancient Near Eastern Iconography and the Book of Psalms* [Winona Lake: Eisenbrauns, 1997], fig. 316).

The second group of divine representations in human shape on Assyrian reliefs consists of tiny, almost invisible images of deities displayed on chariot accessories such as yoke poles, fan-shaped plaques, and tall standards (*šurinnu*). The miniature size of the deities displayed on these objects and the context of the wall reliefs in which they are engaged indicate that they are not shown here as the focus of cultic veneration but as protective icons charged with the care of war chariots. These depictions accord very well with the many other realistic details represented in these sculptured narrative compositions and highlight the growing tendency in Assyrian wall reliefs for realistic display.[91]

The only clear examples of human-shaped cult images depicted in Assyrian wall reliefs actually represent foreign gods and goddesses. These images comprise the third group of human-shaped deities depicted in Assyrian palaces.[92] Their foreign origin is revealed by the contexts in which they are shown: they are carried away as war booty by Assyrian soldiers (fig. 20). Most of the scenes in which such images are shown represent Assyrian campaigns in alien territories located to the west of the Euphrates, where it seems that the tradition of pictorially

---

91. In other contexts, however, the *šurinnu*s were considered as objects of cultic veneration; see B. Pongratz-Leisten, K. Deller K. and E. Bleibtreu, "Götterstreitwagen und Götterstandarten: Götter auf dem Feldzug und ihr Kult im Feldlager," *BaM* 23 (1992), pp. 291–356.

92. Layard, Nineveh I, pl. 65. *Idem*, The Monuments of Nineveh II (London: John Murray, 1853), pls. 30, 50. Barnett and Falkner, *The Sculptures*, pp. xxiv–xxv, 29–28, pls. XCII–XCIII. Barnett et al., *Palace of Sennacherib*, pp. 13, 25–26, 36, 128, 74, pls. 143, 451–53. J. M. Russell, *Sennacherib's Palace Without Rival at Nineveh* (Chicago and London: The University of Chicago Press, 1991), pp. 53, 169–70, fig. 35. Börker-Klähn, *Felsreliefs*, pp. 43–44.

displaying major deities in human form was strong, perhaps continuing the traditions of Hittite imagery.

I would like to conclude this discussion of the increasingly non-anthropomorphic representation of gods in first-millennium Mesopotamia by examining two monuments that hint at the existence of a concurrent Babylonian cult of anthropomorphic and non-anthropomorphic divine images. The first example appears in an Assyrian wall relief of Tiglath-pileser III from the Central Palace at Nimrud (fig. 21).[93] The relief shows the removal of captured cult images by Assyrian soldiers during the campaign of Tiglath-pileser III to Babylonia in 731.[94] The Babylonian locale is implied by the fallen date palm and by the large statue of a bearded god, identified with Marduk by his attribute, the spade-like *marru*, which he holds. The large scale of this statue of Marduk, indicated by the proportions of the statue in relation to the soldiers who carry it, suggests that it was a cult image. Other Assyrian soldiers depicted on this slab carry a large statue of a bird of prey, which according to its scale can also be considered a cult image, possibly alluding to Ninurta.[95] The Assyrian soldiers carry both cult images in a similar manner, and both sculptures are faced by begging females and the fallen tree. This homology within the context of the composition may hint at the equivalent status of these two types of cult statues. The similar status of both types of cult objects is confirmed by the use of the *mīs pî* and *pīt pî* ('mouth-washing' and '-opening' rituals used for the induction of cult images), which were also carried out on divine symbols, e.g., the *uskāru* 'moon crescent'.[96] The parallel roles of the anthropomorphic and non-anthropomorphic cult objects, as reflected for example in the Babylonian ritual procession of the month of *Šabāṭu* discussed earlier, are also revealed in cases where oaths were sworn in front of symbols in lieu of divine statues.[97] These examples support the conclusion that anthropomorphic and non-anthropomorphic representations of deities functioned very similarly, not only in visual compositions, but also in actual worship.

A second monument from the first millennium on which anthropomorphic and non-anthropomorphic divine representations appear side by side is the Sippar Tablet, on whose upper section a sculpted pictorial image depicts a divinity in both guises. The tablet's inscription reports the installation of a new cult statue of Šamaš in the Ebabbar temple in the thirty-first year of Nabu-apla-iddina II

---

93. Layard, *Nineveh* I, pl. 67A.

94. H. Tadmor, *The Inscriptions of Tiglath-Pileser III, King of Assyria: Critical Edition, with Introductions, Translations and Commentary* (Jerusalem: The Israel Academy of Sciences and Humanities, 1994), pp. 239–40, 272.

95. Barnett and Falkner, *The Sculptures*, pp. xvi, 17, pl. VII.

96. Ch. Walker and M. B. Dick, "The Induction of the Cult Image in Ancient Mesopotamia: The Mesopotamian *mīs pî* Ritual," in M. B. Dick, ed., *Born in Heaven, Made on Earth: The Making of the Cult Image in the Ancient Near East* (Winona Lake: Eisenbrauns, 1999), p. 71.

97. Lambert, "Mesopotamian Gods," pp. 123–24.

In the Likeness of Man 123

Fig. 22. The Sippar Tablet. WA 91000. ©Copyright The Trustees of the British Museum.

(fig. 22).[98] This visual composition differs from the relief of Tiglath-pileser in that its two divine representations both refer to the same god—Šamaš. The fact reported in the inscription, that the *nipḫu* sun-emblem had replaced the statue of

---

98. Leonard W. King, *Babylonian Boundary-Stones and Memorial-Tablets in the British Museum*, 2 vols. (London: British Museum, 1912), no. 36. Walker and Dick, "The Induction," pp. 58–63. Slanski, *Babylonian Entitlement narûs*, pp. 196–221. Ornan, "Idols and Symbols," p. 104 (with earlier bibliography).

Šamaš in human form for two hundred years while it had been missing, sheds light on the high status of divine emblems in first-millennium Babylonia. This status is also conveyed by the very large scale of the emblem and its position in the center of the scene. It accords well with the conspicuous role of divine emblems on Babylonian *kudurrus* and in Late Babylonian glyptic, discussed above.[99] Whether or not the visual composition on the Sippar Tablet actually depicts the removal of the emblem from the shrine in favor of the human-shaped cult image as described in the inscription,[100] the placement of the latter within the structure while the former is shown outside the temple, implies the somewhat "inferior" status of the divine emblem in relation to the god's anthropomorphic image. A similarly hierarchical arrangement in which the "lower" rank of the divine emblem is implied can also be observed in the relief of Tiglath-pileser, where Marduk in anthropomorphic form is shown at the front of the scene, while the bird of prey is positioned at the back, farther removed from the beholder.[101] In both of these cases, the positions of the divine emblems suggest the higher status of the human-shaped god in works of art dated to a period when divine anthropomorphic renderings were eschewed, which leads us to examine contemporary anthropomorphic representations of the divine.

II. Anthropocentric perception of the divine as revealed by pictorial renderings

II.1. Preliminary Remarks

When shown in their human form, Mesopotamian deities are regularly represented as having a fully human appearance, with no theriomorphic features such as wings, tails, hoofed legs or long ears. Such pictorial portrayals, however, are not always consistent with the literary descriptions of major deities. For example, the image of Ningirsu envisioned by Gudea in a dream, mentioned above, was

---

99. Ornan, "Idols and Symbols," p. 104.

100. H. Frankfort, *Art*, p. 202. T. N. D. Mettinger, *No Graven Image? Israelite Aniconism in Its Ancient Near Eastern Context*, Coniectanaea Biblica, Old Testament Series 42 (Stockholm: Almqvist and Wiksell, 1995), p. 48. See also E. Reiner, "Suspendu entre ciel et terre . . . ," in H. Gasche and B. Hrouda, eds., *Collectanea Orientalia. Histoire, Arts de l'Espace et Industrie de la Terre: Etudes offerts en Hommage à Agnès Spycket*, Civilisations du Proche-Orient, archéologie et environnement 3 (Paris: Neuchâtel, 1996), pp. 311–13. The possibility that the scene shown on the monument relates to the real historical event documented in the inscription suggests this to be an exceptional case of Babylonian art where an historical event is pictorially depicted. As historical compositions are well attested in contemporary Assyrian palatial imagery, Assyrian inspiration for the Sippar Tablet can be suggested (Ornan, "Idols and Symbols", p. 104).

101. For the hierarchical relationship of human-like deities and "non-human" divinities implied by the (usually) smaller amounts of commodities given to divine objects in contrast to those allocated to (human-shaped) major gods in the third millennium, see Selz, "The Holy Drum," pp. 174–75, and 184.

that of ". . . a god as regards his head, he was a Thunderbird as regards his wings, and a floodstorm as regards his lower body. . . ."[102] This description, on the one hand, may hint at an inconsistency between text and picture with regard to the divine body, or on the other hand, may suggest that the nonhuman divine elements are to be understood as a metaphoric representation of properties.[103] The latter possibility seems preferable to me, since the main organ of the deity—the head—is described as that of a god, most probably referring to the anthropomorphic image of Ningirsu. When animal traits do appear as parts of human-shaped divinities, such images are usually considered to represent apotropaic supernatural entities of a lesser divine status, which are not represented, as a rule, as being the object of cultic veneration. Exceptional cases of images of major deities shown as having theriomorphic features are, however, found in Mesopotamian art, such as the winged, claw-footed goddess depicted on the large, clay, cultic Burney relief,[104] or the noted first-millennium depiction of Ninurta found in the temple of Ninurta at Nimrud.[105] Deities in fully human shape often wear a horned miter, which serves as a general marker of divinity[106] and helps to distinguish them from the figures of human beings. The theriomorphic nature of these horns in no way "reduces" the anthropomorphic substance of the deity, since they are an external component of the divine body. This is evident already in Akkadian glyptics, where the horns are not shown as a physical organ of the divine but are attached to a headdress *worn* by a deity. A unique, unprovenanced late third-millennium bronze headdress adorned with horns, which was used as a head covering for a

---

102. Edzard, *Gudea*, p. 71, iv: 14–19.

103. Suter, *Gudea*, pp. 66–67, 109 (with note 202) and fig. 9.

104. J. E. Curtis and D. Collon, "Ladies of Easy Virtue," in H. Gasche and B. Hrouda, eds., *Collectanea orientalia. Histoire, arts de l'espace et industrie de la terre: Études offerts en hommage à Agnès Spycket*, Civilisations du Proche-Orient, archéologie et environnement 3 (Paris: Neuchâtel, 1996), pp. 89–95 (with earlier bibliography).

105. Layard, *Nineveh* II, pl. 5. Although this portrayal did not serve as Ninurta's main cult image, as is implied by its placement in a side chapel (C) and probably also by its combatant nature, Moortgat-Correns believes that it was very similar to the main cult statue of the god, which stood inside the shrine. U. Moortgat-Correns, "Ein Kultbild Ninurtas aus neuassyrischer Zeit," *AfO* 35 (1988), pp. 117–23. That the wings in this case do not signify a lesser divinity is implied by the two lighting bolts, not otherwise carried by minor divinities. The wings attached to Ninurta in this composition probably reflect artistic inspiration from territories west of the Euphrates, where representations of major winged deities were more common, e.g. W. Orthmann, *Untersuchungen zur späthethitischen Kunst* (Bonn: Robert Habelt Verlag, 1971), pls. 23a, 24b (Carchemish), 40a,b,d (Malatya). See, however E. A. Braun-Holzinger, "Ninurta (B)," RLA 9 (2001), p. 524. For the cult statue of Ninurta as described by Ashurnasirpal II, see A. Annus, *The God Ninurta in the Mythology and Royal Ideology of Ancient Mesopotamia*, SAA XIV (Helsinki: The Neo-Assyrian Text Corpus Project, 2002), p. 42 (with earlier bibliography). See also Collon, *Cylinder Seals* V, p. 141, fig. 4 and Ornan, *The Triumph*, figs. 79 and 134.

106. F. A. M. Wiggermann, "Mischwesen A," RLA 8 (1994), p. 233. J. M. Asher-Greve, "Reading the Horned Crown (A Review Article)," *AfO* 42/3 (1995–6), pp. 181–89.

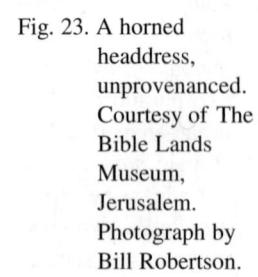

Fig. 23. A horned headdress, unprovenanced. Courtesy of The Bible Lands Museum, Jerusalem. Photograph by Bill Robertson.

cult statue, lends further support to the hypothesis (fig. 23).[107] The horns, imitating those of a wild bull, are to be regarded, then, as an added component that grants greater power and splendor to the divine.

From my short survey of Mesopotamian art in the first part of this paper, it has become clear that during the second half of the second millennium, and in the first half of the first, images of major gods and goddesses in human shape were outnumbered by non-anthropomorphic portrayals of deities. In the following section I wish to show that in spite of the iconographical data that attests to the removal of anthropomorphic deities from visual renderings, the concept governing Mesopotamian perception of the divine remained anthropomorphic. This will be demonstrated by discussing three categories of pictorial representations, as I noted at the beginning: combined anthropomorphic and non-anthropomorphic icons, human-shaped representations of lesser divinities, and a few representations of major deities.

II.2 Combined anthropomorphic and non-anthropomorphic icons

Some of the non-anthropomorphic emblems discussed in Part I.3 seem to betray divine anthropomorphism in their combining of human organs with non-anthropomorphic symbols. This kind of pictorial symbolism is best illustrated by the image of Aššur within a winged disc represented on a glazed tile of Tukulti-Ninurta II, and by the ninth-century Neo-Assyrian wall reliefs from the Northwest Palace at Nimrud.[108] The prototype for the addition of human features to the celestial symbol of the winged disc is found on the Broken Obelisk where, as mentioned earlier, two "human" hands stretch out from the emblem (fig. 18). The

---

107. O. W. Muscarella, ed., *Ladders to Heaven: Art Treasures from the Lands of the Bible* (Toronto: McClelland and Stewart, 1981), pp. 90–91.

108. W. Andrae, *Coloured Ceramics from Ashur* (London: K. Paul, Trench, Truebner, 1925), p. 27, pl. 8. Layard, *Nineveh* I, pls. 13, 21, 25.

human-like "nature" of the god in the winged disc shown in some of the reliefs of the Northwest Palace is further accentuated by the resemblance between the god shown in the disc to the king depicted below it (fig. 19). The monarch and the god, in these compositions, are portrayed with similar or identical gestures. The purpose for such a resemblance was first of all to exalt the royal figure by comparing it to the image of the divine. But concurrently, and as a consequence, the anthropocentric notion of the god is also implicitly revealed. The very image of Aššur fiercely brandishing a bow in a "manly manner" on some of these reliefs confirms the premise that the conceptual icon of Aššur was indeed based on the human model. The fusing of human and non-human features in a single visual icon is a special type of symbolism. Combined with the other data considered here, it strongly suggests a world-view governed by an anthropocentric perception of the divine.

This type of divine symbolism is also attested in Mesopotamian art in visual icons that include other combinations of anthropomorphic and non-anthropomorphic components, such as theriomorphic elements or various inanimate objects. A common type of partially anthropomorphic icon combines the human form with elements representing natural phenomena, such as mountains and streams of water. These elements are blended into the divine body, as if hiding their original non-anthropomorphic form, and are articulated as if "disguised" by the deity's lower garments, as shown, for example, by the male and female lesser divinities depicted on the outer wall of the Eanna temple at Uruk.[109] Such depictions were used in Akkadian glyptics for conveying divine images, in particular in portrayals of Šamaš rising from a mountain, which allude to the natural phenomenon of the sunrise as experienced by the inhabitants of Mesopotamia. In these renderings the god is represented by his torso and head, while the rest of his body is "concealed" by a scaly, mountain-like pattern in such a way that the natural phenomenon appears to become an organic part of the divine body.[110] In other instances, divine figures are shown merging with streams of water, for example, as is depicted on a well-known Akkadian cylinder seal from Mari, where the lower bodies of the two goddesses are fused with a river. The latter portrayal may recall the description of the lower body of Ningirsu as a floodstorm, seen by Gudea in his dream as it is described in Gudea's Cylinder A.[111] The embodiment of the divinity in natural phenomena is enhanced on the seal from Mari by the tree branches growing from the two divine female figures. Depicting the divine in a partially anthropomorphic way is also exemplified in the representation of lesser deities on another Akkadian seal, where a boat-like icon, consisting of a river terminating in

---

109. PKG, pl. 169.
110. E.g., R. M. Boehmer, *Die Entwicklung der Glyptik Während der Akkad-Zeit* (Berlin: Walter de Gruyter, 1965), no. 393.
111. Edzard, *Gudea*, p. 71, iv: 16–18.

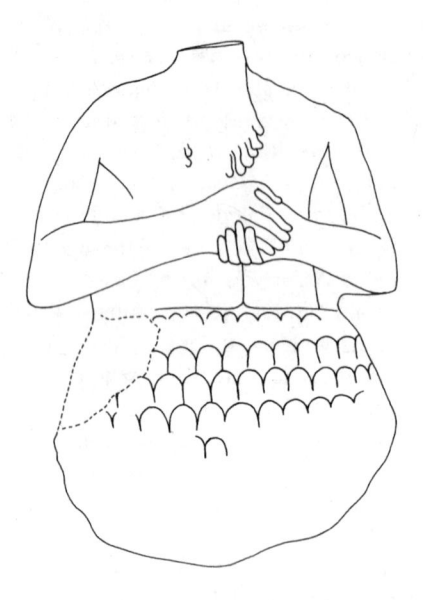

Fig. 24. A limestone statue of Šamaš, attributed to Mari (after PKG, pl. 161).

two human-shaped torsos and heads, represents lesser divinities.[112]

Divine icons composed of both anthropomorphic and non-anthropomorphic elements continue to appear in later Mesopotamian iconography. For example, an image of Šamaš that combines a human-like torso and head with a mountain-like lower body is represented on the so-called Cabane Statue, attributed to Mari and inscribed with a dedication of Yasmah-Adad (fig. 24).[113] The same convention was also used for the representation of other major deities, as is shown in the image of Aššur depicted in the Well Relief from Ashur, an image that supports the suggestion that the god was considered to be a personified manifestation of the hill on which the city of Ashur was located, as noted above.[114] A similar portrayal of a major god with a mountain-like lower body is found on an unprovenanced cylinder seal assigned to Shalmaneser I,[115] and gods with mountain-like lower bodies or lower bodies composed of running water are depicted on lapis lazuli Middle Babylonian cylinder seals discovered at Thebes in Boeotia, Greece, and classified as belonging to the Second Kassite group, discussed earlier.[116] The embodiment of a natural phenomenon within an otherwise human-shaped divine image became a common theme in the imagery of the Hittite Empire, perhaps reflecting some Hurrian traditions.[117]

---

112. P. Amiet, "Notes sur le répetoire iconographique de Mari à l'époque du Palais," *Syria* 37 (1960), pp. 216, 219, figs. 2, 3b, 5. Compare the conquered deities on the Akkadian stone mold of Naram-Sin, D. P. Hansen, "Through the Love of Ishtar," in L. al-Gailani Werr *et al.*, eds., *Of Pots and Plans: Papers on the Archaeology and History of Mesopotamia and Syria presented to David Oates in Honor of his 75th Birthday* (London: Nabu Publications, 2002), pp. 99, 102.

113. PKG, pl. 161. Wiggermann, "Mischwesen," p. 236 (with bibliography).

114. E. Klengel-Brandt, "Bemerkungen zum kultrelief aus Assur," *Akkadica* 19 (1980), pp. 38–47. Lambert, "The God Aššur?" pp. 85–86. See however, Stein, "Mittelassyrische," p. 301. J. E. Reade, "Das Kultrelief from Assur: Glas, Ziegen, Zapfen und Wasser," *MDOG* 132 (2000), pp. 105–12.

115. Matthews, *Principles*, no. 339.

116. E. Porada, "The Cylinder Seals Found at Thebes in Boeotia," *AfO* 28 (1981), pp. 1–78.

117. R. L. Alexander, *The Sculpture and Sculptors of Yazilikaya* (Newark: University of Delaware Press, 1986), pp. 61, 92–93, 98. M. N. van Loon, *Anatolia in the Second Millennium B.C.*, Iconography of Religions 12 (Leiden: Brill, 1985), pp. 12, 20–21, 28, 33.

Another ancient Near Eastern strategy for representing an anthropomorphic deity is to depict a single, isolated human organ that stands for the deity, an approach that I could not find in Mesopotamian imagery. Such an example is found in the late second- to early first-millennium temple at ʿEin Dara in northern Syria, where pairs of huge feet on the thresholds of the temple stand for the deity worshipped in this temple.[118] Divine symbolism consisting of human organs combined with inanimate objects is, however, employed in Mesopotamia in the Early Dynastic foundation pegs that combine the torso of a divinity in human shape with a peg-like lower body to create a single icon (e.g. fig. 25).[119] It also appears on a few other occasions in the art of the ancient Near East during the second half of the second millennium. For example, the image of Nergal in chamber B at Yazilikaya is composed of a human head with a huge and elaborate sword that perhaps alludes to the writing of his name.[120] A possibly similar example of this type of divine symbolism is found on a stele from a small, Late Bronze shrine at Hazor in Israel, on which a pair of hands appears below the images of a full and a crescent moon. The two hands in this case may stand for the blessing hands of the moon god, who is at the same time also represented by the lunar symbol.[121] The "human" element of the moon god conveyed by this stele accords well with an anthropomorphic basalt cult statue of the moon god found in another Late Bronze temple, at Hazor. These two contemporary, but differently articulated, cult images

Fig. 25. Foundation peg figurine, unprovenanced, southern Mesopotamia. IMJ 87.60.563. Courtesy of The Israel Museum, Jerusalem

---

118. R. L. Alexander, "The Storm God at ʿAin Dara," in K. A. Yener and H. A. Hoffner, eds., *Recent Developments in Hittite Archaeology and History: Papers in Memory of Hans G. Güterbock* (Winona Lake: Eisenbrauns, 2002), pp. 11–19.

119. R. Ellis, *Foundation Deposits in Ancient Mesopotamia* (New Haven: Yale University Press, 1968), pp. 50–52, fig. 7.

120. Alexander, *Yazilikaya*, 61–62. I. J. Winter, "The 'Hasanlu Gold Bowl': Thirty Years Later," *Expedition* 31 (1989), p. 95.

121. Y. Yadin, *Hazor, The Head of All Those Kingdoms* (London: The British Academy, Oxford University Press, 1972), p. 73. This example differs from the icon of Nergal from Yazilikaya, as the hands here do not touch the non-anthropomorphic lunar emblems.

exemplify the two possible forms of divine representation and recall the two types of divine representation in the relief of Tiglath-pileser III and on the Sippar Tablet, discussed above. The "human" version of the moon god remained rather common in representations of the moon deity on first-millennium Syrian monuments and also in seventh- to fifth-century Babylonian glyptics, as will be shown below.

II.3 Human-shaped lesser divinities

That the essential Mesopotamian notion of the divine was indeed modeled on the human prototype is further supported by the portrayal of lesser gods and goddesses. The lower status of a deity may be inferred from its placement at the entrance to a building, where it functioned as an apotropaic figure warding off evil, a role comparable to that of animal-like hybrids such as the *aladlammu*.[122] Another criterion that can signal a lesser divinity is its depiction as carrying a container, such as the small *ḫegallu* ('abundance') jar from which water flows,[123] which implies its function as a divine servant. At times horned tiaras with only one or two pairs of horns may signal the secondary status of a deity. Representations of lesser divinities in a human form were common on steles of Gudea, as well as on Ur III cylinder seals, and continued into Old Babylonian glyptics. The most common lesser divinity shown on these latter objects is the goddess Lama, a beneficent protective deity who usually introduces the worshipper into the presence of a major deity.[124] An image of Lama as a protective deity is depicted on a large terracotta plaque that flanked a doorway of a small sanctuary at Old Babylonian Ur, and in a similar function she appears at both sides of the "investiture"

---

122. For example see the anthropomorphic divinities mentioned in texts describing rituals for the protection of the house, such as the 'god of the house' (*il bīti*), Lulal, Meslamtaea, and Narudda, positioned in the outer gate as guardians: F. A. M. Wiggermann, *Mesopotamian Protective Spirits: The Ritual Texts* (Groningen: Styx, 1992), pp. 58–62. A. Green, "Ancient Mesopotamian Religious Iconography," in J. M. Sasson *et al.*, eds., *Civilizations of the Ancient Near East* III (New York: Simon and Schuster and Prentice Hall International, 1995), pp. 1848–49, types 8, 20–22. Compare also the two *laḫmu*s flanking a doorway on the cult pedestal of Tukulti-Ninurta I discussed above and illustrated in fig. 16.

123. CAD 6, 168. R. S. Ellis, "Mountains and Rivers," in L. D. Levine and T. Cuyler Young Jr., eds., *Mountains and Lowlands: Essays in the Archaeology of Greater Mesopotamia*, Bibliotheca Mesopotamica 7 (Malibu: Undena, 1977), pp. 31–33. See, however, a late twelfth-century *kudurru* (J. de Morgan, *Fouilles à Suse en 1897–1890 et 1898–1899*, Mémoires de la Mission archéologique de Perse I. Mémoires de la Délégation en Perse [Paris: E. Leroux, 1900], fig. 383), where the divinity with the *ḫegallu* is mounted on a beast—a scheme typically used for major deities.

124. J. Black and A. Green, *Gods, Demons and Symbols of Ancient Mesopotamia: An Illustrated Dictionary* (London: British Museum Press, 1992), p. 115. Suter, *Gudea*, pp. 67 (notes 147, 148), 199, 350 (ST. 9). D. Collon, *Catalogue of the Western Asiatic Seals in the British Museum: Cylinder Seals II. Akkadian, Post Akkadian, Ur III Periods* (London: British Museum Publications, 1982). Idem, *Catalogue of the Western Asiatic Seals in the British Museum: Cylinder Seals III. Isin-Larsa and Old Babylonian Periods* (London: British Museum Publications, 1986), p. 25.

Fig. 26. Lesser divinities, façade wall of the Eanna enclosure, Uruk (after L. Jakob-Rost, E. Klengel-Brandt, J. Marzahn, R. Wartke, *Das Vorderasiatische Museum, Staatliche Museen zu Berlin Preussischer Kulturbesitz* [Mainz: Philip von Zabern, 1992], p. 97).

mural of Zimri-Lim from Mari.[125] As a protective divinity standing at doorways, Lama was paired with the u d u g/*šēdu*, a human-shaped minor deity whose image was modeled on those of ancient kings and who is frequently depicted on Old Babylonian cylinder seals.[126] The lesser divinities continued to retain a human form during the second half of the mid-second millennium and later, the periods I examine here during which portrayal of anthropomorphic major deities was gradually pushed aside.

Deities of lesser status made of mud brick adorn the façade wall of the Eanna enclosure built by Karaindash at Uruk (ca. 1413 BCE, fig. 26). Each of these alternating and almost three-dimensional male and female figures stands in a niche and holds the *ḫegallu*.[127] Their protective role and low status is indicated by their

---

125. C. L. Woolley and M. Mallowan, *Ur Excavations* VII: *The Old Babylonian Period* (London: The British Museum Publications 1976), p. 173, pl. 64:1 (h. 73 cm). M.-Th. Barrelet, "Une peinture de la cour 106 du palais de Mari," in A. Parrot *et al.*, S*tudia Mariana* (Leiden: Brill, 1950), pp. 6–35.

126. Wiggermann, "The Staff of Ninšubura," pp. 23–26.

127. J. Jordan, *Erster vorlaufuger Bericht über die von der Notgemeinschaft der deutschen Wissenschaft in Uruk-Warka unternommenen ausgrabungen*, UVB 1 (Berlin: Walter de Gruyter, 1930), pp. 30–38, pls. 15–16. PKG, pl. 169. These figures can also be seen as belonging to the category of

position attached to the outer wall of the enclosure, and by their representation carrying a small vessel, as well as by the single pair of horns on their headdresses. Support for this conclusion may be found in the later, twelfth-century composite supernatural hybrids that adorn the outer mud-brick wall of a sacred enclosure at Susa.[128] Figures of Lama depicted in two limestone reliefs from Uruk provide another Middle Babylonian case of a large, anthropomorphic portrayal of a lesser divinity. The two reliefs, one found in the *akītu* house and the other an unprovenaced find, mention Lama in their inscribed Sumerian dedication to the goddess Inanna for the life of Nazi-Maruttaš.[129] The reconstructed location of the two reliefs flanking the entrance of the *akītu* house may confirm the low status of Lama in spite of the fact that in these two renderings she is wearing a headdress with multiple pairs of horns. Representations of Lama are common on early Kassite cylinder seals, where the goddess may appear facing another figure or on her own.[130] These renderings follow the pattern of the Old Babylonian presentation scene, where Lama served as an intermediary figure leading the petitioner before a major divinity. Since the major deity is often missing from Kassite cylinder seals, however, it can be argued at least from a formal, compositional point of view that this minor goddess at times took the place of an image of a major deity.

Among the lesser divinities depicted in human shape used here to confirm the anthropomorphic perception of the divine, we may include the human-shaped pictorial images of the healing goddess Gula, although these seem to contradict the implications of the image of the goddess as she is described in textual compositions, where she is regarded as a prominent goddess—as in the self-praising Bullutsa-rabi hymn of Gula, dating to the second half of the second millennium or later, where she appears as the consort of Ninurta.[131] The high status of Gula is conveyed not only by her important divine consort, but also by her temple and cult center at Isin, the Egalmah, known from the Akkadian to the Kassite periods.[132] In spite of this, the human-shaped Gula usually appears in a lower register on *kudurru*s dated from the twelfth and the first half of the eleventh century,[133] which implies her low status among the deities represented on these stone monu-

---

partially anthropomorphic figures discussed above, since their lower body consists either of a mountain-like pattern or a running water design.

128. Moortgat, *The Art of Mesopotamia*, pp. 93–94, pls. 226–28. PKG, 295. P. O. Harper et al., eds., *The Royal City of Susa: Ancient Near Eastern Treasures in the Louvre* (New York: The Metropolitan Museum of Art, 1992), p. 144. Compare Seidl, *Kudurru*, p. 25, no. 22, pp. 41–42, no. 64, fig. 10.

129. A. Becker, *Uruk, Kleinfunde* I: *Stein,* Ausgrabungen in Uruk-Warka, Endberichte 6, R. M. Boehmer, ed. (Mainz am Rhein: Philipp von Zabern, 1993), p. 59, no. 791, pl. 45.

130. Matthews, *Principles*, pl. II: F, N, P. Collon, *First Impressions*, nos. 236, 245.

131. W. G. Lambert, "The Gula Hymn of Bullutsa-rabi," *Orientalia* (n.s.) 36 (1967), pp. 105–32.

132. Ornan, "Gula and her Dog," pp. 14, 25–26 (with bibliography).

133. Seidl, *Kudurru*, p. 28, no. 29, pp. 143, 196.

ments (above, fig. 6). These renderings contradict the textual evidence, but they do accord well with the observation that in Middle Babylonia, it was usually only lesser divinities that retained their human form in pictorial compositions. Yet, it is not clear to me why it was only Gula, among all the deities displayed in the lower registers of the *kudurru*s, who was represented in human shape. A rare depiction of another anthropomorphic goddess found on one of the *kudurru*s of Meli-Shipak may also be regarded as portraying a lesser deity.[134] The goddess is holding an ear of corn and hence can be identified as Shala, the consort of Adad. Her presumably low status can be inferred from the context in which she is depicted, accompanied by two erect hybrids, and from the absence of any divine headdress.

The tradition of representing lesser divinities in human form continued in first-millennium imagery as is attested by the large Neo-Assyrian stone sculptures in the round recovered at Nimrud, Arslan-Tash and Khorsabad (fig. 27). The sculptures, dated to the reigns of Adad-nirari III, Tiglath-pileser III and Sargon II,[135] can be identified as representing lesser divinities by their placement at doorways and by the containers that they hold. Given the absence of actual large, three-dimensional statues of major gods, on the one hand, and the existence of several large stone sculptures of kings on the other hand,[136] it becomes evident that first-millennium divine anthropomorphism was, as a rule, conveyed pictorially through the depiction of lesser divinities.

Fig. 27. A lesser god, Khorsabad (after Strommenger, *Rundskulptur*, fig. 13).

The tendency to maintain the anthropomorphic visual form of lesser divinities in first-millennium Assyria is further suggested by the human form given to some benevolent apotropaic figures displayed in Assyrian palatial wall reliefs. These figures include the huge, curled *laḫmu*-like "hero" holding a small lion and found at Khorsabad (fig. 28), and in the Southwest Palace of Sennacherib at Nineveh, the *laḫmu* and Lulal from the latter palace, and a figure wielding an axe and dagger and three *sebetti* in

---

134. *Ibid*, p. 24, no. 12. King, *Babylonian Boundary Stones*, pls. XXIX:B, XXX:C, D.
135. Strommenger, *Rundskulptur*, pp. 18–24, 28, 31.
136. *Ibid*, pp. 13–18.

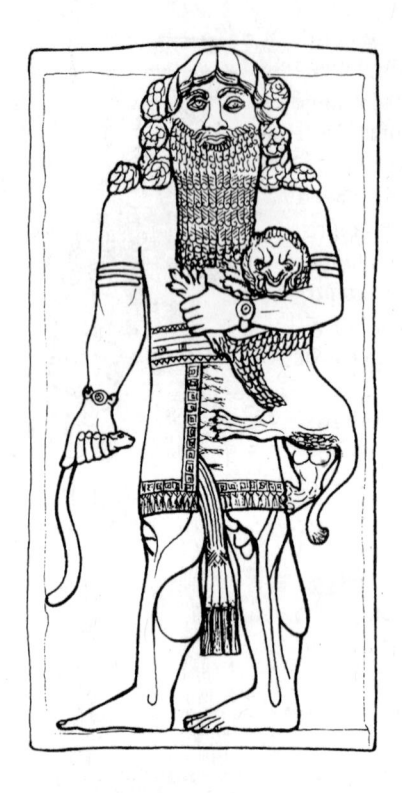

Fig. 28. Laḫmu-like figure carrying a lion, wall relief, Khorsabad (after P. Albenda, *The Palace of Sargon King of Assyria* [Paris: Editions Recherche sur les Civilisations, 1986], pl. 15).

human form from the North Palace, discussed earlier (fig. 1).[137] Human form and affinities also dominate the articulation of the figures of three benevolent and protective figures of the *apkallu* type that are repeatedly depicted in the Northwest Palace (the human- and bird-headed *apkallu,* and the *apkallu* in fish garb).[138] First-millennium apotropaic clay figurines buried in the corners of rooms, below thresholds, and elsewhere in buildings offer further evidence of the tendency to depict lesser divinities in a human form, as can be seen, for example, in the figurines of Ninšubur, Lulal and the figure with the *ḫegallu*.[139] In light of the suggestion that the Mesopotamian pantheon was modeled on the pattern of the earthly royal court,[140] the implication that lesser divinities retained their human form during the second part of the second millennium and in the first millennium is significant. It reconfirms the premise of the anthropomorphic perception of the major deities in Mesopotamia because it seems highly unlikely that at a time when lesser divinities were considered anthropomorphic, their divine masters would have been conceptualized differently.

II.4 Human-shaped portrayals of major deities

As I noted above, it was almost exclusively during the reign of Sennacherib that Assyrian art chose in some monuments to represent major deities in anthro-

---

137. T. Ornan, "Expelling Demons at Nineveh: On the Visibility of Benevolent Demons in the Palaces of Nineveh," in A. George and D. Collon, eds., *Nineveh*: Papers of the XLIXᵉ CRRAI London, 7–11 July, 2003, *Iraq* 66, Part One (2004), pp. 83–92.

138. Wiggermann, *Mesopotamian Protective Spirits,* pp. 65, 75–76.

139. D. Rittig, *Assyrisch-babylonianische Kleinplastik magischer Bedeutung vom 13.-6. Jh.v.Chr.* (München: Uni-Druck, 1977), pp. 36–50, 226–30. A. Green, "Beneficent Spirits and Malevolent Demons," *Visible Religion* 3 (1984), p. 82. Wiggermann, *Spirits,* pp. 60, 63–64, 94, 146–48.

140. Lambert, "Ancient Mesopotamian Gods," pp. 117, 118, 123.

Fig. 29. A procession of anthropomorphic deities, rock relief, Maltai (F. Thureau-Dangin, "Les sculptures rupestres de Maltaï," *RA* 21 [1924], p. 187).

pomorphic form. In the following pages, I will discuss this unique approach of Sennacherib's imagery in order to highlight the underlying Mesopotamian anthropocentric perception of the divine. The emphasis on the anthropomorphic representation of the divine by Sennacherib is significant, for it could not have occurred unless the dominant thinkers of Mesopotamia had always perceived the divine in human terms. Human-shaped representations of deities appear on rock reliefs from Bavian,[141] Faida[142] and Maltai (fig. 29),[143] located north of Nineveh, sites that were connected to the irrigation systems created by Sennacherib. The variety of layouts in which anthropomorphic deities are depicted on these monuments indeed suggests that during the reign of Sennacherib, the representation of major divinities in human shape became almost the norm in monumental royal display, except (as mentioned above) in palace decoration. To the example of these rock reliefs, we may add various small artifacts adorned with anthropomorphic images of major deities that have been dated to the late eighth or early seventh century (e.g., fig. 30),[144] which further underscore the artistic tendency in Assyria to portray prominent divinities in human form during the reign of Sennacherib.

This tendency is well manifested by the cylinder seals selected for endorsing the so-called Vassal Treaties of Esarhaddon recovered in the Nabu Temple at

---

141. Börker-Klähn, *Felsreliefs*, pp. 206–8, nos. 186–88.

142. R. M. Boehmer, "Bemerkungen bzw. Ergänzungen zu Gerwan, Khinis und Raidhi," *BaM* 28 (1997), pp. 248–49, pls. 38–44. T. Ornan, "The Godlike Semblance of a King: The Case of Sennacherib's Rock Reliefs," in J. Cheng and M. H. Feldman, eds., *Ancient Near Eastern Art in Context: Studies in Honor of Irene J. Winter by Her Students*, Culture and History of the Ancient Near East 26 (Leiden and New York: Brill, 2007), pp. 161–78.

143. W. Bachmann *Felsreliefs in Assyrien, Bawian, Maltai und Gundük* (Osnabrück: Otto Zeller, 2nd ed., 1969), pp. 23–27, pls. 25–32. R. M. Boehmer, "Die neuassyrischen Felsreliefs von Maltai (Nord-Irak)," *Jahrbuch des Deutschen Archäologischen Instituts* 90 (1975), (Berlin: Walter de Gruyter, 1976), pp. 42–84. Börker-Klähn, *Felsreliefs*, pp. 210–11, nos. 207–10.

144. *Ibid.*, nos. 187, 188, 200–201, 205, 207–10.

Fig. 30. Aššur and Ninlil on a model plaque, Ashur (after Moortgat, *The Art of Mesopotamia*, fig. 280).

Nimrud. The huge tablets, which deal with the issue of the succession of the king's sons, were impressed with three different cylinder seals, usually regarded as dating to the Old, Middle and Neo-Assyrian periods.[145] On the basis of the inscriptions on the Old and Neo-Assyrian seal impressions, the original seals are considered to be seals of the god Aššur. The portrayal of Aššur and Ninlil on the Neo-Assyrian seal, which according to its legend was used by Sennacherib, on the one hand accords well with Sennacherib's use of anthropomorphic divine images for display (particularly with the representation of these deities on one of the Bavian rock reliefs discussed above), and on the other hand, continues the long Mesopotamian tradition of representing gods in human form. Nevertheless, we should bear in mind that although these seals were presumably kept only temporarily in the annex of the Nabu Temple at Nimrud, anthropomorphic renderings of deities were common on objects that belonged to gods or were part of the sacred paraphernalia kept in temples.

This anthropomorphic approach towards divine representation strongly distinguishes the official imagery of Sennacherib from the art commissioned under

---

145. D. J. Wiseman, "The Vassal-Treaties of Esarhaddon," *Iraq* 20 (1958), pp. 1–28. For the dating of the Middle Assyrian impression, see also Ornan, "On the Dating," (with earlier bibliography).

other Assyrian monarchs and is to be regarded as part of a broader pattern of iconographic innovation introduced by this king. Although most of the innovations introduced by Sennacherib do not relate to religious matters,[146] the representations of the gods in human form, however—like the adoption of the Babylonian *appa labānu* ('nose-rubbing') gesture of veneration by Sennacherib[147] and the depictions of the king in close proximity to Aššur and Ninlil, such as those on the Bavian rock reliefs (see also fig. 45)—represent a change in religious iconography. This modification in cultic iconography was probably associated with other religious reforms carried out by Sennacherib, the most notable of which is the building of the *akītu* temple in honor of Aššur, whom the king attempted to liken to Marduk.[148] Since many of the portrayals of the gods rendered on the monuments and artifacts that are attributed to Sennacherib show them mounted on animals or on fantastic beasts in a manner well known in Syrian imagery, it is conceivable that Syrian monuments that had become familiar to Assyrian through the campaigns of Sennacherib to the west inspired such representations.[149] Anthropomorphic divine depictions continued to a certain degree during the reign of Esarhaddon, as seen on the royal steles from Til Barsip and Zinjirli.[150]

---

146. These artistic innovations include: the expansion of the sculptured relief over an entire wall; use of epigraphs instead of a central inscription; depiction of the colossi with four legs; a reduction in displays of the schematized tree; depictions of new types of protective demons; introduction of large-scale wall reliefs showing construction projects; and images of elite women in a public display. See I. J. Winter, "Royal Rhetoric and the Development of Historical Narrative in Neo-Assyrian Reliefs," *Studies in Visual Communication* 7 (1981), pp. 24–25. Russell, *Sennacherib's Palace*, pp. pp. 180–87, 202–15; *idem*, "The Program of the Palace of Assurnasirpal II at Nimrud: Issues in the Research and Presentation of Assyrian Art," *American Journal of Archaeology* 102 (1998), p. 165. T. Ornan, "The Queen in Public: Royal Women in Neo-Assyrian Art," in S. Parpola and R. M. Whiting, eds., *Sex and Gender in the Ancient Near East,* Proceedings of the 47th Rencontre Assyriologique Internationale (Helsinki: The Neo-Assyrian Text Corpus Project, 2002), pp. 461–77. *Idem*, "Expelling Demons."

147. Magen, *Königsdarstellungen*, p. 62.

148. J. E. Reade, "Shikaft-i Gulgul: Its Date and Symbolism," *Iranica Antiqua* 12 (1977), p. 42. W. G. Lambert, "The History of the *muš-huš* in Ancient Mesopotamia," in P. Borgeaud, Y. Christe, I. Urio, eds., *L'animal, l'homme, le dieu, dans le Proche-Orient ancien: Actes du Colloque de Cartigny 1981, Université de Genève* (Leuven: Peeters, 1984), p. 89. B. Pongratz-Leisten, "The Interplay of Military Strategy and Cultic Practice in Assyrian Politics," in S. Parpola, and R. M. Whiting, eds., *Assyria 1995: Proceedings of the 10th Anniversary Symposium of the Neo-Assyrian Text Corpus Project, Helsinki, September 7–11, 1995* (Helsinki: The Neo Assyrian Text Corpus Project, 1997), pp. 245–46, 251–52.

149. Reade, "Shikaft-i Gulgul," p. 42. I. J. Winter, "Art as Evidence for Interaction: Relations Between the Assyrian Empire and North Syria," in H. J. Nissen and J. Renger, eds., *Mesopotamien und seine Nachbarn: 25th CRRAI, 1978* (Berlin: D. Reimer, 1982), p. 367. Ornan, "Idols and Symbols," pp. 97–98. It should be noted, however, that the theme of deities posed on animals (or fantastic quadrupeds) is found in some second-millennium glyptic groups, including Middle Assyrian cylinder seals (e.g., Matthews, *Principles*, nos. 429, 469, 496, 495, 510, 535, 608, 622, 624–626) and on ninth-century Assyrian cylinder seals (Collon, *Cylinder Seals* V, p. 90, nos. 153, 152. Herbordt, *Neuassyrische Glyptik*, p. 193, pl. 1:1).

150. Börker-Klähn, *Felsreliefs*, nos. 217, 219.

Fig. 31. Veneration of anthropomorphic deities, Neo-Assyrian cylinder seal of Adad-nāṣir, eunuch of Mannu-kī-māt-Aššur, VA 511. Courtesy of the Staatliche Museen zu Berlin, Vorderasiatisches Museum.

The anthropomorphic approach towards divine representation exhibited in the monumental art of Sennacherib is also typical of ninth- to eighth-century Assyrian cylinder seals. These seals, usually cut with the drill technique, show devotional scenes and were mainly owned by court officials (e.g., fig. 31).[151] As demonstrated in Part I, such renderings of anthropomorphic deities in monumental and miniature art are to be considered as an exceptional approach to divine representation, as seen in the larger framework of Mesopotamian art dating from circa the mid-second to the middle of the first millennium. Their very existence shows approval, however, of the underlying anthropocentric concept that governed Mesopotamian thinking regarding the nature of the divine.

---

151. K. Watanabe, "Seals of Neo-Assyrian Officials," in K. Watanabe, ed., *Priests and Officials in the Ancient Near East: Papers of the Second Colloquium on the Ancient Near East—The City and its Life, held at the Middle Eastern Culture Center in Japan (Mitaka, Tokyo), March 22–24, 1996* (Heidelberg: C. Winter, 1999), pp. 313–66. I. J. Winter, "Le Palais imaginaire: Scale and Meaning in the Iconography of Neo-Assyrian Cylinder Seals," in Ch. Uehlinger, ed., *Images as Media: Sources for the Cultural History of the Near East and the Eastern Mediterranean (1st millennium BCE)*, OBO 175 (Fribourg and Göttingen: Vandenhoeck and Ruprecht, 2000), pp. 68–74. Cf. Porada, *Corpus*, pp. 81–85, nos. 678–703. Herbordt, *Glyptik*, pp. 193, 199, pl. 1:1, 5, pl. 2: 1–10. For the origin of these seals see Matthews, *Principles*, pp. 113–14. For the seal of Adad-naṣir, eunuch of Mannu-kī-māt-Aššur, illustrated here in fig. 31, see K. Watanabe, "Neuassyrische Siegellegenden," *Orient* 29 (1993), p. 117, no. 6.8.

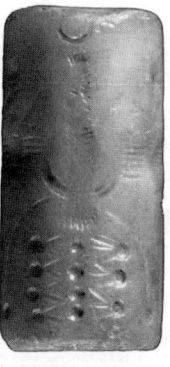

Fig. 32. Human-shaped Sin within a crescent, Aramaic inscribed cylinder seal of *brkhdd*. Harriet Otis Cruft Fund, courtesy of The Museum of Fine Arts, Boston.

Some glyptic representations of the god Sin provide further first-millennium examples of a preference for anthropomorphic depiction of major gods. In addition to the representation of Sin as a crescent moon[152] in the upper part of a seal's picture, and as a crescent mounted on a pole (an image that stands for Sin of Harran), Sin is also portrayed with an image like that of a human in first-millennium cylinder and stamp seals. The latter theme is especially common on seventh- to fifth-century Babylonian seals, perhaps representing the image of Sin worshipped at Ur.[153] In these representations, which are rarely encountered in Mesopotamian imagery before the first millennium, Sin is shown standing within a crescent, which can also be interpreted as a boat.[154] As the theme was popular on Aramaic inscribed seals (e.g., figs. 32, 33), these seals (and in particular, those inscribed with Babylonian names written in Aramaic) may have been used by Arameans living in southern Mesopotamia.[155] The attribution of the seals depicting Sin in human shape to a population originating in Syria is not implausible, considering

---

152. For the identification of the crescent moon, the star and the wingless sun disc on the Sippar Tablet, see Seidl, *Kudurru*, p. 98.

153. MacGinnis, *Letter Orders*, p. 173 (B.12). Collon, *Cylinder Seals* V, p. 120–21, nos. 229–30, 231(?).

154. M. Stol, "The Moon as Seen by the Babylonians," in D. J. W. Meijer, ed., *Natural Phenomena, Their Meaning, Depiction and Description in the Ancient Near East* (Amsterdam, Oxford, New York and Tokyo: Royal Netherlands Academy of Arts and Sciences, 1992), pp. 247–49.

155. Cf. E. Lipiński, *Studies in Aramaic Inscriptions and Onomastics* II (Leuven: Peeters, 1994), pp. 186 (n. 167), 187, 192. For the inscribed Aramaic stamp seal of Nabu-Qagillani, see N. Avigad and B. Sass, *Corpus of West Semitic Stamp Seals* (Jerusalem: The Israel Academy of Sciences and Humanities, 1997), p. 305, no. 816.

Fig. 33. Sin in a crescent, Aramaic inscribed stamp seal of *nbqglny*. IMJ 90.24.21. Courtesy of The Israel Museum, Jerusalem.

that the theme is also encountered in the western regions of the Assyro-Babylonian empires.[156] Although the portrayal of anthropomorphic Sin was already established in Akkadian glyptics and continued in Ur III and during the Old Babylonian periods,[157] his image was well known in second-millennium Syro-Anatolian art,[158] and also in Syrian art of the first millennium.[159] As portrayals of Sin in human form were not common in Mesopotamia during the second half of the second millennium,[160] his first-millennium Babylonian representations can be seen as the result of Syrian inspiration. A specifically Syrian inspiration is also suggested for the only monumental Assyrian depiction of Sin, in the rock relief of Sennacherib from Maltai, where the god, mounted on a horned lion dragon, is identified by a crescent surmounting his horned crown (fig. 34).[161] The prominent position of Sin on the Maltai rock reliefs—third in the row, behind Aššur and Ninlil—highlights the over-all Syrian influence on the steles and rock reliefs of Sennacherib noted above.

The scarcity of anthropomorphic representations of major deities in Mesopotamian art dating from the mid-second millennium onward supports the idea that

---

156. E.g., Herbordt, *Glyptik*, pl. 3:14. Collon, *Cylinder Seals* V, p. 118.

157. J. V. Canby, *The "Ur-Nammu" Stela*, University Museum Monograph 110 (Philadelphia: University of Pennsylvania Museum of Archaeology and Anthropology, 2001). A. Parrot, *Les Palais* II: *Peintures murales. Mission archeologique de Mari* (Paris: P. Geuthner, 1958), p. 76, pls. XVII, XVIII. For Old Babylonian glyptic examples, see Ornan, "The Bull," pp. 6–7, figs. 5, 6 (with bibliography).

158. E.g., in Cappadocian glyptics: Collon, "Moon God," p. 23, fig. 7.

159. Collon, "Moon God," pp. 22–27, figs. 1–18. PKG, pl. 356. K. Kohlmeyer, "Drei Stelen mit Sin-Symbol aus Nordsyrien," in B. Hrouda *et al.*, eds., *Von Uruk nach Tuttul, eine Festschrift für Eva Strommenger: Studien und Aufsätze von Kollegen und Freunden* (Munich and Vienna: Profil, 1992), pp. 91–100, pl. 40.

160. For the cylinder seal from Samsat, which betrays some Middle Assyrian traits and on which Sin in human shape is shown standing in a boat, see E. Porada, "The Cylinder Seal (Appendix A)," in P. Bikai, *The Pottery of Tyre* (Warminster: Aris and Philips, 1978), pp. 77–82.

161. Boehmer, "Maltai," p. 50. Börker-Klähn, *Felsreliefs*, p. 211, nos. 207–10 (with bibliography).

Fig. 34. Sin on a rock relief, Maltai (D. Collon, "The Near Eastern Moon God," in D. J. W. Meijer, ed., *Natural Phenomena: Their Meaning, Depiction and Descriptions in the Ancient Near East* [Amsterdam: Koninklijke Nederlandse Akademie van Wetenschappen, 1992], fig. 20). Courtesy of the Koninklijke Nederlandse Akademie van Wetenschappen.

it was an idea of gods as much like humans that dominates the Mesopotamian concept even in periods when a coherent divine anthropomorphic pictorial tradition is not revealed. For example, the infrequent depictions of human-shaped deities and, in particular, the relatively few identifiable major deities found on Babylonian *kudurru*s, support the conclusion that anthropomorphic depictions of major deities were generally avoided in the Middle Babylonian period. Indeed, examination of the few extant Middle Babylonian portrayals of major deities on *kudurru*s, such as those of Adad, Nanaya and Marduk,[162] reveals inconsistencies in the artistic depiction of anthropomorphic deities that may have resulted from the rarity of such anthropomorphic representations of the divine.[163] These iconographical inconsistencies can be illustrated by the depiction of the traditional horned headdress contemporaneously with the newly introduced feathered crown worn, for example, by the enthroned goddess Nanaya on two twelfth-century *kudurru*s of Meli-Shipak (fig. 35).[164] Variations in divine head coverings shown on other *kudurru*s of Meli-Shipak may corroborate the suggestion made above.[165] Another rendering of the feathered crown in the twelfth to eleventh centuries underlines the evasive character of divine portrayal, since it was concurrently used by royal figures,

---

162. Seidl, *Kudurru*, nos. 7, 21, 23, 24, 25.
163. Ornan, *The Triumph*, Chapter 1.
164. Compare the gods depicted on two steles from Susa, originally worked in the twelfth century: U. Seidl, "Zur Umarbeitung zweier Stelenbekrönungen aus Susa und anderer altorientalischer Reliefs," *Berliner Jahrbuch für vor- und frühgeschichte* 5 (1965), pp. 175–86 with idem., *Kudurru*, nos. 23, 24.
165. Seidl, *Kudurru*, nos. 21, 26, fig. 3, pl. 10b.

Fig. 35. Nanaya on a kudurru of Meli-Shipak (after Ornan, "Gula and her Dog," fig. 14).

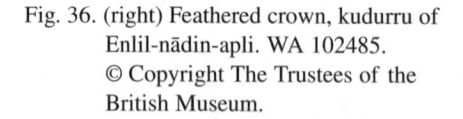

Fig. 36. (right) Feathered crown, kudurru of Enlil-nādin-apli. WA 102485. © Copyright The Trustees of the British Museum.

as on a *kudurru* of Marduk-nādin-aḫḫe I.[166] The ambiguity in the use of the feathered crown is also suggested by its depiction as a divine symbol placed on a pedestal on a *kudurru* of Enlil-nādin-apli (fig. 36).[167] The rather few human-shaped deities found on Middle Babylonian cylinder seals also reveal a somewhat indecisive pictorial tradition of representing gods, yet these glyptic and monumental examples clearly testify to the existence of a cognitive notion of granting the divine an anthropomorphic form.

We may conclude, then, that it was not the human perception of the divine that was modified or eliminated, but rather its pictorial manifestation. Moreover, it

---

166. *Ibid.*, pp. 46–49, 198, nos. 76, 79, and for other images of rulers, see nos. 27, 81(?), 198.
167. King, *Babylonian Boundary Stones*, 11. Seidl, *Kudurru*, p. 44, no. 71.

seems that within Mesopotamian temples the deities retained their human form, and only when it was exhibited outside of the temple was their image modified into a non-anthropomorphic icon. Indeed, the *mīs pî* and *pīt pî* induction rituals confirm that human-shaped cult images were usually housed within Mesopotamian temples, and although these rituals were also performed on divine non-anthropomorphic cult objects such as the *uskāru* emblem of Sin, as mentioned earlier, usually they were carried out as part of the making of human-shaped cult images of major gods. Examination of various portrayals of anthropomorphic gods reveals that their depictions were mostly confined to temples. This is pictorially illustrated on the Sippar Tablet discussed above (fig. 22), where it is the Šamaš in human form who is shown inside the shrine, while the symbol is located outside of the building. That this visual theme does not merely reflect the specific actual event described in the accompanying inscription[168] is sustained by the example of other compositions in which major deities are depicted. For example, a similar cultic distinction is observed in the depiction of Ishtar enthroned within a shrine shown on the White Obelisk from Nineveh, while a ceremony being conducted by the king is depicted outside of the shrine.[169] It is also reflected in some Neo-Assyrian wall reliefs illustrating cultic rituals directed towards *šurinnu* standards that were carried out in military camps.[170] Similarly, the example of the *kakki Aššur*, the god's weapon (and symbol) carried by Assyrian troops in foreign territories and also used as a cult object in conquered cities,[171] sustains the notion that when removed from its sacred abode, the divine image was often modified into a non-anthropomorphic cult object.

A cultic reality in which the worship of an anthropomorphic image kept in a shrine was accompanied by concurrent worship directed towards a non-anthropomorphic object located outside of the temple, is also documented in other areas of the ancient Near East. For example, contemporary worship of both kinds of cult objects is referred to in Hittite cultic inventories, which mention an anthropomorphic image of a certain deity housed in its temple located within the city, and concurrently *ḫuwaši* standing-stones representing the same deity located outside the city.[172] Similar phenomena, revealed by archaeological data, existed in second-

---

168. Reiner, "Suspendu."

169. Börker-Klähn, *Felsreliefs*, no.132a. Ishtar is identified by the epigraph mentioning *bīt natḫi*, which formed part of her sacred enclosure at Nineveh: Grayson, *Rulers of the Early First Millennium*, pp. 254–56 (A.O.101.18).

170. E.g., a slab in room 14 at Khorsabad (P. Albenda, *The Palace of Sargon, King of Assyria* [Paris: Editions Recherche sur les Civilisations, 1986], pl. 137). Pongratz-Leisten, Deller and Bleibtreu, "Götterstreitwagen."

171. S. W. Holloway, "The ᵍⁱˢ*kakki Aššur* and Neo-Assyrian Loyalty Oaths," in T. Abusch, *et al.*, eds., *Historiography in the Cuneiform World, 45th CRRAI, Boston July 1998. Part I, Harvard University* (Bethesda: CDL Press, 2001), pp. 239–66.

172. Van Loon, *Anatolia*, p. 29. D. E. Fleming, *Time at Emar: The Cultic Calendar and the Rituals from the Diviner's Archive* (Winona Lake: Eisenbrauns, 2000), p. 84.

Fig. 37. Marduk, lapis lazuli cylinder, Babylon (after E. Klengel-Brandt, ed., *Mit Sieben Siegeln versehen: Das Siegel in Wirtschaft und Kunst des Alten Orients* [Berlin: Staatliche Museen zu Berlin, Vorderasiatisches Museum. and Mainz: Verlag Philipp von Zabern, 1997], p. 100, fig. 99).

Fig. 38. Adad, lapis lazuli cylinder, Babylon (after D. Collon, *First Impressions: Cylinder Seals in the Ancient Near East* [London: British Museum Press, 1987], no. 563).

millennium Syria and Israel where in various cities such as Qatna, Aleppo, Ugarit, Gezer or Hazor, divine anthropomorphic statues were venerated in temples, while steles representing deities were worshipped in open-air sanctuaries.[173]

Evidence that the human-shaped representations were usually confined to the temple precinct is also provided by several artifacts adorned with portrayals of

---

173. Mettinger, *Graven Image*, pp. 28–32, 79–113, 115–34, 112 (with bibliography).

Fig. 39. Cylinder seal of Mušezib-Ninurta, Babylon (after A. Moortgat, *Vorderasiatische Rollsiegel: Ein Beitrag zur Geschichte der Steinschneidekunst* [Berlin: Mann, 1940], no. 600).

major deities in human shape, which were regarded as "belonging to" or were actually found in or attributed to temples and sacred enclosures. Examples include: the Sippar Tablet (fig. 22), the *perlendepot* hoard's huge lapis lazuli cylinders (figs. 37, 38), the Assyrianized cylinder seal of Mušezib-Ninurta found in Babylon (fig. 39), a huge cylinder from Persepolis (fig. 40), a *kudurru* of Nabu-šuma-iškun (fig. 41), the sketchy rendering of a goddess wearing a horned, feathered crown incised on a limestone stele from the Karaindash temple at Uruk (fig. 42), and probably also the three cylinder seals of the god Aššur dated to the Old Assyrian, Middle (or late) and Neo-Assyrian periods which were rolled on the Vassal Treaties of Esarhaddon discussed above (figs. 43–45).[174]

Indirect evidence corroborating the human perception of the prominent deities of Mesopotamia comes, among other sources, from texts dealing with the divine characteristics of Mesopotamian kings. The human nature of the divine is apparent, for example, in texts describing the family-like relationship existing between the god(s) and the king. The very use of metaphors portraying kings as being conceived, born, suckled, fathered and raised by gods and goddesses is based on a conceptualization of the divine after the human model. Interesting examples are found in the Epic of Tukulti-Ninurta I, where the king is described as being cast into a divine womb and being raised by Enlil, who was considered his natural

---

174. U. Seidl, "Babylonische und assyrische Kultbilder in den Massenmedien des 1. Jahrtausends v. Chr.," in Ch. Uehlinger, ed., *Images as Media: Sources for the Cultural History of the Near East and the Eastern Mediterranean (1st millennium BCE)*, OBO 175 (Fribourg and Göttingen: Vandenhoeck and Ruprecht, 2000), pp. 89–114. E. Unger, "Two Seals of the Ninth Century B.C. from Sahdikanni on the Habur," *BASOR* 130 (1953), pp. 15–21. Becker, *Uruk, Kleinfunde*, p. 61, pl. 50:795.

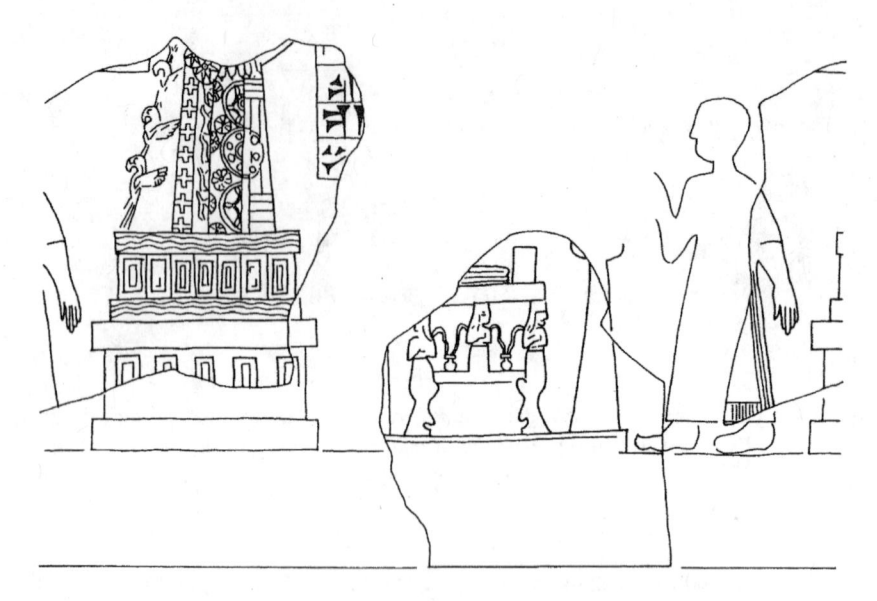

Fig. 40. A huge lapis lazuli cylinder, Persepolis (U. Seidl, "Babylonische und assyrische Kultbilder in den Massenmedien des 1. Jahrtausends v. chr.," in Ch. Uehlinger, ed., *Images as Media: Sources for the Cultural History of the Near East and the Eastern Mediterranean (1st Millennium BCE)*, OBO 175 [Fribourg and Göttingen: Vandenhoeck and Ruprecht, 2000], p. 102, fig. 9).

Fig. 41. Anthropomorphic Babylonian deities, kudurru of Nabu-šuma-iškun (after U. Seidl, *Kudurru*, fig. 22c).

father and treated him as second only to Enlil's first-born, Ninurta.[175] The same kinds of intimate family ties are mentioned in a prophetic text with regard to

---

175. P. Machinist, "Literature as Politics: The Tukulti-Ninurta Epic and the Bible," *Catholic Biblical Quarterly* 38 (1976), pp. 462, 466.

Ashurbanipal, where he is described as being suckled by four-breasted Ishtar.[176] These verbal metaphors are used to describe two Assyrian kings in whose reigns, as shown above, the depiction of large-scale major deities was virtually rejected. Their existence in periods when pictorial divine anthropomorphism was avoided emphasizes that it was not the divine anthropocentric conceptualization that was modified in these periods, but only its pictorial manifestation. These seemingly contradictory approaches shed light on an inherent difference between verbal and pictorial modes of expression[177] and furthermore underscore an inherent resistance in Mesopotamian thinking to giving divine anthropomorphism concrete form.

The reasons for the transformation of the cult image into a non-anthropomorphic icon are highly conjectural, since the ancient records are not explicit about this issue. Thus we can only speculate that it was the awesome sacred status of Mesopotamian deities, or perhaps their sublime splendor, which prevented their visual representations from being viewed by humans.[178] Such a conclusion may be inferred from the fact that the highest position of Enlil among all the gods is expressed in a Sumerian poem with the words, "no god could look upon him."[179] Preventing the portrayal of the human-shaped god from being displayed outside of the temple enclosure may also have had political implications. Limiting the divine statue to the confines of the temple may have been used to exalt the locale of the sacred precinct as being the

Fig. 42. A goddess, stele from the Karaindash temple, Uruk (after Becker, *Uruk, Kleinfunde*, pl. 50:795).

---

176. A. Livingstone, *Court Poetry and Literary Miscellanea*, SAA 3 (Helsinki: Helsinki University Press, 1989), p. 34.

177. Suter, *Gudea*, pp. 1–12.

178. The notion of "concealing" the human-shaped cult image when it moved from its abode is perhaps also reflected in the instruction to cover the head of the cult statue when it is carried away for renovation; see W. Farber, "Singing an *eršemma* for the Damaged Statue of a God," ZA 93 (2003), pp. 208–13.

179. J. A. Black, G. Cunningham, E. Flückiger-Hawker, E. Robson, G. Zólyomi, *The Electronic Text Corpus of Sumerian Literature* (Oxford, 1998–, http://www.etcsl.orient.ox.ac.uk), Enlil in the E-kur (Enlil A), 103.

Fig. 43. Reconstructed Old Assyrian impression found on the Vassal Treaties (Wiseman, "Vassal-Treaties," p. 18, fig. 4). Courtesy of the British School of Archaeology in Iraq.

Fig. 44. Reconstructed Middle Assyrian impression found on the Vassal Treaties (Wiseman, "Vassal-Treaties," p. 21, fig. 6). Courtesy of the British School of Archaeology in Iraq.

only place where a superior (human-like) divine manifestation could be found. In other words, by concealing the "true" (i.e., human-like) appearance of major gods when they were shown outside of the temple, by representing them only in non-anthropomorphic pictorial metaphors, the status of the signified god and his earthly abode was thus elevated.

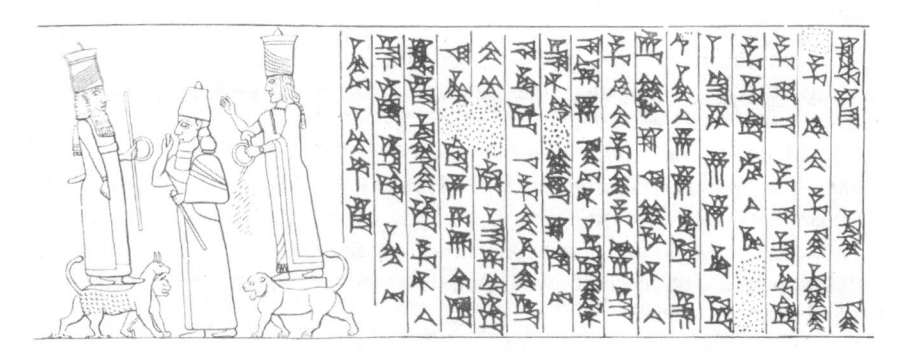

Fig. 45. Reconstructed seal of the god Aššur belonging to Sennacherib, found on the Vassal Treaties (Wiseman, "Vassal-Treaties," p. 16, fig. 2) Courtesy of the British School of Archaeology in Iraq.

The topic of divine anthropomorphism in Mesopotamia was dealt with by Jacobsen, who suggested that the early Mesopotamian divine powers were thought of as natural phenomena, and that these were given concrete form in words and pictures by means of non-human agents. He accepted, however, the notion that concurrently the divine powers were given a human form from very early times (the Uruk period) in Mesopotamia, commenting that "this early tendency to give situationally determined, nonhuman form to the numinous, however, probably at no time excluded attribution also of human form." Further on, he suggested that the human metaphor for the divine was determined and then intensified in response to the increasing role and higher status of earthly rulers during the Early Dynastic period.[180] The ambiguity of Mesopotamian civilization in respect to divine anthropomorphism was discussed in the works of Spycket. Her observations that human-shaped sculptures of gods and goddesses were preceded in early Mesopotamia by emblematic renderings, and that human-shaped cult sculptures in-the-round of deities were not referred to in texts during most of the third millennium, shed light on Mesopotamian civilization's difficulty to give concrete form to its conception of the divine as human.[181] In this regard it should be emphasized

---

180. Th. Jacobsen, "Mesopotamian Gods and Pantheons," in Th. Jacobsen (edited by W. L. Moran), *Toward the Image of Tammuz and Essays on Mesopotamian History and Culture* (Cambridge: Harvard University Press, 1970), pp. 16–18. First published in *The Encyclopedia Britannica* II (1963) s.v. Babylonia and Assyria: religion, pp. 18–29.

181. A. Spycket, *Les statues de cult dans les textes mesopotamiens des origines à la Iere dynastie de Babylone*, Cahiers de la Revue Biblique 9 (Paris: Gabalda, 1968). *Idem, La statuaire du Proche-Orient ancien* (Leiden-Köln: Brill, 1981), pp. 54, 37 (for the inscribed ^{d}Abu sculpture from the Sin temple at Tell Asmar); pp. 144–46, pl. 96 (for what is probably the earliest securely identified large cult sculpture in-the-round: the Akkadian-style stone statue of enthroned Inanna/Narundi from Susa), pp. 185–87, 204. Cf. I. J. Winter, "Review of Spycket 1981," *JCS* 36 (1984), pp. 105–7 (for the ^{d}Abu

that the only known large, human-shaped sculptures, dated from the Uruk period, represent mortals (rulers) and not divinities.[182] This may support Jacobsen's postulate that the image of the divine was based on that of the ruler, exemplified by the use of the term en 'lord, manager', a title of the earthly ruler, in divine names, e.g., Enlil 'the lord of the wind'. The fact that the earliest freestanding sculptures represent mortal rulers, and not deities, lends support to the premise that concretizing the divine in large-scale statuary was already a problematic issue at beginning of Mesopotamian history and that the later sculptured, anthropomorphic representations of gods and goddesses were indeed fashioned in the likeness of man.

Conclusions

Geographically and chronologically remote examples supporting this conclusion may perhaps be found in archaeological finds from the seventh millennium BC discovered in other areas of the ancient Near East. These are the large, plaster, human-shaped statues excavated at ʿAin Ghazal, Jericho and Naḥal Ḥemar Cave.[183] Whether these images represent human beings or supernatural entities is not clear, and it is disputable whether they are to be understood as portrayals of venerated ancestors, such as "ghosts," or as deities.[184] I tend to reject the latter suggestion since it is mainly based on comparisons to Babylonian data,[185] in which, as postulated here, the concretization of major deities was seriously challenged during many periods of Mesopotamian history. These Neolithic statues reveal a resemblance to the plastered, painted or otherwise reworked human skulls that pertain to a cult of mortal ancestors, and hence can be seen as stemming from the cult of the dead.[186] As the earliest known free-standing human-shaped statues were indeed associated in one way or another with human beings, it is possible to reconstruct later developments of divine anthropomorphic imagery as emerging from sepulchral cultic art. This notion is intriguing since it was, after all, mortal men and women who were the protagonists in this kind of a cult, and thus an anthropocentric perception of the divine already present in very early periods of the ancient Near East can be established.

---

sculpture and the enthroned female images from Mari). For a different interpretation of the ᵈAbu sculpture, see Jacobsen, "God or Worshipper," pp. 124–30 (with earlier bibliography).

182. Spycket, *La statuaire*, pp. 29–30. Moortgat, *The Art of Mesopotamia*, pp. 8–9, pls. 6–10, 13.

183. G. O. Rolefson, "Ritual and Social Structure at Neolithic ʿAin Ghazal," in I. Kuijt, ed., *Life in Neolithic Farming Communities: Social Organization, Identity, and Differentiation* (New York: Kluwer and Plenum, 2000), pp. 165–90 (with previous bibliography). K. M Kenyon, *Digging Up Jericho* (London: E. Benn, 1957), pp. 60–64. O. Bar-Yosef and D. Alon, "Naḥal Ḥemar Cave," *ʿAtiqot* 18 (1988), pp. 20–21.

184. Bar-Yosef and Alon, "Naḥal Ḥemar," p. 28. Rolefson, "Ritual and Social Structure," pp. 171–72, 185.

185. D. Schmandt-Besserat, "ʿAin Ghazal 'Monumental' Figures," *BASOR* 310 (1998), pp. 1–17.

Indeed, considering that the gods and goddesses of Mesopotamia—the supernatural entities which governed the ancient mind and behavior—were human-made, fantasized products, it is not surprising that basically these uncanny figures mirrored the men and women who created them. The Mesopotamian conception of the divine can, thus, be considered anthropocentric, since it centered on and was constructed after the human model in form and essence.

The nature of the Mesopotamian divinity is to be determined in accordance with this overall, encapsulating attribution of a human nature to the gods, most clearly manifested in literary narratives and metaphors and in many pictorial representations. This anthropomorphism was probably also in the background, dominating the ancient mental conceptualization of the divine, in cases where the humanly conceptualized deity was not textually or pictorially apparent and was made manifest in a non-anthropomorphic agent. These agents include animals, hybrid creatures, natural phenomena, celestial bodies or inanimate objects, which relate to a personified deity in one way or another and thus are to be seen as emanating from this "higher" personified divinity. They are sometimes signified as a divine recipient of veneration in pictorial renderings by a gesturing worshiper whose encoded role in a visual composition may be compared to that of the DINGIR determinative in a written context. The non-human manifestations of divinities are then to be understood as representing various aspects embedded in the image of a transcendental, conceptually human, multi-faceted, and at times invisible, god.

---

186. R. Amiran, "Myths of the Creation of Man and the Jericho Statues," *BASOR* 16 (1962), pp. 23–25. K. M. Kenyon, *Excavations at Jericho III: The Architecture and Stratigraphy of the Tell* (London: The British School of Archaeology in Jerusalem, 1981), pp. 436–37, pls. VIII-IX. T. Ornan, *A Man and His Land: Highlights from the Moshe Dayan Collection*, The Israel Museum Catalogue no. 270 (Jerusalem: The Israel Museum, 1986), pp. 18–19. Bar-Yosef and Alon, "Naḥal Ḥemar," p. 21. An association between these Neolithic statues in human form and the cult of the dead is also suggested by the Sumerian GIDIM (Akkadian *eṭemmu* 'spirit of the dead'), composed of reed (GI) and picture/statue (DIM); see G. Selz, "Was belibt? Ein Versuch zu Tod und Identität im Alten Orient," in R. Rollinger, ed., *Von Sumer bis Homer: Festschrift für Manfred Schretter sum 60. Geburtstag am 25. Februar 2004*, AOAT 325 (Münster: Ugarit, 2005), pp. 585–86. My thanks to Irit Ziffer for this reference.

Blessings from a Crown, Offerings to a Drum:
Were There Non-Anthropomorphic Deities in Ancient Mesopotamia?

Barbara N. Porter
The Casco Bay Assyriological Institute

> Everything was potentially charged with power,
> and recognizably potent objects were sought for every concern....
> The objects in antiquity were potent because they were animate.
> (Beatrice L. Goff, *Symbols of Prehistoric Mesopotamia*, p. 179)

> The world is charged with the grandeur of God.
> It will flame out, like shining from shook foil....
> (Gerard Manley Hopkins, "God's Grandeur")

The myths of ancient Mesopotamia offer vivid pictures of Mesopotamia's gods in action.[1] In such texts, the great gods appear primarily as great divine persons, quite human in their physical appearance and in their behavior. In a well-known Akkadian myth known as *The Descent of Ishtar to the Underworld*, for example, Ishtar, goddess of love, and her sister Ereshkigal, ruler of the underworld, are represented despite their cosmic powers as much like human queens, wearing crowns

---

Author's note: I am deeply grateful to the other participants in the conference for their thoughtful papers and discussion. In addition, I owe a debt of gratitude to Prof. Stefan Maul and his students and colleagues at the University of Heidelberg for stimulating questions and comments in response to a talk on non-anthropomorphic gods given there in 2004. And I would like to thank Profs. Robert C. Hunt, Theo Krispijn, Michel Tanret, Jeffrey Stackert, Irene J. Winter, and Henk Versnel for long and helpful discussions, and in the case of the latter two, also for their insightful responses to the final manuscript. Above all, I am grateful to my family, Anne Porter, Seth Porter, and especially Michael H. Porter, for unfailing patience and for expert (and tactful) editorial advice.

1. For non-specialists, a few comments on the conventions that distinguish Akkadian from Sumerian words in the essay that follows may be helpful. As a Neo-Assyrian specialist, I have primarily followed the typographic conventions used by Assyriologists, representing Akkadian words in lower-case italics and Sumerian words used for logographic writings in Akkadian language texts in small capitals without italics. Sumerian words in Sumerian language texts are shown in letter-spaced lower-case roman type. Personal names in either language are treated as English words unless their translation or linguistic affiliation is under discussion.

and jewelry, living in palaces, served by viziers and gatekeepers, and subject to quite human emotions.[2] As the myth describes Ishtar's journey to the land of death, the two goddesses emerge as fully realized personalities, conversing, struggling with one another, angry, afraid—and in most respects remarkably human.

Although this highly anthropomorphic concept of the divine is particularly apparent in Mesopotamian myths, it is also quite evident in the hymns and prayers in which Mesopotamians directly addressed their gods, as I noted in the introduction. In these genres, however, the images of gods are more fluid and less consistently anthropomorphic. In hymns and prayers, gods may appear at one moment as anthropomorphic beings who control some powerful aspect of the cosmos, and at the next moment they may be described as if they were that powerful phenomenon itself. In one third millennium Sumerian hymn, for example, Inanna is addressed first in anthropomorphic form as a great divine lady who controls the storm ("O destroyer of mountains, you lent the storm wings! . . . O my lady, at your roar you made the countries bow low"[3]). She is next represented as a wild presence in the storm, separate from it yet almost its personification: "With the charging storm, you charge, with the howling storm you howl." And finally the hymn represents her as the storm itself, "Inanna, the great dread storm of heaven."[4] In another hymn, Inanna is represented as both the bright planet Venus and a queen, "The pure torch that flares in the sky, the heavenly light, shining bright like the day, the great queen of heaven, Inanna," who is praised for "her brilliant coming forth in the evening sky."[5] Similar examples of gods represented as both anthropomorphic and non-anthropomorphic could be cited in hymns and prayers from every period and for almost every great god of Mesopotamia.

Despite such evidence, which seems to suggest that many of Mesopotamia's great gods were imagined at least partly in non-anthropomorphic form, it is the images of Mesopotamia's gods as almost human in their form and nature that have captured the greatest attention. Most Assyriologists have concluded that the ancient Mesopotamians, as Jean Bottéro once put it, were "resolutely polytheistic and anthropomorphist from the beginning," and that "the gods' image was thus basically anthropomorphic."[6] Although Thorkild Jacobsen, in describing the historical development of Mesopotamian religion, hypothesized that Mesopotamia's gods were initially envisioned non-anthropomorphically, he went on to conclude,

---

2. For a recent English translation, see Stephanie Dalley, *Myths from Mesopotamia: Creation, the Flood, Gilgamesh, and Others* (Oxford: Oxford University Press, rev. ed., 2000), pp. 154–62, with bibliographical and philological notes.

3. Thorkild Jacobsen, *The Treasures of Darkness: A History of Mesopotamian Religion* (New Haven and London: Yale University Press, 1976), p. 138.

4. Jacobsen, *Treasures*, p. 136.

5. *Ibid.*, p. 139.

6. Jean Bottéro, *Religion in Ancient Mesopotamia*, trans. Teresa Lavender Fagan (Chicago and London: University of Chicago Press, 2001), pp. 44 and 64.

as we have already seen, that the subsequent "victory of the human over the non-human forms" of gods happened at a very early stage.[7] As Jacobsen understood it, "The situationally determined, nonhuman, forms [that appear in texts and imagery from historic times] . . . are all original or old forms or . . . survivals into a later age. They appear to have had their floruit in Protoliterate or earlier periods, that is to say during the fourth millennium B.C. Even then, however, the human form would seem to have been an alternative, or perhaps a competing, possibility; and with the beginning of the third millennium, from Early Dynastic onward, the human form came to dominate almost completely, leaving to the older forms the somewhat ambiguous role of divine 'emblems' only."[8] Even a cursory survey of handbooks and textbooks on ancient Mesopotamia suggests that most scholars have agreed with Bottéro and Jacobsen in concluding that while each great god was linked to a particular power or phenomenon in the cosmos, the gods of Mesopotamia were nevertheless imagined primarily as anthropomorphic beings, much like humans not only in their physical form, but also in their activities and nature.

Given this widespread emphasis on the anthropomorphic nature of Mesopotamia's gods, it is a little startling to discover in a well-known late Babylonian ritual instruction text, for example, that the gods presented with daily food offerings in the city of Uruk include both familiar gods usually represented in anthropomorphic form, and also what appear to be deified objects that have no anthropomorphic form at all. The text in question gives detailed instructions for preparing and serving four elaborate daily meals to the gods dwelling in temples of the city of Uruk.[9] It begins by instructing the priest to present drinks on golden trays to the god Anu, his spouse Antu, the goddess Ishtar, and other deities of Uruk, and then instructs the temple's bakers in the number of loaves of bread they must prepare for each god's daily meals. In the process, this text provides a list of many gods that were important enough to be honored with daily food offerings in Babylonian Uruk:

---

7. Jacobsen, *Treasures*, p. 9.

8. Jacobsen, *Treasures*, p. 9.

9. In the text's colophon, the scribe identifies himself as writing in the Seleucid period and notes he is copying from a tablet dated to the time of the seventh century Chaldean king Nabopolassar. The text thus appears to reflect ritual practice in the city during the Neo-Babylonian period; whether these same rituals were being practiced unchanged at Uruk when the later copy of the text was made is unclear. I am indebted to Vanstiphout and Ornan for pointing out that in any case, texts giving instructions for performing rituals may not have reflected actual or current cultic practice; they might, for example, describe rituals as their author thought they ought to be performed, or represent (or inadvertently misrepresent) past practices. In many cases, however, contemporary (and apparently ordinarily factual) administrative records of the disbursements of food or animals for offerings seem to confirm that the offerings prescribed by the ritual instruction texts were in fact being made, and on a regular basis.

... the cooks will take 486 liters of barley flour and 162 liters of spelt flour, to cook from it 243 loaves of bread.The cooks should reserve from it 30 loaves, in total, for the Table of Anu: for the big and small meal of the morning, 8 loaves each; and for the big and small evening repast, 7 loaves each. From the same, 30 loaves will be required for Antu; 30 for Ištar; 30 for Nanaya; 12 for the Throne of Anu and for the domestic divinities of the Cella of Anu; 16 for the Tiaras of Anu; 16 for the Temple-tower (the ziggurat) and its domestic divinities; 16 for those of the two Wings of the Sanctuary of Anu and of Antu. This makes a total of 160 loaves. [10]

Among the recipients of daily bread offerings, this passage lists not only familiar great gods of Mesopotamia such as Anu, a ruler-god and the patron deity of the sky, and Antu, his spouse and the divine queen of Uruk, but also a throne, two "tiaras" or crowns, and a building, the ziggurat or 'temple-tower.' These objects appear in the same list with the Uruk temple's anthropomorphic gods and receive food offerings just as they do. Does this treatment imply that they, too, were considered to be gods?[11]

There can be little doubt that the throne and crowns presented here with offerings of bread were actual objects that belonged to the god Anu and were housed in his temple in Uruk, and that the ziggurat was an actual building, the stepped tower of that temple. Throughout Mesopotamian history, texts report that rulers presented thrones, crowns, chariots, weapons and other objects as gifts to the gods, placing them in temples where they were used in rituals or "used" by the gods in their daily lives, serving them for example as furniture, insignia of office, tools, or in the case of chariots, as transportation for the gods' statues when they moved in procession outside the temple.[12] In the third millennium, for example, the ruler Gudea of Lagash celebrates in one of his year names his presentation of

---

10. Jean Bottéro, *La plus vieille cuisine du monde* (Paris: Editions Louis Audibert, 2002), p. 174 (the translation from the French is mine). The standard edition of the text (with a handcopy of the cuneiform) is that of F. Thureau-Dangin, *Rituels accadiens* (Paris: Editions Ernest Leroux, 1921), AO. 6451, pp. 61–86; see esp. I: 21–33, pp. 76 and 82.

11. In introducing his collected edition of Uruk ritual texts, Thureau-Dangin noted that not only are the statues of gods "lent life and movement" in the texts, rising and sitting, coming and going "as if they were animate," but also that "Cette fiction n'est pas limitée aux seules statues: elle s'applique aussi à certains objets sacrés qui n'ont rien de la forme humaine, par exemple à une arme, un sceptre, un trône, une torche" (*Rituels*, p. 61). In these ritual texts, the objects and buildings that receive offerings in our text emerge as part of a larger phenomenon at Uruk in which a variety of sacred objects, both anthropomorphic and non-anthropomorphic, are described and treated as if they are animate deities. For further discussion of deified objects at Uruk, see Paul-Alain Beaulieu, *The Pantheon of Uruk During the Neo-Babylonian Period* (Leiden and Boston: Brill and Styx, 2003), Chapter 8: Non-Anthropomorphic Deities, pp. 351–68.

12. For references in Akkadian texts, see, for example, CAD s.v. *kussu, agû, narkabtu, šubtu* and *kakku*.

a throne to the goddess Nanše,[13] and the giving of such gifts to gods is still frequently attested in the first millennium, when, for example, the Assyrian king Esarhaddon describes a "cunningly made crown ... of red gold and precious stones" that he commissioned for the god Aššur, as well as a seat made of *musukannu*-wood and a footstool of red gold that he ordered to be constructed and placed in the Esagila temple in Babylon for the goddess Tašmētum.[14] As for ziggurats, these were substantial brick buildings whose construction, requiring the making of many hundreds of bricks, is reported in numerous royal inscriptions and letters over the centuries; at Uruk, as elsewhere, the remains of a ziggurat still survive and have been excavated.[15] In the passage we have just looked at, these very real objects and buildings receive food offerings together with more anthropomorphic gods of the city of Uruk; their inclusion in this act of worship suggests that in southern Mesopotamia even in this late period certain material objects were considered to be gods. Was this in fact the case? Was it the case in earlier periods or in other regions? What does it mean to say that such objects were "gods"? Did they function like the more anthropomorphic gods? Were other non-anthropomorphic entities also treated as gods? And if so, did all non-anthropomorphic gods function in the same way, or did they differ?

Before we can pursue these questions further, however, I must clarify how I am using the word "god" here and briefly explore the ambiguities introduced by using that modern term in a discussion such as this one. By asking whether the presentation of offerings to certain material objects at Uruk indicates that they were considered gods in that setting, for example, I am asking whether the ancient Babylonians of Uruk considered those objects to belong in the category of things they designated as DINGIRs and *ilu*s, the ancient Sumerian and Akkadian words that Assyriologists have long translated as 'god.' This modern Assyriological translation of the native terms, however, is problematic because it has encouraged Assyriologists to impose all the baggage of a modern Western cultural concept on an ancient Mesopotamian cultural concept that appears to have been in some ways significantly different. Webster's dictionary defines the word "god" as "a being of more than human attributes and powers, a deity, esp. a male deity;

---

13. Dietz Otto Edzard, *Gudea and His Dynasty*, RIME 3/1 (Toronto: University of Toronto Press, 1997), p. 27, a listing of year-names from Gudea's reign, with discussion and further bibliography.

14. Rykle Borger, *Die Inschriften Asarhaddons Königs von Assyrien*, Archiv für Orientforschung Beih. 9 (Graz: Self-publication by the editor, 1956), pp. 83–84, AsBbA, Rs.: 32–33 and 39–40.

15. CAD s.v. *ziqqurratu* ; for some references in letters, Simo Parpola, *The Correspondence of Sargon II, Part I: Assyria and the West*, SAA 1 (Helsinki: Helsinki U. Press, 1987), nos. 70–71 and 78–79; Henri Frankfort, *The Art and Architecture of the Ancient Orient* (Baltimore, Md.: Penguin Books, 1956), on the remains of the earliest ziggurat at Uruk, pp. 5–7, on the later high terrace and its evolution into a ziggurat still present at Uruk in the Neo-Babylonian period and later, p. 274, and for ziggurats at other sites, see the index, p. 298 s.v. *Ziggurat*.

anything worshipped by man as a deity."[16] In defining gods as "beings" endowed with "more than human attributes" the dictionary implies that gods are entities thought of as living persons, a concept that reflects the influence of the largely anthropomorphic gods of ancient Greek, Roman, Israelite and Norse tradition on modern conceptions of what a god is like, but is not necessarily appropriate for the gods of Mesopotamia. Although the idea that Mesopotamian DINGIRs and *ilu*s were gods is by now deeply entrenched in Assyriological thinking, the Mesopotamian evidence, as I hope to demonstrate, suggests that the Mesopotamian and modern Western concepts of deity are only partially equivalent. It is already clear, for example, that our idea of gods as they occur in a Mesopotamian context must be flexible enough to accommodate a goddess like Ishtar, who is described not only as a living person but also as a planet (and labeled and referred to as a DINGIR or *ilu* in both contexts), and broad enough to encompass the concept of thrones and crowns (not persons at all) as appropriate recipients of divine offerings, as if they too were gods.

One of the dangers in using the word "god" for DINGIRs and *ilu*s is that it leads us to expect of Mesopotamia's "gods" a degree of uniformity in their form and nature that belies the ancient evidence. In discussing Mesopotamian ideas about the role of gods in disease, for example, Marten Stol argues that although the name of the disease known to us as epilepsy (Akkadian *bennu*) was frequently preceded with the DINGIR sign, a sign that was used to label the names of gods, the disease was nevertheless not a "real god," as he puts it, because it lacks "personality."[17] Stol's comment is ambiguous because it fails to indicate whether he is using the word "god" to reflect the modern or ancient concept of deity, and problematic if, as it appears, he means to indicate that Mesopotamians saw epilepsy as something that was not truly a DINGIR or *ilu*. Although Mesopotamian gods were often represented as beings with fully developed personalities, the writing of epilepsy with the label used for gods' names in itself suggests that personality was not considered an essential quality of DINGIRs and *ilu*s. While lack of personality might disqualify *bennu* from being a god in the modern sense, and did differentiate it from many (but not all) Mesopotamian DINGIRs and *ilu*s, it evi-

---

16. *Webster's New Collegiate Dictionary, Based on Webster's New International Dictionary, Second Edition* (Springfield, Mass.: G. and C. Merriam Co., 1956).

17. Marten Stol, *Epilepsy in Babylonia* (Groningen: Styx Publications, 1993). He comments, "Very often the name of the disease is preceded by the sign for 'god,' but this demonic power is no real god; it is just a demon . . . This power, although divine, is still lacking in 'personality' and for that reason the 'deputy' of a higher god, so we assume. Seeking for redress the patient has to approach the real god who is the ultimate sender of his ailment" (p. 6). Although Stol here characterizes the DINGIR determinative as "the sign for god," he nevertheless asserts that Mesopotamians understood only some DINGIRs to be gods, seeing others (such as demons) as different and lesser entities that were "divine" but lacked "personality" and therefore, in Stol's understanding, were not gods after all.

dently did not disqualify it from being a valid DINGIR and ilu.[18] To deny that such disparate entities as Ishtar and epilepsy could both be "gods" from a Mesopotamian point of view is to deny the complexity of the concept of deity that the texts seem to point to.

Bottéro, in characterizing Mesopotamian religion, makes a proposal similar to Stol's, as we saw in the introduction to this volume. He argues that entities such as planets, mountains, rivers, and demons, although labeled and referred to as DINGIRs and *ilu*s and thought to be endowed with "superhuman powers," never received "true divination" and remained "inferior to the gods themselves."[19] Bottéro, like Stol, correctly draws attention here to significant differences among the wide variety of entities that were labeled as DINGIRs and *ilu*s. He also argues persuasively that some deities were higher in status and power than others, more prominent in the pantheon, and more consistently identified as gods in lists, in labeling and in their treatment, but he fails to establish by such arguments, I believe, that such differences disqualified the less prominent DINGIRs and *ilu*s from membership in the category of gods, as Mesopotamians understood it. They were different, and in some cases clearly considered inferior to other gods, but they were not seen as entities of a truly different type. The ancient scribes' persistent use of the DINGIR determinative to label both the great gods and all these other entities suggests instead that the Mesopotamians themselves did not make such a distinction between gods envisioned in anthropomorphic form and gods envisioned as planets, demons, mountains or illnesses, instead including them all in the single category of DINGIR and *ilu*. Despite the reservations of scholars such as Stol and Bottéro, all of these DINGIRs and *ilu*s appear to have been part of the varied group of entities that constituted, for ancient Mesopotamians, "the gods themselves."

Despite the ambiguities using the word "god" entails, its use here is perhaps ultimately helpful—which is convenient because it is in any case unavoidable. As I have already suggested, the translation of DINGIR and *ilu* as 'god' is so deeply rooted in the thinking of Assyriologists that it cannot be eradicated by fiat from a discussion such as this one; even if I had chosen not to use the word "god" here for the Mesopotamian entities, this problematic equation would have hovered in the background all the same. But more significantly, I have chosen to use the word "god" because I am convinced there are indeed real, if partial, resemblances

---

18. Mesopotamians seem to have been of two (or three?) minds about the nature of diseases; the case of *bennu* itself is illustrative of this, since in some cases it is referred to as a demon (itself a type of minor, perhaps supernatural, entity sometimes but not always labeled with a DINGIR determinative), sometimes it is marked as a DINGIR, and sometimes it is not marked or treated as a deity in any way, but discussed as what we might now call an inanimate phenomenon of nature. Although it seems not to have been always understood as a DINGIR, the evidence suggests that it was thought of as a DINGIR at least some of the time, or by some people.

19. Bottéro, *Ancient Mesopotamian Religion*, pp. 62 and 63.

between the gods of modern Western usage and Mesopotamian DINGIRs and *ilu*s; because the equation is partly valid, it is genuinely useful, so long as we remain aware of its complexities and flaws. As we explore the similarities and differences between gods as we (variously) understand them, and DINGIRs and *ilu*s as the Mesopotamians (perhaps also variously) understood them, it will sharpen our understanding of both concepts, making us more aware of our unspoken assumptions about these closely related, but significantly different, cultural concepts. When I use the word "god" for the deities of Mesopotamia in the discussion that follows, however, I mean that they are gods in the sense that ancient Mesopotamians thought of such beings. It is the complicatedly varied deities of Mesopotamia—DINGIRs and *ilu*s as Mesopotamians themselves imagined them—that I have in mind when I speak in the pages that follow of Mesopotamia's deities as gods.

My purpose in the pages that follow is to explore the documentary evidence for the ancient Mesopotamian concept of DINGIR/*ilu* in the light of the complex and varied group of DINGIRs and *ilu*s that appear to have been imagined as non-anthropomorphic in form and nature.[20] The Late Babylonian Uruk ritual text we looked at a few moments ago is far from exceptional, as we are about to see. In every chronological period and every geographic region, Mesopotamian texts of various types refer to material objects, buildings, natural phenomena, and even illnesses in ways that suggest that these and many other non-anthropomorphic entities were thought of, at least at times, as being DINGIRs or *ilu*s. To explore this phenomenon in depth, I will begin by examining the various ways in which Mesopotamian texts identify entities as being gods (as they understood the concept), and will then use these identifying criteria to survey an assortment of texts. This brief survey will provide us with a necessarily incomplete (but re-

---

20. Although I have focused here primarily on textual evidence, I am of course aware that visual images also frequently appear to represent objects or emblems as non-anthropomorphic deities, or perhaps as partially anthropomorphic deities appearing in that instance in a non-anthropomorphic form. Such visual evidence and its interpretation are dealt with ably and in detail by Tallay Ornan in her contribution to this volume.

The ambiguities inherent in much of the available visual evidence make its interpretation to my mind particularly difficult. It is possible, for example, that Mesopotamian gods that were represented visually in non-anthropomorphic form were nevertheless *thought of* as being anthropomorphic, as Ornan argues here, but it is also possible that a particular god *was* in fact imagined in the form in which it was visually represented, or was at least thought of as appearing in that form as well as in others. In addition, it is difficult to decide whether a single image that represents a particular deity in partly anthropomorphic form, for example, should be taken as a rare but revealing glimpse of its usually hidden anthropomorphic form, or as picturing a partly anthropomorphic form in which the god was not usually imagined. The problem here lies in our difficulties in recognizing cases of literal representation of gods as the Mesopotamians imagined them to be, and differentiating these from cases of metonymic representation and from representations of emblems or animal familiars of gods, a problem particularly difficult in dealing with a culture essentially alien to us. Distinguishing between cases of literal and metaphoric description is of course a fundamental problem in assessing the meaning of both visual and verbal representations. It lies behind many of our disagreements in these chapters.

markably ample) list of possible non-anthropomorphic gods for further study. We will then return to the documentary evidence to take a closer look at several different types of non-anthropomorphic gods, searching for similarities and differences among them and also assessing the consistency with which deities of each type are represented as non-anthropomorphic.

Mesopotamian texts identify entities as being gods in three principal ways, and non-anthropomorphic entities are identified as gods by each of them. First, certain material objects or natural phenomena are at times explicitly *said* to be DINGIRs or *ilu*s (not just marked as such with a DINGIR determinative, but actually called a god), and in other cases such entities are said to *behave* in ways characteristic of DINGIRs and *ilu*s, such as conferring blessings or receiving prayers. Second, many non-anthropomorphic entities are labeled as gods by having the cuneiform sign for the Sumerian word DINGIR placed before their names as a determinative, an unpronounced graphic marker used in Sumerian and Akkadian to indicate the category to which the following word belongs.[21] Third, as we have seen in the ritual text from Uruk, some non-anthropomorphic entities are identified as DINGIRs by receiving a treatment reserved for gods: they are formally presented in temples with specially named food offerings such as the *ginû* or the *sattukku*, an honor and form of worship otherwise conferred only upon DINGIRs and *ilu*s typically represented in anthropomorphic form. Many non-anthropomorphic entities are characterized as gods in more than one of these ways.

A good introductory example is the case of rivers, prominent topographic features that are characterized in texts as being DINGIRs in all three of these ways. Many texts refer to rivers quite matter-of-factly as bodies of water.[22] In other cases, however, they are identified as gods. The river Tigris, for example, is described as acting in the role of a DINGIR in Assyrian personal names such as ^{d}IDIGNA-*rēminni* 'Tigris have mercy on me' and $^{MÍ}Tašme$-^{d}IDIGNA 'the Tigris hears.' In both these names, the Tigris River is also usually labeled as a god with the DINGIR determinative (indicated in transcription by a superscript *d*, as in the two examples above), further confirming the Tigris' identity as a god.[23] Significantly, the Tigris is sometimes labeled with both the determinative for god and the determinative for river (ÍD), which suggests that even when it was thought of as a deity, it was thought of as a deity in river form, not as an anthropomorphic god.[24] In other personal names, an entity called simply "River" (probably refer-

---

21. Other determinatives label entities, for example, as plants, stars, body parts, wooden objects, or male humans. For a brief but authoritative introduction to determinatives and their use in Akkadian, see John Huehnergard, *A Grammar of Akkadian*, Harvard Semitic Museum Studies 45 (Atlanta, Georgia: Scholars Press, 1997), pp. 111–12.

22. E.g., CAD s.v. *nāru* A, 1d–f.

23. Helmut Freydank and Claudio Saporetti, *Nuove Attestazioni dell'Onomastica Medio-Assira*, Incunabula Graeca LXXIV (Roma: Edizioni Dell'Ateneo e Bizzarri, 1979), p. 182.

24. Freydank and Saporetti, *Nuove Attestazioni*, p. 71.

ring to a particular unspecified river in each case) is referred to similarly, as a source of protection (*Puzur-Nāri* 'Protection of the River') and as the provider of an heir (*Iddin-Nāru* 'The river gave [an heir]'), actions typical of Mesopotamian deities and attributed to well-known anthropomorphic deities in other personal names of the same pattern.[25] Another specifically named river, the Balīḫ, receives the treatment appropriate for a DINGIR in an Old Babylonian offering list, which reports that animal offerings were presented to it together with other gods[26]; the same river is characterized as a god in the personal name *Kurub-Balīḫ* 'pray to Balīḫ,'[27] where its role as an appropriate recipient of prayers is a further indication of its divinity. In a text from Assyria that gives instructions for the performance of a ritual in which offerings were presented to gods in temples all across Assyria, "rivers" as a collective entity appear as a divinity, marked as divine with the DINGIR determinative and included as part of a long list of gods (VI: 19); at the conclusion of the same text (IX: 41') "rivers of the four corners (of the earth)" (this time written without the DINGIR determinative) appear to be invited to join other gods in conferring blessings such as long life and rule on the Assyrian king, benefits that only gods could confer.[28] Here, as in the personal names cited above, rivers are characterized as active deities, affecting the lives of humans like their more anthropomorphic counterparts. The non-anthropomorphic form of such river gods emerges with particular clarity in texts that describe legal ordeals in which an accused person was thrown into a river to see if he would float, determining his guilt or innocence. In these texts, the river judging the accused is often labeled with the DINGIR determinative, and in several cases it is described quite literally as being a body of water into which the accused person "plunges" or which "submerges" him.[29] Rivers, clearly thought of as bodies of water and parts of the landscape, nevertheless emerge in these texts as divine beings, beings that are in this case as active in the lives of their Mesopotamian worshippers as the DINGIRs and *ilu*s imagined in anthropomorphic form.

The case of rivers is not an isolated phenomenon. A wide assortment of other non-anthropomorphic entities, ranging from harps to city gates, are identified as

---

25. J. J. M. Roberts, *The Earliest Semitic Pantheon: A Study of the Semitic Deities Attested in Mesopotamia before Ur III* (Baltimore and London: The Johns Hopkins U. Press, 1972), p. 46.

26. Ichiro Nakata, "On the Official Pantheon of the Old Babylonian City of Mari as Reflected in the Records of Issuance of Sacrificial Animals," *Acta Sumerologica* 13 (1991), Chart 1, pp. 256–57.

27. Roberts, *Earliest Semitic Pantheon*, p. 17.

28. Brigitte Menzel, *Assyrische Tempel* (Rome: Biblical Institute Press, 1981), II, no. 54 (K. 252), pp. T 113–125; the request for blessings is in col. X *passim*. "Rivers" were almost certainly also explicitly identified as being gods in the missing final lines of this passage in column VI, which probably paralleled the concluding lines of the previous section (VI: 5–10), in which the entities listed before it (and often marked with DINGIR signs) are called upon to accept the offering and are identified as "gods of Nineveh," a pattern repeated often throughout the text.

29. CAD s.v. *nāru* A, 11 2'.

DINGIRs and *ilu*s in one of these three ways (that is, by explicit statement or by descriptions of their characteristically godlike behavior, by the attachment of the DINGIR determinative to their names, or by the presentation to them of the offerings and gifts routinely presented to other types of DINGIRs and *ilu*s), and this occurs in Mesopotamian texts from almost every period and region, as the following brief sampling makes clear.

We will start with a few cases in which a material object or other non-anthropomorphic entity is explicitly named in a text as a deity, or is described as acting in a way that gods typically act. Non-anthropomorphic entities are called gods for example, in the Assyrian ritual text mentioned above in the discussion of rivers,[30] which names the ziggurats of the city of Aššur, together with more anthropomorphic gods such as Anum and Nisaba, as being the "gods of the temple of Anu" (II 23–24). The same text identifies the gate of a particular temple (XI 6') and the walls of Babylon (XI, ll. 18'-19') as being "gods of the temple Esagil and Babylon" (20'-21'). In the Middle Assyrian personal name *Šār-ili* ('the wind is my god'[31]), a natural phenomenon, the wind, is identified as the personal god of an individual. In some Neo-Assyrian personal names, such as *Ešarra-šarru-uṣur* '"O temple Ešarra, protect the king!"' and *Esaggil-idinna* 'the temple Esagil has given [an heir],' temples take the place usually held by anthropomorphic gods in names of that pattern and are said to act in ways characteristic of such gods.[32]

Next we will consider examples of entities that are labeled with the DINGIR sign, the determinative for "gods".[33] My hypothesis here is that labeling a word

---

30. Menzel, *Assyrische Tempel* II, no. 54 (K. 252), T 113–125.

31. Claudio Saporetti, *Onomastica Medio-Assira*, Studia Pohl 6 (Rome: Biblical Institute Press, 1970), II, p. 161.

32. Karen Radner, ed., *The Prosopography of the Neo-Assyrian Empire, Volume 1, Part II, B–G* (Helsinki: The Neo-Assyrian Text Corpus Project, 1999), pp. 405 and 407. For modern readers, it is tempting to see the temple in such instances as simply a *pars pro toto* reference to the chief god who dwelt in it, but since other material objects such as thrones and crowns belonging to gods or closely associated with them sometimes received food offerings independently from those presented to their divine owners, we cannot dismiss the possibility that the temples named here were similarly considered to be divinely charged from their close association with a god and had thus come to be seen as active, independent deities in their own right. W. G. Lambert takes this position, arguing that "the divinity of the deity was seen to have spread to temple, city and accoutrements . . . in such a way that these things also became gods and received offerings as a mark of the fact" (p. 129) in "Ancient Mesopotamian Gods: Superstition, Philosophy, Theology," *Revue de l'histoire des Religions* 207/2 (1990), pp. 115–30. On the concept of temples as active agents in Mesopotamia, see I. J. Winter, "Agency Marked, Agency Ascribed: The Affective Object in Ancient Mesopotamia," in *Art's Agency and Art History*, Robin Osborne and Jeremy Tanner, ed. (Malden, MA and Oxford: Blackwell, 2007), pp. 43 and 55–58.

33. The problem of the use of determinatives, and of the meaning of the DINGIR determinative in particular, emerged as central to our problem and became the focus of intense debate during the conference; for excerpts from this debate, see the discussion chapter, below. The meaning and (varying) use of determinatives in ancient Mesopotamian contexts is a complex issue that will require further detailed studies by both linguists and historians. For a discussion of the meaning and use of the divine

with the DINGIR determinative in Mesopotamia meant that it was understood to *be* a DINGIR, with all that that entailed. Because the precise meaning of each of the determinative labels and the nature of the category each refers to is never explicitly discussed in ancient Mesopotamian sources, however, it cannot be entirely excluded that the DINGIR determinative meant instead, "sharing a quality typical of DINGIRs," perhaps holiness or sacredness, as some participants argued during the conference. Other determinatives, however, do not appear to have functioned in this way; the sign for the word "bird," for example, is used as a determinative preceding the names of birds, not of objects with bird-like qualities, just as the determinative for "female" appears before words naming female persons and female animals, not entities belonging to the world of women or having what was judged to be a feminine quality. By analogy, we would expect the DINGIR determinative to identify entities that were considered to *be* DINGIRs, not just to be DINGIR-like. I can find no evidence to suggest otherwise.

Objects marked with the DINGIR determinative provide the earliest examples in written evidence of probable non-anthropomorphic deities. The texts known as the *Fara God Lists*, copies of which were found at the site of Early Dynastic Fara and in several other early Sumerian cities, are among the earliest surviving Mesopotamian written documents.[34] These texts consist simply of a long list of entries, each of them labeled with the DINGIR determinative without further comment or explanation. Many of the entities named in these lists appear to be objects, suggesting that non-anthropomorphic DINGIRs already played a significant role in early Mesopotamian religion.[35] The Fara texts include in their listing of DINGIRs a wide assortment of non-anthropomorphic entities. Along with more conventional gods, they include, for example, objects of types that figure in later texts as the possessions of gods, such as 'the Crown' (^{d}men$_x$), 'the Princely Ring (?)' (^{d}ḪAR-nun) and 'the staff (of) the Leader' (^{d}ḫendur-sag), objects like those used later to adorn gods' statues, such as 'the Lapis Lazuli Necklace' (^{d}lam-sag-za-gìn), and a weapon, 'the Saw(?)' (^{d}šum), later an attribute of the god Šamaš. The lists also include parts of temples and objects found in temples, such as 'the Holy Foundation Peg' (^{d}temen-kù), and 'the Stag Door' (^{d}ig-alim) belonging to the temple of Ningirsu at Lagash, and various objects and materials that were perhaps used in temple rituals, such as 'the Emblem' (^{d}šu-nir), 'the Incense' (^{d}šem-ki), 'the Fire' (^{d}IZI), and 'the Drum(?)' (^{d}ùb); as well as the name of what appears to be an object representing a lion, referred

---

determinative in ancient Egyptian, see Racheli Shalomi-Hen, *Classifying the Divine: Determinatives and Categorisation in CT 335 and BC 17* (Wiesbaden: Harrassowitz, 2000).

34. For further discussion of the Fara lists, see W. G. Lambert, "Götterlisten," in RLA III, p. 473.

35. Gebhard J. Selz, "'The Holy Drum, the Spear, and the Harp': Towards an Understanding of the Problems of Deification in Third Millennium Mesopotamia," in *Sumerian Gods and Their Representations*, I. L. Finkel and M. J. Geller, eds., Cuneiform Monographs 7 (Groningen: Styx, 1997), pp. 167–209. The transliterations and translations of the items discussed here are those proposed by Selz.

to as 'the Lion(ess) (is) a Protective Goddess' (ᵈpirig:lamma).³⁶ Although these early lists of items, all of them without exception marked with a DINGIR determinative, provide no description of those items beyond their names, leaving us to conjecture about their imagined physical appearance and possible functioning as gods, the marking of all the entities in the list, including these numerous material objects, with the divine determinative suggests these material objects were considered to be non-anthropomorphic gods.

In texts from later centuries, the DINGIR determinative continued to be used as a label for various material objects and other non-anthropomorphic entities. "Stone" is labeled with the divine determinative, for example, in an Old Babylonian juridical text from the vicinity of Larsa, in which "the weapon of the god stone" (ᵍⁱˢTUKUL *ša* ᵈ*Ab-nu-um*) serves as one of the witnesses to an oath, together with the emblem of the god Sin, the bird of the god Ninmar, and the spade of the god Marduk.³⁷ In an important example from northern Mesopotamia, an Assyrian text that describes the performance of a royal ritual known as the *tākultu* uses the divine determinative to label particular parts of temples, such as the pipes (*ratāti*) running from a fermenting vat used to prepare drinks for the temple's resident gods (I:39) and the platforms on which the gods' statues stood (III:15).³⁸ Another Assyrian ritual text attaches the DINGIR determinative to two apparently non-anthropomorphic objects called rather mysteriously 'the Totality of the Lands' (ᵈ*Kippat-māti*) (I:11 and IV:33) and 'Mouth and Speech (or, Tongue)' (ᵈ*Pû-lišānu*, III:7).³⁹ It also affixes the divine determinative to "the Crown" (I 14); to Mount Ebeḫ (the modern Jebel Hamrin range), an entity which it reports as being worshipped in several temples (II:15, II:26, VII:4); to the 'weapon of Aš-šur' (ᵈ ᵍⁱˢ*kakku* [*Aššur*], VI 14); and (as we saw earlier, but this time occurring in a northern, Assyrian context) to "ziggurats" (VII 14). All of these are listed together with more anthropomorphic gods as the residents of one or another temple.

---

36. Selz, "Holy Drum," pp. 171–172.

37. No. 58a:23 and 58a:24 in Dominique Charpin, *Archives familiales et propriété privée en Babylonie ancienne: Etudes des documents de "Tell Sifr"* (Geneva: Droz, 1980), p. 243. For discussion of the god "Stone," attested primarily in Amorite and West Semitic personal names, see Karel van der Toorn, "Worshipping Stones: On the Deification of Cult Symbols," *Journal of Northwest Semitic Languages* 23/1 (1997), pp. 10–11. Attempting to explain the process by which "stone" or "a stone" might have become a god, van der Toorn suggests, "... in the psychology of the believer, the symbol which is the focus of devotion is not an ordinary object. It is a manifestation of the god, and as such divine. It belongs to the realm of the sacred to such a point that it is itself a holy object. And such a holy object can be deified and function in practice as an ultimate object of devotion. From a token of the god, it becomes a god in its own right" (p. 2).

38. Menzel, *Assyrische Tempel* II no. 61 (VAT 10126), T 138–44; for an earlier edition with extensive commentary, see also R. Frankena, *Tākultu: De Sacrale Maaltijd in het Assyrische Ritueel met een Overzicht over de in Assur Vereerde Goden.* (Leiden: E. J. Brill, 1954).

39. Menzel, *Assyrische Tempel* II, no. 54 (K. 252), T 113–125.

Occasionally, a puzzling omission of the DINGIR determinative in situations where we would have expected it to be used raises questions about precisely what its use or lack of use in that case implies. In general, the use of a determinative of any kind seems to have been optional.[40] The DINGIR determinative, however, was in most periods only rarely omitted in writing the names of the primarily anthropomorphic gods, and its occasional omission appears in most cases to have been arbitrary, simply a scribal variation in the writing of that word and not intended to suggest that the entity in question was not, in that particular situation, considered to be a god. In the ritual text from Late Babylonian Uruk with which we began this chapter, for example, the god Anu's name is labeled with the divine determinative but that of his spouse Antum, equally divine, in this case is not. The omission of the DINGIR sign from non-anthropomorphic entities that are identified in other cases as DINGIRs seems in most cases similarly arbitrary. In one Assyrian ritual text discussed above, for example, a temple door appears without the determinative in one copy of the text, but it is marked with the DINGIR determinative when the same passage appears in a parallel text.[41] The case of the god Stone, mentioned earlier, is even clearer. "Stone" is labeled with the DINGIR sign on the envelope of the text, but not in the text inside; since the object, the scribe, and the situation described are precisely the same in both cases, it seems obvious that the Stone was as much a god on the inside, where the determinative is omitted, as on the envelope, where the divine determinative is used. In such cases the use or omission of the divine determinative appears optional and without significance for the nature of the object in question.

In some offering lists, however, the DINGIR sign is omitted for objects but not for the anthropomorphic gods listed before and after them, a pattern suggesting that omission in this case marked a significant difference. Two texts recording offerings presented in the temple of Enlil at Nippur in the Ur III period, for example, begin by listing several well-known anthropomorphic deities, all but one marked with the DINGIR determinative,[42] who each receive an offering of milk; it then lists a throne and bed which receive exactly the same offering but are labeled only with the determinative for wooden objects.[43] Since Enlil's throne is frequently marked with a DINGIR determinative in other offering lists from Nippur in this period, and since the two objects that lack the determinative are treated here

---

40. Huehnergard, *Grammar of Akkadian*, p. 112.
41. Menzel, *Assyrische Tempel* II, no. 54 (K. 252), T 114, I:29 and STT 88 I:34′.
42. The exception, the god An, is probably not significant; despite the rare case mentioned earlier, An's name was normally written with the DINGIR sign read syllabically as the syllable pronounced "an," and customarily omitted the DINGIR determinative before it, presumably because a duplicated sign, meant to be read once as a determinative and once syllabically, might well have confused readers.
43. Walther Sallaberger, *Der kultisched Kalender der Ur III-Seit*, Untersuchungen zur Assyriologie und Vorderasiatischen Archäologie Bd. 7/1 (Berlin and New York : Walter de Gruyter, 1993), II, p. 19.

exactly like the gods marked with the determinative who precede them in the list, it seems likely that the throne and bed were considered to be gods here despite their labeling as wooden objects instead of gods. The different determinative may have been intended to draw attention to the different physical form of these entities, rather than to suggest they were not gods at all.[44] That the scribe in this case apparently felt constrained to indicate a difference in the physical forms of the DINGIRs recorded in his list, however, is itself intriguing. In most cases, however, the DINGIR sign appears to have been used before the names of gods regardless of their physical form, and its occasional omission does not appear intended to signal a change in that designation.

A third indication that a particular non-anthropomorphic entity was considered to be a DINGIR is that it was treated like a god, in the sense that food offerings were ritually presented to it, an honor otherwise reserved for the deities usually represented as anthropomorphic divine persons. Offering lists from the Sumerian city of Lagash shortly before 2300 BCE, for example, record the presentation of food offerings to what appear to be various possessions of anthropomorphic gods, including "the Punting /Steering Oar (of) (the god) Nindar" and "the Scepter"; to objects probably used in temple rituals, such as "the Harp," "the Holy Drum," and "the Chariot"; and to parts of temples, such as "the Stag-door." [45] (Some other objects to which offerings were presented in Lagash at this time, however, seem more likely to have been emblems representing a particular anthropomorphic god, rather than independent non-anthropomorphic deities in their own right, such as the "Bronze Date-palm," a tree sometimes identified with the goddess Inanna/Ishtar, and with her lover, the god Dumuzi.[46]) Somewhat later, at Nippur under the Ur III dynasty, regular offerings were presented in the temples of Enlil and Ninlil to the throne of Enlil (^{d}gu.za ^{d}en-líl-lá), to Hursagkalamma (the name of the ziggurat of Enlil's temple), to the harp of the goddess Ninlil, and to a chariot and plow belonging to the temple.[47] In the city of Girsu in the same period, a harp (^{d}balag) received offerings of meal during a ceremony in which it was paraded around the city,[48] and in Umma another harp received monthly

---

44. In his perceptive recent study of the garments of gods, Stefan Zawadski suggests that the divine determinative was sometimes omitted in listing offerings presented to the ziggurat of Sippar because "there was evidently some doubt as to whether it should be treated only as a divine power (and for this reason the divine determinative was omitted) or as a divine being, whose name should be preceded by the determinative" (p. 168). This is an interesting and attractive hypothesis for which, however, I can find no supporting evidence in my material. See Stefan Zawadski, *Garments of the Gods: Studies on the Textile Industry and the Pantheon of Sippar According to the Texts from the Ebabbar Archive*, OBO 218 (Fribourg, Academic Press, and Göttingen,Vandenhoeck and Ruprecht, 2006), pp. 167–69.

45. Listed in Selz, "Holy Drum," p. 173.
46. Selz, "Holy Drum," pp. 173–4.
47. Listed and discussed in Sallaberger, *Kalender*, pp. 99–100.
48. Sallaberger, *Kalender*, p. 297.

offerings at the dark of the moon.[49] In the Old Babylonian period, beer was offered on one occasion at Nippur both to the god Ninurta and to two thrones.[50] In the Neo-Babylonian period, a chariot belonging to the god Anu received daily offerings in Uruk of sheep, lambs, turtledoves, duck and geese, in amounts equal to those presented to important anthropomorphic gods of that city,[51] while a star-shaped branding iron of the goddess Ishtar, evidently a less important divine object in Uruk at that period, received an offering only once, on the eve of a great festival.[52] At Sippar in the same period, the city's ziggurat was presented daily with a bull, sheep, lambs, geese, ducks, and turtledoves, almost equivalent in amount to the offerings presented to important anthropomorphic gods such as Marduk, Bunene and the Queen of Sippar.[53] Such offerings point to the persistent and sometimes quite important role of non-anthropomorphic DINGIRs and *ilu*s as objects of worship in many different periods and regions.[54] Although the particular objects and non-anthropomorphic entities worshipped varied in different cities in any given period, as our examples make clear, and while there are also changes over time in a given city as well, the principle that non-anthropomorphic entities could be gods remains a constant.

The wide array of objects and entities identified as DINGIRs or *ilu*s even in this far from exhaustive survey of the documentary evidence can be divided into different categories, which often appear to have had different characteristics and functions as gods. We will now return to the documentary evidence to take a closer look at some of the many categories of non-anthropomorphic gods and at the surprising variations among individual gods, sometimes even within a given category.[55] As we will also discover on closer examination, some of the objects identified as deities in our initial sampling may not have been non-anthropomorphic deities after all, since descriptions of them suggest they were imagined as more anthropomorphic in form than their names had suggested, or because they appear to be alternative forms of an anthropomorphic great god rather than independent non-anthropomorphic deities in their own right. When these more dubi-

---

49. Sallaberger, *Kalender*, p. 298.

50. René Marcel Sigrist, *Les sattukku dans L'Ešumeša durant la période d'Isin et Larsa* (Malibu, Calif.: Udena Publications, 1984), p. 93.

51. Beaulieu, *Pantheon of Uruk*, p. 295.

52. Beaulieu, *Pantheon of Uruk*, p. 353.

53. Jennie Myers, "The Sippar Pantheon: A Diachronic Study" (Ph.D. diss., Harvard University, 2002), pp. 213–14, and 241–46.

54. The latter two examples also make it clear that quite different non-anthropomorphic entities were important as divinities in particular cities in the same region and period.

55. Because of limited space, I have been able to discuss only a few of these categories. Other candidates for designation as categories of non-anthropomorphic deities include, for example, illnesses, animals, fantastic composite beings (e.g., scorpion-men), demons, and non-material powers or abstractions (e.g., justice). Examples of each of these are sometimes marked with the DINGIR determinative or appear to be identified as deities in other ways.

ous candidates have been weeded out, however, we will find remaining a substantial number of objects and other non-anthropomorphic entities of many kinds that appear to have been understood by Mesopotamians to be members of the class consisting of DINGIRs, although in some cases viewed as DINGIRs of a special kind. In the pages that follow, we will examine several different types of non-anthropomorphic deities to see how (and whether) deities of each type "functioned" as gods, how each type may have come to be considered divine in the first place, what qualities the non-anthropomorphic deities of different types shared with one another or with the more anthropomorphic gods, and also how they differed.

Both rivers and mountains, important topographic features in Mesopotamia, are widely attested as gods and would appear to represent one category of non-anthropomorphic deity. A number of different rivers, as we saw earlier, are represented as being active non-anthropomorphic gods that took care of worshippers, determined guilt or innocence, and received offerings. Although we can only speculate, rivers (like storms, grain, or particular planets, perhaps) may have been understood to be gods because of their own inherently awesome qualities: such as the powerful force of their flowing waters and the ability of their waters to sustain life, to purify, or to destroy. A number of individual mountains, as we have also seen, are, like rivers, referred to and treated as gods. It seems likely that mountains also were perceived to be gods because of their inherent qualities; perhaps the looming, lofty presence of mountains conveyed to Mesopotamians a sense of remote, awesome, supernatural power that led to their veneration as gods. In exploring the nature of mountains as gods, I will focus on Mt. Ebiḫ (also written "Ebeḫ" and "Abiḫ"), known in modern times as the Jebel Hamrin, since it is one of the best documented examples of a divine mountain range. It is explicitly identified as a god in the theophoric personal name *Abiḫ-il* (written EN.TI-il) 'Abiḫ-is-God', and it is characterized as a god actively involved with worshippers in personal names such as *Ir'e-Abiḫ* (written Ir₃-e-^{d}EN.TI) 'Abiḫ-shepherded', *Ur-Abiḫ* (Ur-^{d}EN.TI) 'Man (or dog?)-of-Abiḫ'[56] and *Ebiḫ-nāṣir* 'Ebiḫ is a protector.'[57] In one Assyrian ritual, as we saw earlier, an image of ^{d}Ebiḫ was presented with offerings in the temple of Sin and Šamaš in Aššur, while two images of the god received food offerings in the same city's temple dedicated to Anu and Adad (K. 252, II 15 and 28), suggesting that this mountain was a deity of some importance in Assyria.

These references establish that Ebiḫ was viewed as a living and active divine entity. They do not refer, however, to the physical form in which Ebiḫ was represented in temples or to how he (or it) was envisioned, although they seem to imply a non-anthropomorphic form by giving the deity the name of the well-known mountain range. For most mountain deities, this is all the information we have

---

56. Roberts, *Earliest Semitic Pantheon*, p. 12; on EN.TI as a writing of A/Ebiḫ, note 7.
57. Freydank and Saporetti, *Nuove Attestazioni*, p. 110.

about the form or forms in which they were imagined. Ebiḫ, however, is an exceptional case, because he/it is one of only two non-anthropomorphic DINGIRs to play a prominent role in a myth, a literary genre that is characterized in ancient Mesopotamia by rich description and by the interaction of its characters in a dramatic setting. In the Sumerian myth known as *Innana and Ebiḫ*, Ebiḫ rather surprisingly appears in two different physical forms: as a topographic feature and as a man. He (or it) is described in the myth primarily in non-anthropomorphic form as an animate topographic feature, an opponent of the goddess Inanna repeatedly referred to as "this mountain" or "this country." In one brief passage, however, the deity is represented in anthropomorphic form as "Ebiḫ" who "has not kissed the ground before me nor with his beard swept the dust before me."[58] Although the myth promptly returns to describing Ebiḫ as a mountainous, wooded country, and while the appearance of the mountain in anthropomorphic form may occur here only to satisfy the dramatic requirements of the genre, this very brief single appearance as a bearded man means that we cannot dismiss the possibility that he was occasionally envisioned as an anthropomorphic deity in other settings as well. Whether or not we should extrapolate from this single example that other divine mountains were also at least occasionally envisioned as anthropomorphic, remains unclear.

Mountains as a collective entity appear to have been a collective deity in Assyria, where mountains were a prominent feature of the landscape, although the evidence for this collective deity is somewhat ambiguous. In one of the Assyrian rituals we have discussed, for example, "mountains, springs, rivers of the four quarters (of the world)" appear to be called upon, together with various anthropomorphic gods, winds, parts of temples, and chapels, to bless the king, but a break in the text of some nine lines separating the reference to mountains from the subsequent request for blessings makes their inclusion in the appeal for blessings not

---

58. I quote here (in my English translation) from S. N. Kramer's translation of the Sumerian in Jean Bottéro and Samuel Noah Kramer, *Lorsque les dieux faisaient l'homme: Mythologie mésopotamienne* (Paris: Editions Gallimard, 1st ed. 1989, second corrected edition 1993). The text appears on pp. 219–226, and the passage quoted here, on p. 220. Ebiḫ is discussed on pp. 226–27. For a transliteration and a somewhat different translation based in part on Kramer's earlier work, see "Inana and Ebiḫ," c.1.3.2 and t.1.3.2, in J. A. Black, G. Cunningham, J. Ebeling, E. Flückiger-Hawker, E. Robson, J. Taylor, and G. Zólymi, *The Electronic Text Corpus of Sumerian Literature* (http://etcsl.orinst.ox.ac.uk/), Oxford, 1998–2006. In this translation, the mountain (kur.re), also referred to as "the mountain range of Ebiḫ, the mountain" (ḫur.sag ebiḫ^{ki}-a-ke$_4$ kur.re), is said to be berated by Inanna "because it did not act appropriately on its own initiative, because it did not put its nose to the ground, because it did not rub its lips in the dust" and so on (ll. 89–95). Whether Inanna is referring here to the mountain's beard or to its lips, however, and whether she is lamenting its lack of initiative or its lack of respect, both these renderings of the Sumerian reflect the sense that the text describes Ebiḫ here both as a human-like person and simultaneously as a mountain range. For an argument that the god Ebiḫ is envisioned as a mountain, not a divine person, even here, see Roberts, *Earliest Semitic Pantheon*, p. 12.

entirely certain.⁵⁹ Earlier in the same text, however, "mountains," along with "rivers," the Anunnaki gods, and non-anthropomorphic entities such as "brick" and "palace," are asked to "grant life, hear prayers, bless the city of Aššur, the land of Aššur, (and) our king" and are then characterized as "gods of the city of Tua."⁶⁰ In Assyrian personal names, "mountains" collectively (*šadâna*, also written ᵈKURⁿᵃ, a collective noun that is plural in form, but receives a singular verb and pronouns⁶¹) appear as an active DINGIR that plays a role in the lives of humans and other gods, in names such as, "'mountains' has given a brother," "'mountains' is lord of his people" and "'mountains' is king of the gods."⁶² Several anthropomorphic gods, however, are also called "mountain" on some occasions, such as in the personal names "Adad (also, Aššur) is the mountain of his people," "Pappsukal (also Sin, Šamaš, and Tašmētum) is our mountain"⁶³; it is possible that the references to "mountains" as divine may refer to a grouping of these primarily anthropomorphic gods rather than to an independent non-anthropomorphic collective deity. The extent to which individual divine mountains such as Ebiḫ, or mountains collectively, were non-anthropomorphic and the extent to which references to "mountains" in the plural were not metaphors referring to a quality of certain anthropomorphic deities cannot be firmly established, although it seems likely from the way in which he is represented that even Ebiḫ (and thus other individual divine mountains as well) was in most cases imagined in mountain form.

A second large group of non-anthropomorphic gods is composed of a wide assortment of material objects, ranging from plows and crowns to thrones and chariots, which appear to have been the possessions of gods, objects which their divine owners "used" or which were used in their service. Many such objects (although not all of the belongings of gods by any means⁶⁴) are identified or treated as gods in their own right in many periods and places, as emerged in our initial survey of the documentary evidence; they receive their own individual offerings,

---

59. Menzel, *Assyrische Tempel* II, p. T 122 (K. 252), IX: 40′–41′.
60. Menzel, *Assyrische Tempel* II, p. T. 121 (K. 252), VIII: 1′–13′.
61. On this somewhat rare form of the plural, perhaps used to refer to a number of individuals rather than a simple plurality, see the discussion by Wolfram von Soden, *Grundriss der Akkadischen Grammatik*, Analecta Orientalia 33/47 (Rome: Pontifical Biblical Institute, 1969), section 61i, p. 77.
62. Saporetti, *Onomastica Medio-Assira*, II, pp. 190 and 197; for further references to personified or deified mountains, see also CAD s.v. *šadû* A, sections 1, m, n, and o.
63. Saporetti, *Onomastica Medio-Assira*, II, p. 157; for the argument that the god Aššur was a mountain deity, anthropomorphized only in a rather cursory fashion and never acquiring a full humanoid personality or biography, see W. G. Lambert, "The God Aššur," *Iraq* 45 (1983), pp. 82–86.
64. For example, there is so far as I know nothing to suggest that the *paššūru* tables on which food offerings were presented to gods were deified, nor the linens used on gods' beds, nor items of gods' clothing, nor the dishes and cups used to serve food and drink offerings to them. The dais on which the statue of the god stood (Akkadian *parakku*), however, was often deified. The operative principle here remains obscure to me.

are labeled with DINGIR determinatives, and are sometimes referred to explicitly as DINGIRs or *ilu*s. In exploring the nature and function of such objects as gods, I will focus first on the example of gods' chariots and boats, two kinds of objects that served their divine owners as means of transportation when they moved (in the form of statues or emblems) outside their temples, either in formal processions or on journeys to visit other temples or cities. Both chariots and boats are treated and referred to as deities in their own right in some periods and places.

The role of chariots as non-anthropomorphic deities is the more clear-cut case, so we will consider it first.[65] The gods Anu, Baba, Bēl, Maḫ, Ea, Enlil, Ninlil, and Marduk are among the many deities referred to in texts as owning chariots;[66] the widespread nature of divine chariot-owning is indicated by the fact that the fourth tablet of the lexical list known as ḪAR.RA = *Ḫubullu* devotes almost 60 lines to recording the names of chariots belonging to various gods.[67] A chariot, almost certainly one belonging to a god, takes the position of a god in a theophoric personal name in the Ur III period, UR-GIGIR 'man (or, dog) of the chariot'; that it was envisioned as being an actual chariot in this case, and not as some kind of chariot-spirit in anthropomorphic form, is suggested by the fact that in writings of this name the chariot is sometimes preceded by both the divine determinative and the determinative identifying a wooden object.[68] The presentation of offerings to chariots is attested in many periods and places. In the Early Dynastic period, for example, offerings to "the chariot" (^{giš}gigir) are included in the lists of offerings made in the temple of Nanše.[69] In the Akkadian period, sheep and other animals are offered to Ningirsu, his chariot, and his statue, while items of clothing (a gift that raises further interesting questions) are presented to the chariot of Šataran.[70]

---

65. For a further discussion of gods' chariots, with additional references, see Pongratz-Leisten, Ina šulmi īrub: *Die kulttopographische und ideologische Programmatik der akītu-Prozession in Babylonien und Assyrien im I. Jahrtausend v. Chr.*, Baghdader Forschungen 16 (Philipp von Zabern: Mainz am Rhein, 1994), pp. 193–95 (= appendix 2.1, "Götterwagen"); A. Salonen, *Die Landfahrzeuge des Alten Mesopotamien*, Annales Academiae Scientiarum Fennicae (Series B), 72/III (Helsinki: Finnish Academy of Sciences, 1951);. CAD s.v. *narkabtu*, 1d and 1f.

66. A. Salonen, "Prozessionswagen der babylonischen Götter," Studia Orientalia XIII.2 (Helsinki; Societas Orientalis Fennicae, 1946), p. 7

67. Salonen, "Prozessionswagen," p. 4.

68. Salonen, "Prozessionswagen," pp. 9–10.

69. G. Selz, *Untersuchungen zur Götterwelt des altsumerischen Stadtstaates von Lagaš*, Occasional Publications of the Samuel Noah Kramer Fund 13 (Philadelphia: 1995), p. 137; Selz proposes that we understand these offerings as being made to the place, rather than the chariot, which is also possible, but an alternative for which I can find no convincing evidence.

70. Salonen, "Prozessionswagen," p. 5. The question here, of course, is whether the presentation of items of clothing or jewelry to a deified material object such as a chariot implied that this chariot was at least sometimes envisioned as anthropomorphic in form, or whether such a gift was offered to this deity by analogy because other gods at times received gifts of clothing or adornment and because items of clothing such as sashes or necklaces could in any case be hung on an object that was not human in shape.

In the Ur III period, offering lists from Ninlil's temple at Nippur record frequent offerings to a chariot that had been given to the goddess by King Shulgi.[71] In Assyria, in the Middle and Neo-Assyrian periods, offerings were presented in the course of the *tākultu* ritual to a specialized chariot known as a *nubālu* (written ^{d}*nubālu*), whose divine owner is not mentioned.[72] At Sippar in the Neo-Babylonian period, the chariot of Šamaš (written variously as ^{d}GIGIR, $^{d\,giš}$GIGIR, ^{giš}GIGIR, and ^{giš}GIGIR ^{d}UTU) received regular daily offerings of sheep alongside important gods,[73] and at Uruk in the same period, a chariot (again written both with and without the DINGIR and wooden object determinatives) stands toward the top of the list of entities receiving daily offerings, a position that suggests the importance of chariots as deities in those two cities in this late period.[74]

The chariots of gods are spoken of as material objects that belonged to a god and were separate from him; in royal inscriptions, letters, and administrative texts gods' chariots are referred to in terms that suggest they were real objects made of wood, leather, gold, silver, and precious stones,[75] and they are spoken of as items "belonging to the god X" (e.g., *ša* ^{d}*Adad*), not as being an emblem or alternate form of that anthropomorphic god.[76] In rituals, they move and stand together with other gods and are treated as separate from the god to whom they belong; in one Assyrian ritual instruction text, for example, a chariot (^{giš}GIGIR), probably belonging to the god Aššur, appears at the top of a list of gods including ^{d}Haja, ^{d}Kittu, ^{d}Tishpak, and ^{d}Istar of Nineveh, which is summed up at the end of the passage as "total: 15 gods (DINGIR.MEŠ) of the right," an entry followed immediately by a list of "gods on the left of the god Aššur." The chariot appears here as one of several independent gods that stand on either side of Aššur on this occasion, suggesting it was, like them, thought to be an independent deity belonging to Aššur's entourage.[77]

Although they are labeled as gods and presented with offerings from early times until the final days of Mesopotamian civilization, the chariots belonging to gods appear to have been thought of as being deities of a rather limited kind. In contrast to rivers and mountains, for example, chariots are never referred to as

---

71. Sallaberger, *Kalender, Teil 1*, p. 100.
72. Menzel, *Assyrische Tempel* II, T. 138, VAT 10126, Vs. I: 14; see also *AHw* s.v. *nubālu*.
73. Myers, "Sippar," pp. 217, 265 and 292.
74. In the offering lists of Beaulieu's Group A, the chariot receives sheep, lambs, turtledoves, ducks and geese, apparently one each daily as part of the regular offerings (*ginû*): Beaulieu, *Pantheon of Uruk*, p. 295.
75. Salonen, "Prozessionswagen," p. 6, and Myers, "Sippar," p. 359, where oil is alloted for greasing (*ana liptu*) of the leather cover (^{kuš}*kutummu*) of the chariot's wooden horn-shaped parts (^{giš}SI-*te*), indicating that it was not represented in the temple at Sippar in the form of an anthropomophic "chariot-man" statue, for example, but as an actual chariot (BM 62951, a text from the accession year of Cyrus, cited in Myers, "Sippar," p. 359).
76. Salonen, "Prozessionswagen," p. 7.
77. Van Driel, *Cult of Aššur*, BM 121206, V. 4'ff., p. 86.

acting on behalf of worshippers, nor are they called upon in hymns or prayers; their activities are confined to serving the gods as a means of transportation, they show no sign of personality, and they have no apparent impact on the lives of worshippers or on the functioning of the cosmos.

Boats, the gods' second means of transportation, were probably also considered deities in early times, but the evidence for their nature as non-anthropomorphic in nature and as independent divinities in their own right is less conclusive than the evidence for divine chariots, and disappears entirely after the Old Babylonian period.[78] Offering lists record that offerings of animals, or of meal, oil, beer, and other foods were presented to boats on seven occasions in the Ur III period and once in the Old Babylonian period.[79] "Boat" (^{d}má) and the specialized *makurru*-boot (^{d}má-gur$_8$) are both marked with the DINGIR determinative in Sumerian personal names, where they serve as the name's theophoric element. Since the moon god (called Nanna or Suen in early texts and Sin later on) is at times referred to metaphorically as being both kinds of boat, however, it remains possible that the references to divine boats in such Sumerian personal names are to be understood as referring to that god (either metaphorically or literally) as the boat-shaped crescent moon traveling across the sky. It is equally possible, however, that such names indeed refer to one of the boats belonging to an anthropomorphic god as being itself a deity.[80]

Visual images offer evidence that seems initially to resolve this question, so I will make an exception and discuss them here, although they prove to contribute further ambiguities of their own. On seal designs of the Early Dynastic and Akkadian periods, the boats that are shown carrying a seated anthropomorphic god such as Šamaš or Sin are sometimes depicted as having a prow that ends in the torso and head of a man, himself wearing the horned crown of a god and often shown poling the boat along through the water. This recurrent image seems to

---

78. For further discussion of gods' boats, with additional citations, see A. Salonen, "Die Wasserfahrzeuge in Babylonien," Studia Orientalia VIII.4 (Helsinki: Societas Orientalis Fennicae, 1939), pp. 58–59; Nikolaus Schneider, *Götterschiffe im Ur III-Reich*, Studia Orientalia XVIII/5 (Helsinki, 1946), pp. 1–13; A. Salonen, "Götterboot A. Nach sumerischen und akkadischen Texten," RLA III, pp. 463–64; R. Opficius, "Götterboot B. In der Archäologie," RLA 3, pp. 464–66.

79. A. Salonen, "Götterboot," RLA III, p. 463; Schneider, *Götterschiffe im Ur III-Reich*, pp. 10–11. In his study of local pantheons, Thomas Richter proposes, however, that the offering presented in the Old Babylonian period to a má-an-na (either 'boat of heaven' or 'boat of the god Anu'), which is said to be "for Ishtar" should be understood as presented for use during the "boat of heaven (festival)" rather than as an offering to the boat itself, an argument that if correct, might affect the Ur III evidence for divine boats as well: Thomas Richter, *Untersuchungen zu den lokalen Panthea Süd- und Mittelbabyloniens in altbabylonischer Zeit*, Alter Orient und Altes Testament 257 (Münster: Ugarit Verlag, 1999), p. 239.

80. Salonen, *Wasserfahrzeuge*, p. 9; Richard L. Litke, *A Reconstruction of the Assyro-Babylonian God-Lists, AN: ^{d}A-nu-um and AN: Anu šâ amēli*, Texts from the Babylonian Collection 3 (New Haven: Yale Babylonian Collection, 1998), Tablet III, nos. 24 and 25, p. 119.

represent the boats of gods unambiguously as gods in their own right, separate from their divine riders.[81] These images, however, at the same time raise the possibility that the boats of gods may have been envisioned as "boat-men," entities that were at least half anthropomorphic, which would remove them from the category we are examining. It is of course also possible that this way of representing such boats was not meant literally, but was a metaphoric visual convention intended to indicate that the boats were living, moving beings but still considered to be boats in their form and nature. While gods' chariots are quite clearly seen and treated as independent non-anthropomorphic deities in many periods and places, the boats of gods in contrast are not treated as gods ritually after the Old Babylonian period, and their status as non-anthropomorphic deities even before that time remains ambiguous. It seems from this example that closely related deified objects belonging to a single category may have been treated and envisioned quite differently as Mesopotamian gods.

Another type of object belonging to gods that appears to have been, at least at times, understood as independently divine is the musical instruments, in particular, the harps (or lyres) and drums, that were used by cultic musicians in performances before gods in temples. Instruments of both types, as we will see, were at times labeled with the divine determinative, and both were presented with offerings. Both drums and harps played an important role in temple life. Perhaps it was because they regularly played an intimate role in the lives of more anthropomorphic gods, these objects came to be thought of as divinities themselves, gods by association or "contagion" which had become gods in their own right through a transfer of divinity from their divine owners. Not all objects used in the daily life of the gods came to be labeled or treated as divine, however; the special tables set up to hold food offerings in temples, for example, seem to have been considered simply tables, despite their close daily association with the gods. Drums and harps, however, may have seemed more inherently god-like because they were experienced as awesome, the rumble of the drums filling the temple and the notes of the lyres or harps vibrating so that the temple's "harp chamber is (like) a roaring bull," as Gudea's Cylinder A inscription puts it.[82] In addition, these musical instruments may have been felt to be different from other possessions of gods because they made sounds, suggesting they had voices and could speak for humans to the gods, an idea implying these instruments to be themselves animate beings.

---

81. Ralph Hempelmann, "*Gottschiff*" *und* "*Zikkurratbau*" *auf vorderasiatischen Rollsiegeln des 3. Jahrtausends v. Chr.*, AOAT 312 (Münster: Ugarit-Verlag, 2004), with drawings of the examples on 3rd millennium seals. For the debated identity of the god (or gods) who are depicted riding in these boats, pp. 86–87. A. Green, "Mischwesen.B," RLA, Bd. 8, p. 259. Jeremy Black and Anthony Green, *Gods, Demons, and Symbols of Ancient Mesopotamia* (Austin: University of Texas Press, 1992), p. 45 and fig. 36.

82. Dietz Otto Edzard, *Gudea and His Dynasty*, RIME 3/1 (Toronto, Buffalo, London: University of Toronto Press, 1997), xxviii 17–18, p. 87.

Even today, it is not unusual for a flutist, for example, to feel that his flute has suddenly and unexpectedly "spoken" in a warmer, freer voice, as if it were for a moment a being with a mind and musical gifts of its own. Such experiences may help to explain the apparent conviction of Mesopotamians that at least some of the harps and drums used in the service of the gods were themselves living deities.

Although both are in many cases labeled as divine, such harps and drums played somewhat different roles in the lives of more prominent gods and also had different careers as deities, both chronologically and in different regions. The harp or lyre (^{giš}ZÀ.MÍ, *sammû*) was often used by *nâru*-singers to accompany hymns of praise to the gods.[83] Such a scene is described in King Assurbanipal's *Acrostic Hymn to Marduk and Zarpanītum*, for example, which reports that "offerings, incense, censers, stringed *inu*-instruments, harps and ... are set out; they glorify the builder of Esaggil (i.e., the god Marduk)."[84] A similarly cheerful scene involving a harp is described in a hymn of Sargon II to the goddess Nanāya, in which the goddess sits in her temple while "skilled musicians are seated before her, the players of the lyre, the small harp, the clapper, the flute, the oboe, the long (pipes)."[85]

The drum, in contrast, was the preferred instrument of *kalû*-priests, who specialized in lamentations. As such, it played an important role in efforts to appease and reconcile angry gods, and was used to purify possibly contaminated areas, although it was also used on some happier musical occasions.[86] The evidence for its divinity is sparse, but seems conclusive. A drum (^{d}ùb), as we saw earlier, is identified as a deity with the divine determinative in the *Fara God Lists*. In Early Dynastic Lagash, an object called the "Holy Drum" (ub$_5$-kù) received small offerings, such as oil and dates, on several occasions and was once presented with "one crown and one necklace" for its adornment.[87] Nothing that I can find suggests that drum gods were ever envisioned in any form but that of a drum.

The evidence for how harp gods were envisioned is more complex and more ambiguous. For example, Gudea of Lagash presented to the god Ningirsu two harps for his temple, one named Ušumgal-kalamma 'Dragon-of-the-land,' and the other named Lugal-igi-ḫuš 'King-with-the-fierce-face'.[88] Their names

---

83. CAD s.v. *sammû*.
84. Alasdair Livingstone, *Court Poetry and Literary Miscellanea*, SAA III (Helsinki: Helsinki University Press, 1989), p. 8, ll. 28–29.
85. Livingstone, *Court Poetry*, p. 13, ll. 7'–10'.
86. CAD s.v. *lillisu* a; AHw s.v. *uppu* III; Simo Parpola, *Letters from Assyrian and Babylonian Scholars*, SAA X (Helsinki: Helsinki University Press, 1993), nos. 340–42, 345, and 347, for performances of the kettledrum before various gods.
87. Selz, *Götterwelt*, p. 284; for the text, see Selz, "The Holy Drum," p. 175.
88. Edzard, *Gudea*, in the list of year-names, p. 27; Gudea Cylinder A vi 24 and vii 24; Gudea Cylinder B, xi 1–2, xv 21, and xviii 22. Jacobsen, in the notes to his eloquently poetic translation of Gudea's two cylinder inscriptions (Thorkild Jacobsen, *The Harps that Once . . . : Sumerian Poetry in*

suggest that both these instruments were thought of as living beings, but whether these names also indicate that the two deified instruments were actually envisioned as sometimes having the form of a dragon (or more accurately, horned serpent) in the one case, and that of a fierce ruler in anthropomorphic form in the other, is unclear. Whether the images their names evoke describe the appearance of the harp deities literally or were understood as figurative descriptions is here again an issue, an issue that is impossible to resolve on the basis of the Gudea hymn alone. In visual images, however, harps from the Ur III period are sometimes represented as musical instruments decorated with the head of a bull, or with a base shaped like a kneeling bull. In addition, actual harps from the Early Dynastic period at Ur have been excavated which incorporated a carved bull's head, suggesting that harps might have been envisioned as being a living divine musical instrument, a living divine person, and a real or mythic divine animal simultaneously.[89] In Gudea's inscriptions, the harps are sometimes referred to simply as harps (balag), and at other times are described as moving to stand before Gudea, perhaps implying an anthropomorphic form.[90] The dragon harp is once referred to in the text as the god's "beloved bard" and both harps are said to be "going about their duties for the Lord Ningirsu," again implying that they were

---

Translation [New Haven and London: Yale University Press, 1987], pp. 386–444), comments on the reference in Cylinder A to Ushumgalkalamma as being Ningirsu's "(well-) beloved harp..., his counselor," that "Harp music was effective in calming emotional turmoil and so made rational action possible. Temple harps were therefore considered the counselors of the deitities to which they belonged, and they were often deified" (p. 396, note 33). This suggests the musical instrument may have been envisioned at times as being an anthropomorphic being who counselled the god. As for the second harp, Jacobsen suggests that Lugaligihuš, whose name he translates as "the wroth-faced king," would "come into play when Ningirsu's face was glowering, the god still full of the wrath of battle" (n. 36, p. 434, re Cylinder B). Selz ("Holy Drum, p. 178) translates the name more literally 'red-eyed lord.' Both translations, and Jacobsen's characterization of the harp as "coming into play" seem to imply the instrument was envisioned, at least at times, as having an anthropomorphic form and nature, in addition to its appearance and activities as a musical instrument.

89. See, for example, plates 27, 31, 37 (top right), and 38 in Frankfort, *Art and Architecture*. See also the comment of Thorkild Jacobsen, in *The Harps that Once*, that the verb used for the instruments in a passage in Cyl. B x, which he translates "lie down," is "the term characteristically used for sheep and cows lying down." He adds, "The sound boxes of harps were often decorated with bovine heads so that when the harp was placed on the ground it would look as if the bull or cow were lying down. See, e.g. the various harps found at Ur. The deep tone of the harp suggested, of course, the voice of a bovine" (p. 434, n. 35). For a photograph of an actual reconstructed Sumerian harp with bull-head protome, found in a twenty-fifth century tomb at Ur, see p. 2602 in Jack M. Sasson et al., eds., *Civilizations of the Ancient Near East* (reprinted: Peabody, Mass.: Hendrickson, 2000: first edition, Farmington Hills, Mich.: Charles Scribner's Sons, 1995). For a close-up photograph of the golden bull's head from such a harp, with lapis lazuli beard attached, see Black and Green, *Gods, Demons and Symbols*, p. 44, fig. 35.

90. E.g., Jacobsen, *The Harps that Once*, Cyl. B col. xviii, l. 22, p. 441: "Ushumgalkalamma took its stand among the tigi-harps."

envisioned partly in anthropomorphic form, or even in a kaleidoscopic series of different forms, both anthropomorphic and non-anthropomorphic.[91]

If the form of such harps is unclear, their divinity is not. Whatever form they may have been imagined to take in their role as gods, a "great harp" was presented with offerings of oil and dates in Lagash, a second harp was offered a goat, and a group of seven harps received offerings of oil and dates.[92] In the Ur III period, drums were no longer labeled with the divine determinative or presented with offerings, to the best of my knowledge, but numerous offerings are still said to be presented to harps, and the names of harps are sometimes written with the divine determinative.[93] Even more significantly, "the Harp of the day," as we saw earlier, its name sometimes preceded with the DINGIR determinative, was the focus of a ritual performed in the city of Girsu several times per year in which it was paraded around the city and presented with offerings, a treatment that seems to mark it as an important divinity there, while in the city of Umma offerings were presented to a harp every month as part of rituals marking the dark of the moon.[94]

After the Ur III period, however, no musical instruments of any kind receive offerings, nor are they marked with the divine determinative, so far as I have been able to determine. Much later in eighth-century Assyria, when King Sennacherib dedicates "a kettledrum (LI.LI.EŠ, *lilissu*) of red copper" to the god Aššur to "quiet his heart," it is discussed in the text simply as an object.[95] This behavior was typical of Assyria, where musical instruments are never, so far as I know, treated as divine, but in Babylonia, where offerings to divine harps had once been commonplace and divine drums had occasionally received offerings in earlier times, offering lists and temple records after the third millennium no longer mention offerings to musical instruments of any kind.[96]

There is, however, one puzzling and significant exception. A Babylonian text composed sometime before the Hellenistic period gives instructions for an elaborate ritual to be performed when a new head was placed on a temple kettledrum;

---

91. Jacobsen, *The Harps that Once*, Cyl. B, col. x, 14–15 and xi 1, p. 434; cf. the different understanding of this line, with Gudea as the subject of the verb, of Edzard, *Gudea*, Cyl. B., col. x 14–15: "he (Gudea) brings along with himself (and introduces) to the lord Ningirsu (e n ᵈn i n - g i r - s u - r a m e - n i - d a m u - n a - d a - d i b - e) his beloved musician (n a r k i - á g - g a - n i), the Dragon-of-the-Land." See also the comments and translations of these passages by Selz, "Holy Drum," p. 178 and notes 218–220, in which the other harps "kneel before . . . the attentive hero" (i.e, Ningirsu) and the two named harps "go about their duties" as quite animate entities. I am grateful to Theo Krispijn for the intriguing comment that in Sumerian, the same word could mean 'singer', 'song', and 'harp', which creates further difficulties.

92. Selz, *Götterwelt*, p. 103.

93. Selz, "Holy Drum" p. 178 and Sallaberger, *Kalender*, p. 297.

94. Sallaberger, *Kalender*, pp. 297–98.

95. Daniel David Luckenbill, *The Annals of Sennacherib*, OIP II (Chicago: U. of Chicago Press, 1924), p. 149, ll. 9–12.

96. Myers, "Sippar," pp. 268 ff.; Beaulieu, *Pantheon of Uruk*, pp. 351–68.

as the ritual reaches its completion on the fifteenth day, the newly covered kettledrum is brought before the god Šamaš and is presented with offerings of sheep, beer, wine, and milk, together with the gods Ea, Šamaš, Marduk, and Lumḫa.[97] At this point, as the drum stands beside those other gods and is honored together with them, its name, like theirs, is marked with the DINGIR determinative for the first and only time in the text.[98] Although the text then continues at some length, describing a series of purifying actions performed on the drum before it is led before the temple's gods to assume its duties, the drum is referred to repeatedly— but never again labeled with the divine determinative. Before and after this moment, the drum is simply 'the copper drum' (*lilis siparri*) and is not identified as divine. The consistency with which the other gods are labeled with the DINGIR determinative in this text and the drum is not, except at this single moment, suggests the use of the determinative for it at this point, and the discontinuation of its use throughout the rest of the text, was not accidental.

To the best of my knowledge, the brief moment when the newly covered drum stands with the other gods and receives offerings with them is the only instance in which a musical instrument of any kind is labeled or treated as a god after the Ur III period. It is tempting to argue that musical instruments (drums included) had continued to be seen as divine despite the lack of attestations to support it, but the disappearance of instruments from offering lists in Babylonia, and the absence of divine determinatives on instruments over a very long period of time in contexts in which the determinative had formerly been used, suggests there had indeed been a change. The case of drums and harps is significant, first because it appears to illustrate that a category of objects once considered to be DINGIRs might come to be considered simply material objects in later periods, although their religious use, functions, and close association with a god or gods remained unchanged. In addition, the oddly temporary deification of the drum in the late Babylonian ritual text seems to suggest that objects could acquire a numinous quality in the course of a ritual and then promptly lose it or set it aside, perhaps

---

97. The tablet is a copy of an older text (dating back at least to the Neo-Babylonian period) and was made in Hellenistic Uruk. Edition with cuneiform hand-copy in F. Thureau-Dangin, *Rituels accadiens,* pp. 1–20; English translation by A. Sachs in *Ancient Near Eastern Texts Relating to the Old Testament,* James B. Pritchard, ed. (Princeton, N.J.: Princeton U. Press, 1955, 2nd ed.), Text A, pp. 334–36. For a discussion of rituals involving kettledrums, see Marc J. H. Linssen, *The Cults of Uruk and Babylon: The Temple Ritual Texts as Evidence for Hellenistic Cult Practices,* Cuneiform Monographs 25 (Leiden: Brill, and Boston: Styx, 2004), pp. 92–100.

98. *5 riksu ana ^{d}E-a ^{d}Šamaš ^{d}Marduk ^{d}Lum-ḫa u ^{d}Lilissi tarakka-as ^{immer}niqû tanaq-ki* (Thureau-Dangin, *Rituels accadiens,* p. 16): "5 ritual preparations you set up, for the gods Ea, Šamaš, Lumḫa and Lilissu; you (then) make an offering" (III, 16–18). In the lines that precede these, and in all the lines that follow, however, the drum is simply "the copper drum" (*lilis siparri*), neither referred to or marked as a deity (e.g., lines 15 and 25, the latter being the first time the drum is mentioned again).

when they returned to situations in which their association with the more anthropomorphic gods was less intense.

These sometimes-divine musical instruments of Mesopotamia were humans' tools, used by humans to communicate with gods and please them. Tools thought of as being used by the gods themselves constitute a different, perhaps more animate, category of non-anthropomorphic deity, a category with its own peculiar complexities. One of the most interesting cases of such a deified tool is that of gods' weapons, such as the "weapon of Aššur," the "weapons of Ninlil," "the weapon of Adad," and the "weapon" and "saw" of Šamaš, all of which appear to have been considered gods in their own right.

Divine weapons belonging to gods are most frequently attested in the Sumerian world, although a few are still mentioned in texts in Neo-Assyrian times. An entity called simply "Saw" is listed in the *Fara God Lists* with a DINGIR sign, as we have already seen, and seems likely to have been the weapon of a god, like the saw of Šamaš in later times.[99] In Neo-Sumerian Lagash, a weapon presented to Ningirsu by Gudea is labeled with the divine determinative and given the name dLugal-kur-dub 'the Lord who Smashes the Mountains' or 'the Lord who Smashes the (foreign) Lands,' a name that suggests this object was imagined not just as alive and active, but as energetically violent.[100]

Somewhat later, in the Ur III period, this same dLugalkurdub was presented on a particular occasion with an offering designated as being "for the mouth-opening (ritual)."[101] This comment is striking, because it seems to indicate that on this occasion, the mouth-opening ritual, a rite normally used to transform the statue of a god into a functioning, living locus of that god, had also been performed on a god's weapon to transform it from a material object into a living DINGIR.[102] A second weapon of Ningirsu named Šar-gaz '(the one that) smashes everything,' was presented with offerings during the Ur III period on the occasion when it was installed before its divine owner; in the same tablet, a mouth-opening ritual is mentioned, but whether it was performed on this weapon is not made clear and remains conjectural.[103] These two cases involving weapons raise the

---

99. Selz, "Holy Drum," p. 171; note, however, that Selz indicates that the translation as 'saw' is not certain.

100. For this translation, see Selz, "Holy Drum," p. 173–74 and note 209.

101. Selz, "Holy Drum," p. 177. Selz suggests that Lugalkurdub is a second name or epithet for another weapon of Ningirsu, known as Šar-ur, but this is uncertain.

102. On the mouth-opening ritual, see Selz's discussion, p. 177 with further bibliography in note 199; Irene J. Winter, "'Idols of the King': Royal Images as Recipients of Ritual Action in Ancient Mesopotamia," *Journal of Ritual Studies* 6 (1992), pp. 13–42; and Christopher Walker and Michael Dick, *The Induction of the Cult Image in Ancient Mesopotamia: The Mesopotamian Mīs Pî Ritual*," SAALT 1 (Helsinki: Neo-Assyrian Text Corpus Project, 2001). Winter argues that as a result of the performance of this ritual "the material form [of the statue of a god or of a king or ruler] was animated, the representation not standing for but actually manifesting the presence of the subject represented" (p. 13).

possibility that material objects in some cases became deities through a deliberate ritual transformation of their status, rather than simply because they were understood to be innately divine or were understood to have become divine through intimate association with an anthropomorphic god. The evidence for the transformation of objects into living gods by the performance of this ritual is quite sparse, however; this suggests that the performance of the mouth-opening ritual on ᵈLugalkurdub (and its possible performance on Šargaz as well) was exceptional, and not a standard practice.[104]

After these instances in the Ur III period, there are no further records of offerings made by residents of southern Mesopotamia to divine weapons, so far as I know. Farther north in Assyria, however, the worship of weapons as gods is now attested, beginning in the Middle Assyrian period and continuing into Neo-Assyrian times. The "weapon of Aššur," as well as Šargaz (now transferred to the god Ninurta, who had by this time replaced Ningirsu, and occasionally to other gods as well) and a second weapon of Ninurta (also sometimes belonging to other gods) named Šar-ur '(the one that) flattens everything,'[105] are all marked with the divine determinative and listed among the gods to whom offerings are presented by Assyrians from the Middle Assyrian period on in temples of Assyria and Babylonia. In a text listing Assyrian gods and their temples, usually referred to as the "Gods' Address Book," an apparently different divine weapon named simply "weapon" (ᵈ ᵍⁱˢ*kakku*) is listed among gods resident "in the temple of Ninlil" in Aššur.[106] The idea that gods' weapons were themselves independent divine entities was clearly enduring and widespread, attested in the south from very

---

103. Selz, "Holy Drum," p. 177.

104. In the Ur III period, the mouth-opening ritual was also performed on a copper bath pitcher that belonged to the god Nanna and that was used for lustration rituals (Jacobsen, *Treasures*, p. 124). Walker and Dick (*Induction*, p. 13) also list performances of the ritual on apotropaic figurines, a leather bag used in divination, a footstool and standard of Šamaš at Mari in the Old Babylonian period, a river, and on jewels used to protect the king's chariot in the Neo-Assyrian period.

105. This is the translation of the name proposed by Selz ("Holy Drum," p. 177). Edzard translates Šarur's name as 'Mow-down-a-myriad': Edzard, *Gudea*, Cyl. B, col. vii 19, p. 92.

106. For the weapon of Aššur, Frankena, *Tākultu*, K. 252 (= III R 66): p. 7, col. VI 14. In the parallel text K. 9925, l. 15', this weapon appears simply as ᵍⁱˢTUKUL 'weapon' without the explicit attribution to Aššur or the DINGIR determinative (see the edition of Menzel, *AssyrischeTempel* II; T. 119, text 54). For Šarur, Frankena, *Tākultu*, K. 252 (= III R 66) p. 8, col. XI 31, and for Šargaz, p. 8, col. XI 32, 10. Frankena discusses these two gods on p. 113, nos. 206 and 208, noting that in V R 46:32, both weapons are said to belong to Marduk, and that in the Assyrian version of *Enūma eliš* (Luckenbill, *Annals*, p. 142, K. 1356, rev. 11), both weapons go out before the god Aššur when he goes forth to fight Tiamat (in this version, Aššur assumes Marduk's traditional role in the myth). For further discussion of these two divine entities as weapons of Ninurta, see Jerrold S. Cooper, *The Return of Ninurta to Nippur: An-gim dím-ma*, Analecta Orientalia 52 (Rome: Pontifical Biblical Institute, 1978), p. 122. The god identified simply as 'weapon' appears in line 10 of the "Gods' Address Book," edited by Frankena, *Tākultu*, p. 123 (for a more recent edition, see Menzel *Assyrische Tempel* II, text 64, T. 147).

early times and surfacing in the north, in Assyria, in the Middle Assyrian period and perhaps even earlier. Whether the apparent end of such veneration of weapons in the south and its subsequent appearance in the north represent actual changes in religious practice or are simply a reflection of gaps in our evidence, remains unclear.[107]

That such weapons of gods were not emblems representing the more anthropomorphic god who owned them, but were thought of as deities in their own right, is suggested not only by their receipt of their own offerings, separate from those given their owners, but also by the way they are described and represented.[108] This emerges most clearly in the case of the weapon Šarur. Gudea's Cylinder A inscription represents the Šarur weapon as a material object, describing the collecting of cedar to make it and later describing its presentation to the god Ningirsu to serve as his tool; the weapon is referred to there as "the floodstorm of his master," that is, an entity used by Ningirsu and clearly separate from him.[109] Like Mt. Ebiḫ, Šarur is an exceptional case in that he (or it) appears as an active character in a myth; in the Old Babylonian myth known as *Lugal.e*, the weapon Šarur is depicted as an independent-minded being quite separate from his divine master (here, Ninurta), whom he advises, debates with, gathers information for, and warns.[110] As in the case of Mt. Ebiḫ, however, this stubborn, loquacious, and in many ways quite anthropomorphic weapon may be represented in this way here so that he can participate in the myth as a fully developed animate character, as the conventions of the genre often seem to demand, and not because this is how Šarur was usually envisioned.

Further descriptions of Šarur suggest he/it may have been imagined as having both anthropomorphic and non-anthropomorphic form, although some of the terms used for him may be intended as metaphoric descriptions of his activity as a weapon. In Gudea's Cylinder B inscription, for example, Šarur is called a warrior and a general (which may, of course, be functional descriptions of the weapon

---

107. Cooper, *Return of Ninurta*, p. 122, comments, "Judging from the number of occurences in late texts, Šarur and Šargaz alone among the deified weapons of Ninurta seem to have achieved independent stature in the pantheon of the first millennium theologians."

108. Krecher explores this question in reference to weapons and other objects that he takes to be symbols or emblems of gods, pointing out that these often appear beside the god itself or are otherwise treated as independent entities. He suggests this makes it difficult to know whether they were considered to be dependent on the god to whom they belonged for their authority, or were understood as themselves independently active and effective divine entities ("von sich selbst aus wirksam und gültig"), as I argue here: J. Krecher, "Göttersymbole," RLA III, pp. 496–97.

109. Edzard, *Gudea*, p. 78, Gudea Cyl. A, xv 22–26 and p. 92, Gudea Cyl. B, vii 19–23.

110. For an edition with transliteration, translation, and transcription of a composite text of the myth, see J. van Dijk, LUGAL UD ME-LÁM-bi NIR-GÁL: *Le récit épique et didactique des Travaux de Ninurta, du Déluge et de la Nouvelle Création* (Leiden: Brill, 1983). The quotations here are from the lively translation of Kramer in Bottéro and Kramer, *Lorsque les dieux*, pp. 338–68 (their English translation is mine).

rather than physical descriptions of this god as an anthropomorphic being), and he is also referred to non-anthropomorphically as a cudgel, a floodstorm, and a bird. In the Old Babylonian *Lugal.e* myth, as we have seen, he is often represented as a rather anthropomorphic weapon that speaks with its master, but he is also represented as an object and as an animal, described in turn as Ninurta's "magic weapon" (e.g., l. 23), his "deadly weapon" (l. 79), and "his lion-headed weapon" (l. 109), and then as an entity that is at first said to be "like a bird" (mušen-gim) (l. 110) but then seems to have actually been envisioned as a bird that "takes flight and stations himself over the Mountain" on a military reconnaissance mission for its master (l. 110), and that has "wings" on which it rises and turns in the sky (ll. 112–113). This panoply of different descriptions suggests that in this case, Šarur was thought of as a god of shifting forms and nature. Šarur makes a second appearance in another Sumerian myth composed in the Old Babylonian period, *The Return of Ninurta to Nippur* (known to the Sumerians as AN.GIM), but here the weapon is not a talkative being but simply a material object, one of the many weapons that Ninurta carries during his triumphant return to Nippur (e.g., "On my right, I bear my Šarur; on my left I bear my Šargaz[111]). The persistence with which Šarur is referred to in texts as a weapon suggest the deified object was primarily envisioned in the form of a weapon, perhaps one shaped to resemble a predator bird or decorated with a bird image, rather than as an anthropomorphic deity, although the question cannot be clearly resolved.

An additional complication in assessing the nature of gods' weapons as independent gods arises from the fact that certain objects that are identified as being the weapons of gods such as Adad, Marduk, and Šamaš were sometimes used in the Old Babylonian period in conjunction with the standards, or portable emblems, of gods (Akkadian *šurinnu*) that were employed for oath-taking and other juridical proceedings taking place outside the temple precincts, and that during the Old Assyrian period, oaths were taken similarly in Assyrian contexts on the "dagger (*patrum*) of Aššur."[112] Since "weapon" is given as a synonym of *šurinnu*

---

111. Cooper, *Return of Ninurta*, p. 77, l. 129. The list of Ninurta's extraordinary weapons continues through line 152, where it concludes with "my fifty-headed mace." On the divinity of these weapons, Cooper comments, "Note that in the late lists [of gods], the divine determinative is used with the mace, but it is used in neither the NA manuscript of Angim, nor, in all probability, in the incantation K. 9336+." (pp. 130–31). Cooper's edition shows that the DINGIR sign is written before the name of Šargaz in one of the three Sumerian copies of the text; it is also used in the Akkadian version of the myth, preserved on a Neo-Assyrian tablet (p. 78). This variation in the use of the determinative for the weapon is also the case, for instance, with the weapon referred to in line 131 as "my heavenly mace" (^{d}ud.zú ninnu). The presentation of offerings to Šargaz and Šarur, which continued into the Neo-Assyrian period, suggests the inconsistency in the use of the determinative here is probably not significant as an indication of their divinity, or lack of it.

112. See CAD s.v. *šurinnu* and *kakku* 3; J. Spaey, "Emblems in Rituals in the Old Babylonian Period," in J. Quaegebeur, ed., *Ritual and Sacrifice in the Ancient Near East*, Orientalia Lovaniensia Analecta 55 (Uitgeverij Peeters and Departement Oriëntalistiek: Leuven, 1993), pp. 411–20, and

in some lexical lists, it has sometimes been argued that the "weapon of the god X" on which oaths were taken was not actually a weapon, but took the form of a standard bearing an emblem representing a particular great god.[113] The consistent reference to these objects in juridical texts as "the weapon of the god X," however, suggests the simpler explanation that the "weapon" on which such oaths were taken was in fact the divine weapon, or a standard visually representing it, not just an emblem representing a great god; perhaps these weapons were chosen for oath-taking because it was the weapons of gods, divine and active in their own right, that would actually enforce the oath at the command of their divine owners, should the oath-taker fail to keep his word.[114] If actual weapons or images of them were in fact used, as I have suggested, these juridical references provide evidence of a special function of this particular type of deified object.

As a final look at some of the different ways in which the possessions of gods functioned as independent deities, we will consider the case of gods' crowns, which are labeled and treated as deities in certain contexts. Unlike weapons, these crowns were not tools used by anthropomorphic gods, but belong instead to the category of objects that served them as marks of their divinity or as insignia

---

B. Pongratz-Leisten, K. Deller, and E. Bleibtreu, "Götterstreitwagen und Götterstandarten: Götter auf dem Feldzug und ihre Kulte im Feldlager," *Baghdader Mitteilungen* 23 (1992), pp. 291–356. On the use of the weapon of Aššur for oath-taking, see Steven W. Holloway, *Aššur is King! Aššur is King! Religion in the Exercise of Power in the Neo-Assyrian Empire* (Leiden: Brill, 2001), p. 167.

113. See, for example, Steven W. Holloway, "The ᵍⁱˢ*kakki Aššur* and Neo-Assyrian Loyalty Oaths," in Tzvi Abusch et al., eds., *Historiography in the Cuneiform World, Part I*, Proceedings of the XLVᵉ Rencontre Assyriologique Internationale (Bethesda, MD: CDL Press, 2001), pp. 239–66. He notes that the references to an "iron arrow" inscribed with the "might of Assur" and erected in a provincial center in the Zagros by Tiglath-pileser III are perhaps the only Neo-Assyrian example in which textual parallels make it clear that the "symbol of Assur" was in this case actually an object in the form of a weapon (pp. 243–44). Holloway concludes that in the second millennium, ŠU.NIR/ *šurinnu* and GIŠ.TUKUL/*kakku* frequently appear jointly and are sometimes used as interchangeable terms and that "the lexical equivalence between *kakku* and *šurinnu* continued into the NA period. . . ."(p. 256). See also the discussion of the word *kakku* in the CAD, which offers several definitions of the word ("weapon," "weapon [metaphoric for military strength . . .]," "standard with divine symbol," "tool, shaft, barb, thorn," and "[a formation on the exta . . .]": significantly, only one of these definitions ("weapon") supposes that a *kakku* was necessarily an object in weapon shape. The section discussing *kakku* as a "standard with divine symbol"(CAD s.v. *kakku* 3a) consistently translates GIŠ.TUKUL (the logographic writing of the word) not as 'weapon,' but rather as 'symbol' (of the god DN), implying recognition that evidence for its physical form as a weapon or picture of a weapon in such settings is absent in almost all cases, as Holloway indicates. The problem, then, is to decide whether the term *kakku* was still understood to refer to a weapon, even when the object was used as just another *šurinnu*, or whether that overtone had essentially disappeared in such contexts.

114. CAD s.v. *kakku*; Toufic Solyman, "Die Entstehung und Entwicklung der Götterwaffen im alten Mesopotamien und ihre Bedeutung" (Ph.D. diss., Frei Universität, Berlin, 1964); B. Pongratz-Leisten, K. Deller, and E. Bleibtreu, "Götterstreitwagen"; Steven W. Holloway, "The ᵍⁱˢ*Kakki Aššur* and Neo-Assyrian Loyalty Oaths," pp. 239–66.

of their authority, much like the scepters and thrones of gods, which were also treated as deities in their own right. In visual imagery, crowns with horns were used to identify gods in general and were also used as the visual emblem representing several anthropomorphic ruler gods.[115] In texts, the gods' crowns are described as emblems of their lordliness and their divinity. The king Agum-kakrime refers to a crown he presented to Marduk, for example, as "the crown with mighty horns, crown of lordship, symbol of divinity."[116] Like chariots, weapons, thrones, and other objects, real crowns were presented to gods by kings in order to please the gods and get them in a positive mood; the Assyrian king Esarhaddon, for example, reports, "a cunningly made crown, symbol of the rule [of] Aššur, king of the gods, my lord, I caused to be made of red gold and precious stones, and I returned it to its place. That crown—clothed in fearsome brightness, adorned with magnificence, glowing with an awesome radiance, enveloped in splendor—greatly pleased Aššur, the great lord; his heart was contented and his face glowed."[117]

Although the crown described in Esarhaddon's inscription is described here simply as a beautiful object made for a god, in other contexts, particularly in Assyria, the crowns of gods are at times treated and labeled as DINGIRs. This appears to have been the case in the Mesopotamian south only in very early times, however. While a crown marked with a DINGIR determinative (^{d}MEN) appears in the *Fara God Lists*, the crowns of gods are not treated as gods thereafter in Babylonia, although they are described as playing an active role in rituals there. In Assyria, in contrast, crowns of gods, particularly the crown of Aššur, are labeled with the divine determinative and treated as deities of some importance. In an Assyrian ritual text listing gods to whom offerings were to be presented, for example, an object referred to simply as "The Crown" (^{d}*A-gu-u*) is labeled with the divine determinative and is listed among the gods of two different temples, once following a composite form of Aššur (^{d}Dagan-Aššur) and once following Nabû, presumably the gods to whom the crowns in question belonged.[118]

We are better informed about the crown of Aššur than about most non-anthropomorphic DINGIRs because it appears several times in texts giving instructions

---

115. See s.v. horned cap, Black and Green, *Gods, Demons and Symbols*, pp. 102–03. For particular gods, see e.g., Frankfort, *Art and Architecture*, pl. 71, which shows a Babylonian *kudurru* depicting in its upper register emblems of various gods, including two pedestals bearing horned crowns.

116. For references to the crowns of gods, see CAD s.v. *agû* 1a; see also CAD s.v. *bēlūtu* 1a.

117. Borger, *Asarhaddon*, AsBbA rs., ll. 32b–34 (my translation from the Akkadian). The size of this crown is unclear. The Assyrian king is sometimes referred to as taking the crown of Aššur from his own head and placing it before the god, suggesting a human-sized crown, but statues of gods were also equipped with crowns and these may have been smaller; see for example Parpola, *Letters from Assyrian and Babylonian Scholars*, SAA X, no. 349, in which the statue of a goddess that is to be repaired is described as having a face, hands, feet, robe, and golden crown.

118. Frankena, *Tākultu*, K. 252 = IIIR 66 i 14 and xi 25.

for performing royal rituals, and unlike the offering lists, these ritual texts provide a glimpse of the Crown "in action" and acting in relationship to other gods.[119] In these rituals, Aššur's Crown, referred to alternately as "Crown" and "Lord Crown," receives its own individual offerings and moves independently of its divine owner, implying that it had its own identity as an independent god and was not simply an emblem of Aššur. In a ritual performed on the sixteenth of Šabāṭu, for example, the king goes to the Aššur temple, kisses the ground before Aššur, lights an incense censer, and then (after a few missing cuneiform signs), turns to Lord Crown and sets up an offering table before him. After the priest puts a cloth of some kind on the king, the ruler presents something (again missing) to Aššur, sprinkles salt, and then presents "water for the hands" separately to Lord Crown.[120] The Crown's independent identity, separate from that of Aššur, is further indicated when it appears as one of sixteen gods referred to as "the gods who went with Aššur into the temple of Dagan."[121] It is also implied in a ritual performed on the twentieth of Šabāṭu in which the king goes to the temple of Aššur, makes offerings before Aššur and his spouse, seats them on the "cult pedestal of fate," circles it once, and then "removes the Lord Crown from his (own) head and causes it to sit on the 'cult pedestal of fate'," as if it were being presented to the two deities.[122] The separate identity of the crown from that of its divine owner, and the fact that the king initially wears this crown on his own head, suggest that Aššur's Crown might perhaps represent "ruling" or "sovereignty" as exercised at Aššur's command, an activity closely related to Aššur but not identical with him. This could explain why "Lord Crown" or "the Crown" was venerated in his company but recognized as an independently powerful divine entity,[123] perhaps similar in nature to the gods that appear to have been living divine embodiments of abstract concepts or powerful human activities, such as the gods 'Justice' (^{d}*mišarum*) and 'Truth' (^{d}*kittum*).[124]

---

119. On the Crown of Aššur and on the interchangeability of its two names, see Menzel, *Assyrische Tempel* I, pp. 136–37 and II, p. 57* n. 698. Its names are written with and without the divine determinative as "Crown" (AGA, ^{d}AGA, MÉN, ^{d}*A-gu-u*, and *A-gu-u*) and as "Lord Crown" (EN AGA and ^{d}EN AGA).

120. A. 125, text no. 24 in Menzel, *Assyrische Tempel* II, pp. T 32–33, Vs. I 11–23.

121. A. 485+3109, text no. 28 in Menzel, *Assyrische Tempel* II, p. 44, rs. 19–24.

122. Menzel, *Assyrische Tempel* I, pp. 54–55 and Menzel *Assyrische Tempel* II, p. 57* n. 698 and A. 125, p. T. 35, Vs. II, 19′–25′.

123. The fact that a crown literally worn by the king bears the name "Lord Crown" here supports Menzel's contention that both "Crown" and "Lord Crown" were names of a single deity represented and imagined in the shape of a crown. The presentation of water "for the hands" to Lord Crown may imply an anthropomorphic shape and nature, or may simply be given to him (or it) because it was given to other gods in the same circumstances.

124. Both these divinities, however, are referred to at times as "daughters" of other gods, perhaps suggesting a primarily anthropomorphic concept of them as deities.

Having examined some of the widely assorted types of entities that are referred to or treated in texts as DINGIRs or *ilu*s, we are in a better position to address the basic question with which we began: what *was* a god in Mesopotamian eyes? First of all, it has by now become rather clear that gods were not necessarily anthropomorphic beings in ancient Mesopotamia. Our initial sampling of the documentary evidence, focusing on offering lists, instructions for performing rituals, juridical texts, personal names, and royal inscriptions, revealed a surprisingly large number of material objects, topographical phenomena and other non-anthropomorphic entities in every period of Mesopotamian history that although not celebrated as gods in hymns and prayers and not listed as gods in the great god-lists that were compiled after the Fara period are nevertheless presented with offerings, labeled with the DINGIR determinative, and simply referred to as being DINGIRs or *ilu*s. Although handbooks on Mesopotamian religion still assert that, "The gods of the ancient Mesopotamians, in historical times, were almost without exception anthropomorphic, male or female,"[125] we have now confirmed on closer examination that exceptions to this rule occur in every period and region. It is hard to avoid the conclusion that for Mesopotamians, non-anthropomorphic entities of widely assorted types were as much gods (in the Mesopotamian sense) as were the larger number of DINGIRs and *ilu*s that they imagined to occur primarily in anthropomorphic form.

In the light of this somewhat marginal group of deities, what qualities were basic to being a god in ancient Mesopotamia? Our survey suggests that the concept of deity in Mesopotamia was remarkably complex and varied. Not only did Mesopotamians in every period imagine DINGIRs in widely assorted forms, some anthropomorphic and some not, they also imagined even the DINGIRs in the non-anthropomorphic category as having a variety of different natures, functions and behavior as gods. To further complicate the picture, Mesopotamians in different cities or regions, and in different chronological periods, as we have seen, clearly had different ideas about whether a particular non-anthropomorphic entity was a deity or not, and if it was, about its importance in comparison to other members of the pantheon.

It is probably significant that it is so often difficult to establish whether a particular entity was imagined as anthropomorphic or not. The shifting forms and the ambiguities in the representation of gods suggest that unlike modern researchers, ancient Mesopotamians were not particularly interested in whether a god was anthropomorphic or not. Indications that there was something significantly different about the gods of non-anthropomorphic form are very rare in Mesopotamian documents. Our own greater interest in the issue probably reflects the importance of largely anthropomorphic deities in the dominant modern Western religious traditions, but may also reflect the apparent preference of modern Western cultures

---

125. Black and Green, *Gods, Demons and Symbols*, p. 93.

for binary thinking, including categorizing in terms of "either/or," a preference that is not universally shared.[126] Mesopotamian descriptions of some gods as having many forms or aspects (e.g., Ishtar as a star, love, war, a queen, etc.) suggest that the Mesopotamian model of god was not construed in binary terms, and that Mesopotamians tended instead to envision a particular god as moving fluidly within a set of alternate forms. Although this way of conceptualizing the divine may seem odd to us, it resembles the way gods were understood in some Latin American cultures as Levi-Strauss and other anthropologists have characterized them, that is, as entities imagined as existing in a series of "transformations," alternating forms not necessarily directly related to all of the other forms, but each evoking some aspect or quality attributed to that god, and each functioning as an equally valid form of that god.[127] If the distinction between anthropomorphic and non-anthropomorphic gods was of only minor interest to Mesopotamians, however, it is of major importance for us because the characteristics of this somewhat marginal minority group help us to identify qualities that Mesopotamians saw as basic to the entities belonging to the category of DINGIR/*ilu*.

Despite their differences, a special treatment shared by DINGIRs and *ilu*s of every kind, whether anthropomorphic or non-anthropomorphic, is that food offerings were presented to them, a common characteristic that implies that even those gods that were not "divine persons" with fully developed personalities and biographies were nevertheless understood to be in some sense quite alive. DINGIRs such as thrones and chariots, for example, which had no families, no social life, and not even the faculty of speech, nevertheless received food offerings, a gift appropriate only for living creatures. The presentation of food offerings further implies that material objects such as divine chariots or ziggurats were thought of as cognizant beings, aware that gifts were being presented to them and, like other gods, able to take pleasure in those gifts (whether or not the food was seen as necessary for their sustenance).[128] The elaborately ritualized presentation of food offerings even to gods that entirely lack personality suggests that all Mesopotamian gods were understood to be living beings endowed with awareness and feelings.

---

126. For further discussion, see Benson Saler, *Conceptualizing Religion: Immanent Anthropologists, Transcendent Natives, and Unbounded Categories*, Studies in the History of Religions LVI (Brill: Leiden and N.Y., 1993), pp. 12–13. I am grateful to Robert C. Hunt for discussing with me some current anthropological approaches to the problem of modelling (and defining) religion and whether any of these approaches might be helpful in analyzing the religious beliefs and practices of ancient Mesopotamians.

127. For a persuasive example, see Eva Hunt, *The Transformation of the Hummingbird: The Cultural Roots of a Zinacantecan Mythical Poem* (Ithaca, N.Y. and London: Cornell U. Press, 1977).

128. Gods are often said both to eat their food and enjoy it; see, for example, the reference to the gift of a drink container to Ningirsu "so that Ningirsu may savor his beer from it" (Bottéro, *La Plus Vielle Cuisine*, p. 171, English translation mine). For an example of gods eating (*i-ka-lu*) a sheep offering, see Richter, *Lokalen Panthea*, p. 114, note 471. Whether gods such as divine chariots "needed" food is, however, not clear.

The conviction of Mesopotamians that material objects such as thrones, harps, and chariots could be living, cognizant divine beings may have its roots in a Mesopotamian understanding of the world in some ways fundamentally different from our own. In her study of visual symbols used in prehistoric Mesopotamia, Beatrice L. Goff proposes that Mesopotamians in prehistoric times and later "saw the world more than we do today as 'redundant with life'" and that in ritual they saw themselves "as handling living things."[129] She cites a letter in which Thorkild Jacobsen argues that while there is "not the slightest evidence they confused animate and inanimate," nevertheless "in moments of specific religious receptivity . . . objects became a Thou" for the ancient Sumerians (p. 166). Citing Mesopotamian lists of the potent properties of particular semi-precious stones and noting the selection of particular types of stone for use as amulets, Goff concludes, "Everything was potentially charged with power, and recognizably potent objects were sought for every concern. . . . The objects in antiquity were potent because they were animate" (p. 169). Whether or not one accepts Goff's essentially animistic characterization of Mesopotamian ideas of the natural world, or Jacobsen's more nuanced position that in certain situations particular objects were perceived as living beings, the presentation of food offerings to certain selected material objects as well as to anthropomorphically conceived gods indicates that for Mesopotamians, objects were at least sometimes felt to be charged with life. By extension they were in some special circumstances recognized as living divinities.

Although they were alive, not all gods appear to have been able (or inclined?) to affect human lives or influence the workings of the cosmos. While some non-anthropomorphic gods (like most of their more anthropomorphic divine colleagues) are quite active, such as the divine mountains that provide families with an heir, or the divine weapons that smash enemies' heads or guarantee oaths, other DINGIRs, such as chariots and thrones, appear almost inert; they are active only as objects used by or for other gods and do not themselves have agency. The same could be said for the divine parts of temples, such as pipes or doorways, or for holy drums. It would appear that neither agency nor the ability to have an impact on human life or on natural phenomena were seen as essential to the nature of DINGIRs and *ilu*s.

What qualities distinguished DINGIRs and *ilu*s from other living things and put them in the special category of things that were divine? Or to put the same question a little differently, why and how did particular entities come to be seen as gods? When non-anthropomorphic DINGIRs and *ilu*s are added to the category of DINGIR/*ilu*, it becomes clear that current theories about how entities became gods in Mesopotamia explain only part of the phenomenon. In his study of the history

---

129. Beatrice Laura Goff, *Symbols of Prehistoric Mesopotamia* (New Haven: Yale University Press, 1963), p. 169.

of Mesopotamian religion, for example, Thorkild Jacobsen follows the hypothesis of Rudolph Otto about the origins of early religious belief lying in an initial experience of certain things as being innately and awesomely "holy."[130] Jacobsen proposes that the entities perceived as gods in Mesopotamia had at some early time been experienced as so awesome, powerful, and mysterious that they were felt instinctively to be 'wholly other,' as Otto put it, belonging to a category of things beyond and above the mundane and the human, the category for which Otto coined the term the *numinous*.[131] Jacobsen finds it probable that the gods of Mesopotamia originated in humans' early experiences of natural phenomena such as storms, or floods, or the appearance of a star in the heavens as being inherently awesome and terrifying, and that these initial experiences of the uncanny and tremendous gradually led Mesopotamians toward the concept of a complex system of numinous beings, largely anthropomorphic in form, that they understood to be present and active in the world and sky, and also present in supernatural realms in the heavens and the underworld.

Jean Bottéro, less willing to hypothesize about the undocumented experiences of prehistoric humans, posits no such initial terrifying experience of the numinous, but like Jacobsen, argues that the fundamental characteristic of Mesopotamia's divine entities was the perception of them as being "everything that by its position or nature was 'above,' 'elevated,' 'superior,'" a concept that he suggests is reflected in the star-shape of the cuneiform sign used for writing the word "god" and the divine determinative.[132] The basic quality of a god, Bottéro argues, was "*superiority*—his superiority over everything else, but especially over humans...." (p. 58). Bottéro goes on to identify power, sublimity, and omnipotence as the basic characteristics of Mesopotamian gods (pp. 59–61), qualities that made them "fascinating and terrible at the same time" (p. 61).

Jacobsen and Bottéro's arguments for the innately terrifying, awesome, and superior nature of the entities that were understood to be gods in Mesopotamia are plausible in the case of divine entities that were associated with powerful natural forces or inherently awesome and dangerous phenomena, such as Ninurta, the storm god, or Anu, the sky god, or Ishtar, the goddess of love, war, and the morning and evening star, but their explanations of the origin and nature of Mesopotamian gods are less persuasive in the case of entities such as chariots, boats, or drums, objects that seem in themselves neither innately terrifying nor awesomely superior. Such objects must have become gods for Mesopotamians in a different way or ways. In a few cases, as we saw earlier, material objects asso-

---

130. Rudolph Otto, *The Idea of the Holy*, trans. John W. Harvey (New York: Oxford University Press, 1958, 2nd ed.), and Jacobsen, *Treasures*, pp. 3–4.

131. On the 'numinous,' see Otto, *Idea*, pp. 5–11; on the initial terrifying experience that Otto posits, p. 32; on the 'wholly other', pp. 25–30.

132. Bottéro, *Religion*, p. 58.

ciated with gods seem to have been deliberately transformed into gods by the performance of the mouth-opening ritual, more commonly used to transform a god's statue into a living locus or repository of that deity, but instances of this practice are rarely attested and appear to be exceptional. A few other non-anthropomorphic deities, such as mountains, rivers, or even the harps that "sang" to gods, might have seemed to Mesopotamians to be inherently charged with awesome supernatural power and thus have become gods in the same way as the more familiar anthropomorphic deities (if Jacobsen's hypothesis is correct), but how did other, less charismatic non-anthropomorphic objects or natural phenomena become DINGIRs?

Although we can only conjecture, it seems likely, as I have already suggested in discussing particular types of deities, that objects such as ziggurats, and the boats, weapons, and thrones of gods became deities by "contagion," by a transfer of divinity to them from the inherently numinous god that owned them and with whom they were in frequent intimate contact. This idea of the transfer of qualities from owner to object is not as odd as it may initially seem. Rather in the way that a bed slept in by Queen Elizabeth I, or a book owned by Margaret Mead, or a dress worn by Jacqueline Kennedy may have a special status in modern eyes, as if it had in some undefined way acquired something of the aura of its famous owner, in similar fashion the chariots and thrones belonging to great gods in Mesopotamia seem to have been seen as sharing something of the divine nature of their owners.[133] Perhaps the closest modern analogy to this idea of a transfer of divinity is the case of objects said to have been owned or used by Christian saints, such as the Veil of St. Veronica or the cloak of St. Martin, which are recognized by some worshippers (if not by the official doctrine of the Church) as being charged with miraculous divine powers, so that help or healing can sometimes be acquired in their presence when it cannot be found elsewhere. Although in similar fashion, certain objects such as the weapons of gods seem to have been regarded by Mesopotamians as living, independent centers of numinous power somehow transferred to them through their intimate association with a particular god, the full range of divine powers and responsibilities of that owner god were not transferred to these objects in Mesopotamian settings (the chariot of the sun-god Šamaš, for example, receives offerings but does not act as a divine judge like its owner), but such possessions were nevertheless treated and labeled as belonging to the same category of beings as their owners, the category of DINGIRs and *ilu*s.

Along with their divinity, such objects seem also to have acquired something of the disquieting, uncanny aura of the gods who were their owners, suggesting that an ominous, supernatural "chargedness" was felt to be fundamental to Mesopotamia's DINGIRs and *ilu*s. The clearest evidence for this lies in two odd letters

---

133. On the transfer of divinity from a god to his temple, its parts, and the implements used in it, so that all of these became gods, see Lambert, "Ancient Mesopotamian Gods," pp. 128–29.

written by the state treasurer of Assyria, a certain Ṭâb-šar-Aššur, to his king, Sargon II (721–705 BCE), in the course of transporting two beds by boat to the holy precincts of the city of Aššur. These letters offer a rare glimpse of Mesopotamians in the throes of dealing with objects that they almost certainly considered to be non-anthropomorphic deities.[134]

In the first of the two letters (no. 54 in Parpola's edition), our author, one of the most powerful officials of Assyria, is in the midst of a boat trip on the Tigris to Libbi-ali, the temple quarter of the city of Aššur and the seat of the god Aššur, Assyria's chief patron deity. The boat has put in to shore for the night and Ṭâb-šar-Aššur is seizing the opportunity to send a quick progress report to the king. He assures the king that if all goes well, they will reach their destination on the following day. He then lays out his plans, for which he requests the king's approval. The text is somewhat broken here, but he refers to bringing something golden into Aššur's temple. He then mentions a bed and goes on to say that after delivering the golden object, he will assemble things for "decorating and washing" and then bring something (evidently the bed) into the temple, where he proposes to "perform our rites together." The bed has apparently come to Aššur to play a role in a ritual to be performed in the state temple. He now says that if the king permits, he will bring the bed into the house of the temple's treasurer, "where," he reports, "the gods of Dūr-Šarrukēn," Sargon's new capital city, "are staying" (rev. ll. 9–10). He informs the king that he himself will stay on board ship with the bed on the river to "watch over it" until he receives instructions from the king about moving it, which he urges the king to send quickly.

It is an extraordinary account, and it is clearly an extraordinary bed. Throughout Mesopotamian history, kings gave beds to gods to please and placate them, and this bed, apparently associated with the gods of the new capital, may be such a gift to one of them.[135] The treasurer's solicitous concern for the bed is so acute, however, and the king's personal interest in its every movement so great, that one begins to wonder if this bed is itself already seen as a god. The letter ends at this point, however, without providing sufficient information to resolve the question.

In the second letter (no. 55), the situation is clearer. Ṭâb-šar-Aššur is engaged in traveling by boat with a different bed and has just arrived, after a longer journey this time, at the city of Aššur, where the inhabitants have greeted the boat's

---

134. The letters are nos. 54 and 55 in the excellent revised edition by Simo Parpola, *The Correspondence of Sargon II, Part I: Letters from Assyria and the West*, SAA 1 (Helsinki University Press: Helsinki, 1987), pp. 50–52. For more detailed discussion, see Barbara N. Porter, "Feeding Dinner to a Bed: Reflections on the Nature of Gods in Ancient Mesopotamia," *State Archives of Assyria Bulletin* 15 (2006), pp. 307–31.

135. On the presentation of elegant beds to gods as a means of pleasing them and obtaining their support, see Barbara N. Porter, "Beds, Sex, and Politics," in S. Parpola and R. M. Whiting, eds., *Sex and Gender in the Ancient Near East*, CRRAI 47/II (Helsinki: The Neo-Assyrian Text Corpus Project, 2002), pp. 530–34.

arrival by setting up tables and presenting offerings, perhaps thanking the gods for the boats' safe journey (to ensure which, the king himself had already presented special offerings). The state treasurer reports that their boats are now anchored on the river, just outside the Aššur gate, and that his canopy has been set up aboard his boat, so that he can remain with the bed. He notes, "I am staying on the river and keeping watch until the day I depart. The king my lord can be greatly pleased." He then adds matter-of-factly, "As long as the bed is aboard, regular sheep offerings are being made in front of it" (l. 13′–rev. l. 1). Regular sheep offerings (UDU.*dariu*) are otherwise attested as being presented in Assyria to the great gods Aššur, Nabû, and Marduk; their presentation to the bed in this instance appears to mark it not only as divine, but as a god of considerable prestige.[136] As we have seen, the bed in the first letter clearly had religious significance, enough to suggest that it might itself be divine; this second bed is treated explicitly as a god in its own right.

As we are by now well aware, there is nothing particularly surprising in the discovery that the second bed, and perhaps the first as well, were considered to be gods in their own right. What is more significant about these letters' reports is the profound uneasiness with which the state treasurer and his king appear to have approached these two objects. As we have seen, possessions of gods that were used in their service, such as thrones and chariots, although often understood to be themselves deities, do not seem to have been active gods beyond serving as seats or means of transportation for their owners, so it is unlikely that the king and his treasurer expected the beds themselves, if neglected or displeased, to "flame out" at them in some dangerous way.[137] These beds may have been intended to be the possessions of a great god, but there is no suggestion here that it was the divine owner of the beds whose wrath the king and his official actually feared; it is the bed itself that is solicitously escorted and placated with its own offerings. Its presumed divine owner is never even mentioned. What the letters reveal is a vague fearfulness and sense of awe, a feeling that if you should treat these beds in the wrong way, bad things will happen. It is the clearest indication we are ever given that even the least active of non-anthropomorphic gods were truly seen as divine beings in the fullest sense, silent and inert, lacking any trace of personality or agency, yet somehow charged with an ominous aura of living divinity that appears to have been basic to the nature of all of Mesopotamia's gods.

---

136. See Porter, "Feeding Dinner," note 12. Offerings were presented to beds (probably belonging to gods) on two occasions in the Ur III period (*idem*, note 62) and at least once in the Late Babylonian period (Zawadski, *Garments*, pp. 181 and 186).

137. Like the earthly things "charged with the grandeur of God" that will "flame out like shining from shook foil," as the nineteenth century English poet Gerard Manley Hopkins put it in his poem "God's Grandeur," quoted at the beginning of this paper (W. H. Gardner, ed, *Gerard Manley Hopkins: A Selection of His Poems and Prose* [Harmondsworth, Middlesex, England: Penguin Books, 1953], p. 27.

Mountains that protect, harps that sing, weapons that fly, and beds that receive food offerings were not just items belonging to the divine sphere, but rather, a part of the wide spectrum of DINGIRs and *ilu*s that together constituted Mesopotamia's gods, evidence of the intriguing complexity of ancient Mesopotamian concepts of the divine.

Highlights of the Discussion

In the four essays the reader has just examined, the gods of Mesopotamia appear in many different forms and guises. Focusing on the different images of gods presented in the different sources on which each concentrated, and guided by different methodological approaches and different intuitive understandings of the evidence, the authors came to somewhat different conclusions about how Mesopotamians envisioned their gods. In order to explore the ambiguities and apparent contradictions in this wide body of evidence, and to compare and perhaps reconcile our often different conclusions, the participants spent more than twenty-three hours in discussion during the four days of the conference. The excerpts below offer glimpses of those often intense conversations.

As we became more familiar with the specialized evidence presented in the other participants' papers and with each others' assessment of that evidence, our own understandings of the Mesopotamian concept of deity changed and evolved. As a result, the reader (like the participants) will find him or herself pursuing a moving target in this chapter. Positions that were hotly defended in the discussion sessions were often gradually modified and sometimes disappeared entirely in the final published version of the papers. In a few cases, statements made in the discussions have been omitted or have been slightly revised here at a participant's request. In many cases, new arguments were added to the chapters in response to questions or disagreements. To further complicate matters, we also grappled in the discussion sessions with one unpublished earlier talk and three essays published elsewhere. Since Stefan Maul was unfortunately prevented by injury from completing his paper or attending the conference, his ideas were represented at the conference by an unpublished lecture,[1] and by two previously published essays which had approached aspects of the problem from other directions.[2] After

---

1. Presented to the Harvard University workshop "Religions of Ancient Mesopotamia and Adjacent Areas" in 1999 and entitled "Constructions of Divinity: Thoughts on the Notions of God in the Ancient Near East." The original plan was to publish that talk here, since it played a significant role in the conference discussions. Maul's position on these issues, however, has since evolved, and research since the time of the conference has led him to revise his ideas about the specific metal to which Ishtar was linked. Since this would require extensive changes in the discussion of Ishtar advanced in the Harvard lecture, it will not be published here, although the thesis it advanced that many of the gods of Mesopotamia were closely linked to particular metals, stones, or other material objects and at times appear to have been represented by such objects, or in some sense even equated with them, is unaffected by these changes and had a significant impact on the conference.

2. Stefan M. Maul, "Das Wort im Worte: Orthographie und Etymologie als hermeneutische Verfahren babylonischer Gelehrter," in Glenn Most, ed., *Commentaries Commentare*, Aporemata Bd. 4

reading these, Hermann Vanstiphout responded by distributing an unpublished lecture of his own, "The *n*th degree of Writing at Nineveh," which also influenced the discussions.[3]

As the excerpts from the discussions make clear, the complicated evidence for how Mesopotamia's gods were envisioned led us to confront some fundamental problems in reconstructing the religion and world view of an ancient society. The discussions also led us each to reexamine our understanding of basic religious terminology and our own varied understandings of the nature of religious belief and practice. It is my hope that as readers follow our steps in this endeavor, they will be prompted to join the fray themselves, contributing to a growing understanding of Mesopotamia's gods, and perhaps also to a better understanding of our own ideas about the nature of the divine.

Literal depictions or metaphoric descriptions?

ROCHBERG: I would prefer not referring to a god as a "package" or asking "What is a god?" because it invites a certain answer. It forces us into a kind of literal framework, that a god *is* this or a god *is* that. Thinking of a god as a conglomeration of things starts this way of thinking.

What I would rather say is something like this: a god is not a thing of this world (unknowable or not). It is a fabrication of the human mind. As such, it is necessarily spoken of in terms of things of this world, with ourselves being the operative reference point for the ancient Near East. So trying to describe a god requires the use of emblems.

If you substitute "the thing used to describe" for "the thing itself," you commit a category mistake, as Ryle argues. What you are defining is something that is definable only through its manifestations, universals such as love, or substantive things. . . . If you say "Ishtar is the bow," or "Ishtar is love," it tells us not what she *is*, but only how she is represented. And that is where the power of metaphoric language lies. The emblems themselves, they cannot become gods, they *represent* gods. . . . I can't possibly say what it meant to say that a star was a god, or a god was a star: I don't know. Gods are *spoken of* as stars, some gods have astral images, stars are spoken of as images of gods. Or stars are personified as gods, so the interpretation of personified stars is that they are still *images* of gods.

* * *

(Göttingen: Vandenhoeck and Ruprecht, 1999), pp. 1–18; *idem,* "The Ancient Middle Eastern Capital City: Reflection and Navel of the World," Stanford Presidential Lectures and Symposia in the Humanities and Arts, http://prelectur.stanford.edu/lecturers/maul/ancientcapitals.html.

3. Since published in Dominique Collon and Andrew George, ed., *Nineveh: Papers of the 49th Rencontre Assyriologique Internationale, London, 7–11 July 2003,* vol. I (London: The British School of Archaeology in Iraq, 2005), pp. 51–54.

PORTER: To take an example from another culture, Mount Fuji is not a metaphor for something else. It is holy in its own right, and people go there and get cured. There is no anthropomorphic figure associated with it.

* * *

ORNAN: Recognizing a metaphor in a text is highly dependent on the context, and this is true visually also. See, for example, this cylinder seal showing the image of a deity in humanlike form with two objects behind her; these stand for her. The distinction Seidel makes between an attribute and a symbol is important to note here.

* * *

ORNAN: The visual representation does not necessarily tell us about the concept of the deity.

What visual criteria identify an image as representing a god?

ORNAN: Although in verbal texts, there are descriptions of Ningirsu with wings and other theriomorphic features, visual descriptions may differ from the textual ones. There is a visual representation of the Imdugud-headed bird with two stags where the bird is shown as a deity "on its own." It cannot be regarded in this case as an attribute of an anthropomorphic deity. The bird is here the deity itself.

In another case, there is a depiction of a deity in anthropomorphic form on one Old Babylonian seal. The deity is represented as a nude female. The signifier here is the worshipper, whose gesture toward the figure indicates that the context is a setting of cultic veneration.

A seal from the Morgan Collection shows a worshipper with raised hand standing before a bird on an emblem and a horse-head, both placed on an altar in a pavilion. The hand gesture indicates the scene is cultic. So these images represent deities.

* * *

ORNAN: In Middle Assyrian glyptics, in contrast to the Old Babylonian and early Kassite periods, the representation of gods as human figures is eschewed. Many seals show combat scenes with human-shaped figures and animals, but it is unclear if the figure is mortal or divine. The fact that we can't tell says something about the decline of anthropomorphic renderings of the divine.

Another Middle Assyrian seal shows a winged dragon, an empty chair or a pedestal, a winged disk, and a star. But in this case we know it is a divine scene because of the kneeling, gesturing worshipper. The star might represent Ishtar, or it could be there to "dingirize" the whole scene.

Objects as symbols of gods? As forms of gods? As non-anthropomorphic gods?

ORNAN: Objects can symbolize gods. Objects are not always objects in their own right, but are instead symbols pointing beyond, references to an anthropocentrically conceived god. But in some cases, objects appear not to refer to an anthropocentrically conceived god.

* * *

ORNAN: If a god is represented ever as anthropomorphic, or as having human attributes, we should conclude that it is therefore anthropomorphically conceived.

PORTER: I would say instead that if a god is represented as a bird, or as a moon crescent, perhaps these are equally important forms of the same god. We shouldn't assume the anthropomorphic one is central. It is there, of course, but so is the bird form of the storm god, so is the crescent of Sin. I would argue that an object or planet or animal in visual representation might not necessarily be an emblem of a deity; this assumes deity cannot exist primarily in the form of an object, which is the very question we must address.

* * *

ROCHBERG: There is evidence of ^{d}*iskaru* 'the crescent' as independent of Sin.

* * *

VANSTIPHOUT (on the relationship of minerals, etc., to gods): In the dreams of Gilgamesh, tin is referred to as the "stone from heaven." It is a manifestation of a god. But some plants and minerals are *not* manifestations of a god. Is the tamarisk, for example, divine? Only sometimes.

* * *

VANSTIPHOUT: There is the idea of Jesus' consubstantiality, the idea that he has the same substance as God the Father. Is this helpful? Are objects perhaps consubstantial with gods?

* * *

VANSTIPHOUT (to Porter): Does it weaken your argument if the statue of the king is given a DINGIR sign, but the king's name is not?

Was observation of stars a natural science or a religious activity?

ROCHBERG: I am very leery of literal interpretations of the stars as gods, of stars as corporeal forms of gods. Worship of the stars is object worship, stellar worship. I wonder whether that is the correct interpretation of, say, the prayers to the stars.

* * *

ROCHBERG: How did the notion that stars were divine originate in the first place? Is it because there was the notion of divine radiance, and when they looked at the heavens and saw the divine radiance of the stars, they understood them to be gods, or was it the other way around, that in the beginning, stars were gods and so there was an association of radiance with gods?

Why is there divine radiance? It is a natural, obvious, empirical explanation: there is divine radiance because it *is*, there is astral luminescence.

But let's consider the possibility that what they [think of themselves as] observing is not exactly something astral in our terms. Nevertheless, their observation of the stars is pure natural science. They're not talking about gods.

PORTER: Is it natural science or is it religion? It's both. Because stars are objects that are ominous, frightening, luminous, they are DINGIRs, have qualities that characterize DINGIRs. In that case, to observe them is neither natural science or religion, it's both; the ancient Mesopotamians didn't make a separation between the two as we do.

ROCHBERG: Of course they didn't make the separation. But *we* have to talk in our terms to elucidate what is going on.

VANSTIPHOUT: Yes. Then the question is, what are the things that they are viewing [in our terms]? We owe that to ourselves. But that does not change their observations, or *their* descriptions of them.

PORTER: My question is precisely to try to understand what a DINGIR is in our terms. If some DINGIRs are at least in part natural phenomena, say, planets that move, and some DINGIRs are objects, then for *them*, for the ancient Mesopotamians, there is not quite the division in the world that we understand to exist between inanimate objects and living things. The world we see is different from theirs, which they see as full of objects that are living DINGIRs.

Was the thing itself believed to be present in the sign representing that thing?

VANSTIPHOUT (*re* "Das Wort im Worte"): This is just scribal cleverness. It is like alliteration, a purely literary device. Stefan Maul goes too far here.

ORNAN: If we look at Rabbi Hillel, he says you can take the same text *both* ways: practically *and* symbolically.

* * *

ORNAN (discussing an Assyrian stamp seal showing a person worshipping a divine creature): Creatures such as this scorpion man are now for the first time shown worshipped as the focus of cult. I think the cosmos is now seen as composed of multifaceted visual emblems, like the multifaceted cuneiform signs that Maul discusses in "Das Wort im Worte."

The role of politics

PORTER (to Ornan): Could the removal of great gods from representation in palace decor have been primarily politically motivated?

ORNAN: The removal of anthropomorphic representations of gods reflects a religious concept or behavior, or rule of behavior. And then the removal of the anthropomorphic representation of the god is *used* by political thinkers in the design of palaces.

* * *

ORNAN: One of the pedestals of Tukulti-Ninurta shows two composite beings with stars. They flank an entranceway, and inside it is the king. Where is the temple's deity? It is unseen. The king is standing where the god should be. This is the dominant message of first millennium art. The god is eliminated from the picture in order to elevate the king.

The god is the competitor; he is the missing competitor. The knowledgeable viewer knows that there is something which is not shown, and in the mind, the god is present. But on the other level, it is the king who is actually shown here. This tension . . . they couldn't show it, but in this way, they manage to imply it visually.

* * *

ORNAN: There is a profound ambiguity in visual representations of the king that are perhaps divine.

VANSTIPHOUT: It is the *office* of kingship that is divine, not the king.

ORNAN: In the case of Shulgi, I call it "flirting" with deification.

VANSTIPHOUT: In the same texts in which he presents himself as partly a god, he insists on his actual humanity.

ORNAN: So he was not really deified in his lifetime?

VANSTIPHOUT: The problem is, when were the hymns written? After his death, or during his lifetime?

Different genres and how they represent gods

VANSTIPHOUT: We must take literary stuff *as* literary stuff, not as a relation of religious beliefs. I trust the literary material. What it reflects may not have been the ideology of the state, but it *was* the ideology of those who could read and write.

* * *

VANSTIPHOUT : The *tākultu* text has the form of a list. And these lists reproduce themselves. Are these *tākultu* texts really cultic texts in Mesopotamia?

ORNAN: That is, do these texts reflect religion as it is conceptualized, or as it is practiced? In the Hebrew bible, there is a big distinction between cult and concept, that is, they don't actually worship God as their worship is represented in the bible.

* * *

PORTER: I want to suggest that there are differences in the way gods are represented in different genres. In particular, there is a big difference in the way gods are represented in myths (where they are almost entirely anthropomorphic) and in rituals.

VANSTIPHOUT: These are not so far apart. I think not everything that is in the ritual texts is actually enacted. Ritual texts and myths are both fictional to a large extent.

ORNAN: Would you make two completely different registers that are saying the same thing?

PORTER: If not, which register, which way of representing the gods, is the essential one in Mesopotamia? *Is* there a single ancient Mesopotamian genre that best represents how Mesopotamians imagined the gods? And is there one that includes all the aspects of how they imagined the gods to be? Or do different genres represent several different ways in which gods were envisioned?

* * *

ORNAN: In eighth and seventh century Assyria, the glyptic stays with the older, anthropomorphic representation of gods, while monumental art goes to the non-anthropomorphic. The change in the way they are represented doesn't indicate a change in how they were conceived. And Marduk and Nabu are sometimes represented non-anthropomorphically in Assyria because they were borrowed from Babylonia, where *kudurrus* represented such gods non-anthropomorphically.

* * *

PORTER: (to Vanstiphout) You restricted yourself to myths.

VANSTIPHOUT: Because that's all there is!

PORTER: Jacobsen also used Sumerian hymns, and quotes texts that suggest the gods were not only a single, anthropomorphic phenomenon, but that there was already a play between the two forms.

ORNAN: And then there is the question, what is the literary and what is the true?

VANSTIPHOUT: What is the respectability of hymns? Can you put a hymn to a minor god, say Nusku, on the same level as a text for which you have forty manuscripts, all coming from the scribal tradition?

PORTER: It's difficult to say, because you are dealing with texts written for two different purposes . . . I think all texts have agendas, different types of texts, different agendas. The myth about Enlil losing the MES seems designed to make him look foolish. Perhaps one function of mythology in Mesopotamia is to permit discussions that are speculative, or not complimentary to gods.

VANSTIPHOUT: That is exactly right. It is an expression of the Mesopotamians' humanity that is basically against a system of gods that intimidate. They *won't* be intimidated. Gilgamesh is the first manifestation of humanism: he has beaten death by accepting it.

God, DINGIR, divinity, deity, holiness, sanctity: Defining key terms

PORTER: There are basic questions of terminology that we all share, but that are not always clearly addressed in our position papers. For example, what do *we* each mean when we use the word 'god'? And what are the criteria in Mesopotamia for recognizing a god? How did gods function there, and are there gods that don't function at all but simply are? And when an Assyriologist suggests, for example, that epilepsy, although it is often marked with a DINGIR determinative, is not a "real" god, do we mean by that that epilepsy is not a Western-style god? (And if so, just what is *that*?) I think we are coming to the word 'god' with a lot of cultural baggage.

What does DINGIR mean? *Does* it mean 'god'? Or are the sometimes shifting Assyriological translations of DINGIR justified, such as translating ^{d}Adad as 'the god Adad,' but translating ^{d}Harp as 'the holy harp,' as Selz does, for example? I would contend that these are both real gods for Mesopotamians because they are labeled and treated in the same way, but that they are nevertheless quite different kinds of things.

* * *

PORTER: Should we distinguish between the terms 'god', 'divinity' and 'deity'? In our papers we often used them as if they were synonyms, but we quietly changed from using one to using another one in certain situations, as if we meant to imply a difference. My Webster's dictionary defines 'god' as "a being of more than human attributes and powers; a deity; . . . the ruler or sovereign embodiment of some aspect, attribute, or department of reality; . . . a person or thing deified." It defines 'divinity' as "the state or quality of being divine, a deity, a celestial being inferior to a god."

VANSTIPHOUT: I think therefore we should have made a distinction between divinity and gods; gods are able to do things, to work on the world.

* * *

VANSTIPHOUT: What if *we* differentiate between deity, divinity, and holiness, but to them, the idea of DINGIR is a unity with different aspects, a DINGIR is something that has the property of holiness *and/or* power?

ROCHBERG: DINGIRs are perhaps things that have sanctity.

ORNAN: We should differentiate between godliness and holiness. Divinity and sanctity are different things. A divinity or deity is a supernatural entity, while sanctity is something you can apply to a whole *range* of entities. Sanctified objects, their relation to the divine is very complex. They are sometimes divine, sometimes associated with the divine. The same entity may change its role. The distinction is functional.

VANSTIPHOUT: The distinction is also fluid. Take the example of transubstantiation in the Catholic Mass: that piece of bread becomes holy, but you need a ritual to *make* it holy.

PORTER: In Mesopotamia, some things are ritually transformed to become gods. Other things may be gods because they are seen as somehow inherently charged with a kind of ominous, numinous potential power, others become gods by association. And some objects take on divine coloring independently.

Saints' relics are a possible partial analogy, but they are of several kinds. Some are inherently part of the saint, like the finger bone of Saint Anthony, and some are divine by association because they were worn by a saint, for example.

ORNAN: But there is a difference between holiness and divine nature.

VANSTIPHOUT: The official teaching of the Catholic church about relics is that you should just revere them. The official teaching of the Catholic church was strongly against the idea that something miraculous had happened at Lourdes, for example.

PORTER: But there is often a difference between official doctrine and ordinary people's belief.

* * *

ORNAN (to Porter): Could DINGIR be precisely those practical objects, a concretizing?

Changes over time

ORNAN: *Kudurru*s offer the most abundant non-anthropomorphic representations of gods. This represents a shift in the way of representing gods. With the emergence of the Kassites to power, representation of gods becomes less anthropomorphic. (The exception is the goddess Gula, who is always represented anthropomorphically. Why? It is perhaps significant that while she is not a minor goddess, she always appears in a lower visual register.) Aside from Gula, major gods are always represented in non-anthropomorphic form.

* * *

ORNAN: A change in the way things are represented doesn't indicate a change in how they are conceived.

What identifies a deity as conceived of in anthropomorphic terms?

ORNAN: The Broken Obelisk of Ashur-bel-kala represents the king and his pleading enemies. Above him, two hands holding a bow emerge from a winged disk. This is a fused image, combining inanimate and human features. The hands clearly designate it as standing for a divinity conceptualized in humanlike terms.

The inferior status of non-anthropomorphic images of deity

ORNAN: The weapon of Assur goes out to battle. The stamped image of the god on a standard goes to your house. But within the temple, they prefer the anthropomorphic representation of the god. This implies a hierarchy in the forms of representation. In the Sippar plaque, the anthropomorphic god is shown inside the building and the non-anthropomorphic image outside. This suggests the inferiority of the non-anthropomorphic rendering.

The meaning of the DINGIR determinative

ROCHBERG: Determinatives have a classificatory function. For example, the sign GIŠ means 'wood.' As a determinative, it means trees, different types of wood, and objects made of wood. It is a term that marks a class within which you have different kinds of things, things sharing a particular quality. As a determinative, the LÚ sign marks a class of human males of different kinds; so you can have different kinds of things in a class designated by a determinative: a man, a male professional, people from Elam.

MUL as a word means 'star.' As a determinative, it represents a class. For example, the $^{mul\,(lú)}$ḫun.ga ('hireling') constellation is a celestial object envisioned in the shape of a hireling. The 'hireling' itself is not by definition a star, but when envisioned as a constellation, the hireling is then brought into the class of stars. Then you have the celestial chariot. By definition, MAR.GÍD.DA ('chariot') is not a MUL. Only as the celestial chariot does it belong to the class of MUL, but by definition it is a chariot.

Then we come to example four: DINGIR. It is a word that means 'god.' As a determinative, it is a classificatory term for anything that has been classified as divine. It is a class including gods, or a kind of divine thing, or a supernatural thing.

PORTER: What did you mean earlier by saying that some gods are "gods by definition"?

ROCHBERG: ^{d}Sin is a god by definition. I would offer as a provisional answer that we are stuck with the evidence of the god lists. The gods that satisfy the criteria for "gods by definition" are all apparently from the god lists, not because I say so, but because of the evidence of proper names.

And if it's the case that all the gods that we know are divine by definition have proper names, and if they have duties to perform, then it seems to me they are anthropomorphic, that is, they act with agency the way human beings do.

PORTER: Why?

ROCHBERG: Well, because they have names, because they have mythologies . . . . I'm talking about what we can identify as gods by definition, the evidence that provides us with things that are identified as gods by definition. In other words, they don't exist apart from . . . .

PORTER: DINGIRs by definition?

ROCHBERG: No. I'm trying to make a classification of things that can be written with the divine determinative. Dingirized objects are not gods. The divine determinative can cover both gods and dingirized objects. Dingirized objects are not conflated with the class of divine names. For example:

Gods by definition	DINGIRized things
^{d}Marduk	^{d}MAR ('spade')
^{d}Sin	^{d}30 ^{d}uskaru ('crescent moon')
^{d}Ištar	^{d}15 ^{mul}DILBAT (the planet Venus) ^{d}nūru ('light')

The things in column one tend to be anthropomorphic. The things in column two tend to be non-anthropomorphic. Without the divine determinative, all of the things in the second column, without exception, would return to a quotidienne, mundane existence with no divine aspect. They have no bearing whatsoever on the divine realm. But for the class of things in the first column, that cannot happen. There is no possibility of reducing them to something non-divine. Sin does not exist except as a DINGIR. All of these things are DINGIRs, but that does not mean that they are all gods. The things in the second column are divine manifestations and can exist in ways that are not divine. They work as gods because of this relationship between the idea of a god and the manifestation of something divine. The function and meaning of the DINGIR sign depends on this relationship.

VANSTIPHOUT: Let's look again at the differences between the two categories:

personal	not persons
have proper names	no proper names
are multifunctional	are uni-functional
multi-morph	uni-morph
social	completely isolated
no existence in mundane world	separate existence in mundane world
many representations	no set of different representations
independent	dependent

But it remains one category. The Mesopotamians have no separate name or category for these two things.

ORNAN: I think the concept is dominated by the persons, while the evidence can be more dominated by the articulations, and I think this changes in different historical periods.

PORTER: Some objects are not DINGIRs because they are manifestations of a particular god. It's not always due to a relationship. Some objects have become independently divine as the *result* of a relationship to a god, and some others are DINGIRs because they are seen as individually energy-filled objects. Maul's evidence suggests this. And the case of mountains and rivers suggests this.

ORNAN: Some material objects are divine?

PORTER: Yes. At least at times. Some mountains and rivers, for example, and other things when they have been used in close association with a god, or are used in rituals, as Maul describes. Those same types of things can also be everyday objects, everyday chariots, say, or metals.

ROCHBERG: I would say, yes, the Mesopotamians do think like we do when they are not thinking in a magical way.

PORTER: Maul doesn't use the word 'magical,' and I think we shouldn't. It's so negatively charged. What I want to say is that I think Maul is right when he says that some objects, some plants, some stones, and so on, are understood both ways. For us, that is magical, I suppose. But for them, it is just a different way of thinking about the world. I would say that stones and minerals and so on are used in rituals as objects charged with a kind of power, but in other cases, may just have a quotidienne existence. I think that for Mesopotamians quotidienne existence involves both objects that we would call "just things" and objects that in themselves also have power, energy. As evidenced by the way they are used in certain contexts.

ROCHBERG: I'm not saying that their culture and ours are the same; that's very dangerous. But you are saying that the Mesopotamians are irrational.

PORTER: No, no!

ROCHBERG: That they don't think like we do, that they think every object in the material world has magical properties.

PORTER: No, not magical. Living, often. I don't think that is irrational. A different spiritual viewpoint, or a slightly different world model, maybe.

ROCHBERG: They had magic, they had their everyday things.

PORTER: Yes. I think there are two things. I think some Mesopotamians understood certain objects to be alive, at least at certain times, in certain contexts.

The nature of Mesopotamian gods

VANSTIPHOUT: If you are omnipotent, you don't have to know anything. If you know everything that will happen, you don't have to have any power. My argument is that the Mesopotamians *never* attribute omniscience to gods.

* * *

VANSTIPHOUT: Mesopotamian gods have three kinds of being substantial, of being real. First of all, the gods do have a kind of human-like appearance, physicality. And they do things that humans do—especially wrong things! But they also have a kind of substantial essence, being, that is purely immaterial: that is the abstract thing. In this way they do seem to be immanent all over the world. A third way is that some of them, not all of them, seem to have an astral or celestial being. These three substantialities do not always conform, and texts as we have them do not always keep them apart. Mostly, they do not keep them apart.

* * *

PORTER: (to Vanstiphout) In one footnote, you talk about the god Enki as sweet water. Isn't that another kind of substantiality? If so, doesn't that open the door to all the others, suggest that the third substantiality might not just be a celestial form, but could be water, or maybe lead as Ishtar?

VANSTIPHOUT: No. I meant that they have a part of the universe where they have that third substantiality. Not always celestial; for Enki, for example, that is the *apsu*, the subterranean sweet water.

ORNAN: Can we widen this and say that all natural phenomena have a god who represents them?

VANSTIPHOUT: No, I don't think so. There is no god of trees, for instance. But there are, for example, Ašnan for grain, Šakkan for writing and administration.

PORTER: I'm moving in the same direction as Tallay, I think, that this third substantiality characteristic of many gods could be not only celestial but also in the form of . . .

ORNAN: Yes, terrestrial!

VANSTIPHOUT: Yes, and Iškur and Enlil as well, who are the storm gods, the heavy cloud . . . .

ORNAN: What about another category, man-made things, like metals?

VANSTIPHOUT: Yes, it's quite good, what you are suggesting. Perhaps I should make a fourth category, or really, split the third category in two, into stellar and earthly. I want to keep the stellar existence separate because that is by definition cyclical.

PORTER: And the stellar is tied to only a few gods, and may be a special category.

* * *

PORTER (to Vanstiphout): Why do you think gods are thought of as having these three substantialities? What drives Mesopotamians to see planets or other immaterial things as gods? Are there different usefulnesses for these?

VANSTIPHOUT: Why do they treat them in many texts as if they were humans? Well, what else could you do? How can you write a novel of ideas without personifying ideas, humanizing the ideas? They use the anthropomorphic form because it is hard for us to find other models for entities we can communicate with. The thing I can talk to, and feed, they want to attribute this to gods.

PORTER: But aren't there gods in this and other cultures that are large stones?

ORNAN: But what is behind those stones? That is the question. It is the station of the entity that is protecting the place.

PORTER: In the past, I've always seen Mesopotamian gods as anthropomorphic primarily and the divine objects as being emanations or emblems of those gods, but when I look at some texts, they seem to treat objects, abstract ideas, etc., as being gods themselves. If I'm being true to the evidence, the idea of gods as anthropomorphic is not true in all cases. Certain chariots, for example, are marked with the DINGIR determinative, have their own temples, are presented with offerings. It seems to me the *Mesopotamians* are putting things like this, along with other gods, in one category, and *we* are resisting that. I'm moving toward a formula in which I think great gods are a package, and a package in which the anthropomorphic form may not in every case even be the dominant one. And some other gods are entirely non-anthropomorphic. Perhaps in literature, you have to personify gods, but did they think of the stone god or the chariot as humanlike persons? Nothing suggests it.

* * *

ORNAN: We think of gods in anthropocentric terms because we don't have any other metaphor to use.

PORTER: Well, perhaps we do have some, actually. Cognition, volition don't have to be thought of as only human traits.

VANSTIPHOUT: You must talk about emotion as well.

PORTER: What about my dog? It understands me very well, it has desires, emotions, certainly volition, but it is not human. I am well aware it is not human.

ORNAN and VANSTIPHOUT: But you treat it as a human.

PORTER: No. As alive and responsive. And what about boats? These have names, they are referred to as feminine, for their owners in many cases they have personalities and seem in a sense alive, are talked to and appealed to in moments of stress, but their owners are well aware they are not human, not even like humans. They do perhaps think of them as alive, although they might not ordinarily admit it.

ORNAN: The visual image of the boat god is anthropomorphic, with a human head.

PORTER: I'm not sure. Maybe that is an image of a boat as living and cognizant? Half of it, after all, is boat.

* * *

VANSTIPHOUT: The Mayans had a very abstract system, just numbers in their calendar system. They *had* to write stories about them. You *have* to visualize it as human, or perhaps an animal, or you have nothing, you can't talk to it. You have to have stories to understand *why* the gods have numbers.

* * *

PORTER: Why did the Mesopotamians link, say, Venus, lapis lazuli, love, war, the number 15, and so on, as being Ishtar, and link numerous other things with other particular gods?

VANSTIPHOUT: It is a way of thinking. "Mythological thought." In Levi-Strauss's sense, a *machine à penser*, which is very ancient. Just as a myth consists of all its versions, not just one text, so they envision Ishtar as made up of all these things. It is the thing therefore that they envisage.

ORNAN: It is an essence!

ROCHBERG: I think mythopoeic thought is a literary creation, not a form of cognition. It is clear that phenomena were understood in empirical ways, too.

VANSTIPHOUT: Yes, yes, they are very expert. What the astronomical reports are describing is pure natural science.

ROCHBERG: How do they look at the heavens? The question is the degree to which they identify the planets with gods. Yes, they identify these things with deities, and it looks contradictory to us. But at the same time they are capable of carrying out empirical investigations. Stars and statues are both corporeal forms of a god. The difference is that the statue is made by human beings and undergoes the mouth-opening ritual, but the planet is part of the cosmos. Both statue and star lend themselves to anthropomorphic language. Both can be spoken of in an anthropomorphic way. When the protases say the stars "see" or "approach," this is metaphor.

* * *

VANSTIPHOUT: My idea is that the gods are not anthropomorphic, but anthropoid.

ORNAN: Meaning that they are human-like but not human in form?

VANSTIPHOUT: No, human in form but not completely like humans. The term was used for early pre-humans that looked like humans. And for robots.

PORTER: Wonderful! Because it carries out your final idea that these gods are sort of robots created to carry out an *idea*.

VANSTIPHOUT: Yes, "Die Geschöpfe des Prometheus."

* * *

PORTER: Do you think the Mesopotamians themselves had an abstract concept of the nature of gods?

VANSTIPHOUT: Abstraction was invented in Mesopotamia. The Sumerian language prescribes a form for naming abstract ideas, NAM, from NA.AM, 'to be.' But no, the word NAM.DINGIR.RA doesn't exist.

PORTER: In Akkadian, you do have the word *ilūtu*.

VANSTIPHOUT: Yes, but in Sumerian, no.

ORNAN: But I don't think it is necessary. You don't have to have the word. Such a conception would be there mentally.

green press INITIATIVE

Eisenbrauns is committed to preserving ancient forests and natural resources. We elected to print this title on 30% post consumer recycled paper, processed chlorine free. As a result, for this printing, we have saved:

2 Trees (40' tall and 6-8" diameter)
963 Gallons of Wastewater
1 million BTU's of Total Energy
58 Pounds of Solid Waste
200 Pounds of Greenhouse Gases

Eisenbrauns made this paper choice because our printer, Thomson-Shore, Inc., is a member of Green Press Initiative, a nonprofit program dedicated to supporting authors, publishers, and suppliers in their efforts to reduce their use of fiber obtained from endangered forests.

For more information, visit www.greenpressinitiative.org

Environmental impact estimates were made using the Environmental Defense Paper Calculator. For more information visit: www.papercalculator.org.